Better Homes and Gardens®

1994
Best Recipes
YEARBOOK

© Copyright 1994 by Meredith Corporation, Des Moines, Iowa.
All Rights Reserved. Printed in the United States of America.
First Edition. Printing Number and Year: 5 4 3 2   98 97 96 95 94
ISSN: 8755-3090
ISBN: 0-696-04634-2

Better Homes and Gardens® Books

An Imprint of Meredith® Books
President, Book Group: *Joseph J. Ward*
Vice President and Editorial Director: *Elizabeth P. Rice*
Executive Editor: *Nancy N. Green*
Managing Editor: *Christopher Cavanaugh*
Art Director: *Ernest Shelton*
Test Kitchen Director: *Sharon Stilwell*

1994 Best Recipes Yearbook

Project Managers: *Jennifer Darling and Shelli McConnell*
Contributing Designer: *Mike Burns*

Better Homes and Gardens® Magazine

Food Editor: *Nancy Byal*
Senior Editor: *Joy Taylor*
Associate Editors: *Lisa Holderness, Julia Malloy, Kristi Fuller R.D.*

Meredith Corporation

Corporate Officers: Chairman of Executive Commitee: *E.T. Meredith III*
Chairman of the Board, President, and Chief Executive Officer: *Jack D. Rehm*
Group Presidents: *Joseph J. Ward,* Books; *William T. Kerr,* Magazines;
Philip A. Jones, Broadcasting; *Allen L. Sabbag,* Real Estate
Vice Presidents: *Leo R. Armatis,* Corporate Relations;
Thomas G. Fisher, General Counsel and Secretary; *Larry D. Hartsook,* Finance;
Michael A. Sell, Treasurer; *Kathleen J. Zehr,* Controller and Assistant Secretary

Our seal assures you that every recipe in the *1994 Best Recipes Yearbook*
has been tested in the Better Homes and Gardens® Test Kitchen.
This means that each recipe is practical and reliable, and meets
our high standards of taste appeal. We guarantee your satisfaction
with this book for as long as you own it.

WE CARE!

All of us at Better Homes and Gardens® Books are dedicated to
providing you with the information and ideas you need to create tasty foods.
We welcome your comments and suggestions.
Write us at:
Better Homes and Gardens® Books,
Cookbook Editorial Department,
RW-240, 1716 Locust St.,
Des Moines, IA
50309-3023

*If you would like to order additional copies of any of our books,
call 1-800-678-2803 or check with your local bookstore.*

Contents

Introduction

Remember the last time you paged through your high school yearbook or family photo album? Did the reminiscing bring back precious memories of good times and good people?

In many ways, paging through this 1994 BH&G Best Recipes Yearbook is like that for us food editors. It reminds us of the good times we had creating and photographing the 1993 magazine stories for you, and the good people we met along the way. For our February Valentine feature entitled "A Taste of Romance from Historic Inns," Julia Malloy met with the head chefs from three of the best inns in America to present luscious recipes that are perfect for your special dining occasions. For the September story, Kristi Fuller, our staff Registered Dietitian, counseled the Hollingsworth family for nearly a year and a half so she could show them—and you—how to eat right while still enjoying the favorite foods families love.

These stories also remind us of you, our readers. We remember the thoughtful letters that you wrote to us with notes of praise or suggestions for improving upon a story. We remember your telephone calls asking for a misplaced recipe or for culinary advice. Ultimately, it's your responses and your enthusiasm for good food that make our jobs rewarding and fulfilling. Every food story in every issue is planned so that it meets your interests and your needs. Likewise, the recipes are thoroughly tested in the BH&G Test Kitchens until we are confident that they will satisfy you and your family.

As you page through and use this book, we hope the stories and the photographs and the recipes—be they brand-new discoveries for you or delicious rediscoveries—bring as much pleasure to you, your family, and friends as they do to us.

The Editors—Kristi, Lisa, Nancy, Julia, and Joy

January

Dollar Dinners

Prize Tested Recipes

Dollar Dinners

By Lisa Holderness

Hearty, family-pleasing, and under 99 cents per serving—now that's a meal worth coming home to. These 10 dinners keep your grocery bill low, yet deliver the home-cooked flavor your family expects. Cutting cost, not quality, calls for careful planning and smart shopping. Our recipes and tips will get you started.

$.71
PER SERVING
Deep-Dish Tuna Pie

Tuna casserole has been a budget stretcher for decades, using low-cost canned tuna and soup. Update this dish with colorful vegetables, dill, and a pastry topper.

Deep-Dish Tuna Pie

USE CONVENIENT PIECRUST MIX TO MAKE A FLAKY TOP CRUST FOR THIS TASTY TUNA PIE—

½ of an 11-ounce package piecrust mix (1⅓ cups)
1 cup chopped onion
1 medium potato, peeled and diced (about ⅔ cup)
¼ cup water
1 10¾-ounce can condensed cream of mushroom soup
⅓ cup milk
⅓ cup grated Parmesan cheese
1 tablespoon lemon juice
¾ teaspoon dried dillweed
¼ teaspoon pepper
1 6-ounce package assorted loose-pack frozen vegetables
1 9¼ ounce can tuna, drained and broken into chunks
1 beaten egg

Prepare piecrust mix according to package directions, *except* do not roll out. Cover dough and set aside.

In a large skillet cook onion and potato in water, covered, about 7 minutes or till tender. Drain off liquid. Stir in soup, milk, Parmesan cheese, lemon juice, dillweed, and pepper. Cook and stir till bubbly. Stir in frozen vegetables and tuna. Spoon into an ungreased 2-quart casserole.

On a lightly floured surface roll pastry into a circle 2 inches larger than the diameter of the top of the casserole and about ⅛ inch thick. Make 1-inch slits near center of pastry. Center pastry over top of casserole, allowing ends to hang over edge. Trim pastry ½ inch beyond edge of casserole. Turn pastry under; flute to the casserole edge, pressing gently. If desired, use pastry scraps to make small decorations.*

Brush crust with beaten egg. If using pastry decorations, place atop crust and brush with some of the beaten egg. Bake in a 400° oven for 40 to 45 minutes or till crust is golden brown. Serve immediately. Makes 6 servings.

*Note: For pastry leaves as shown on page 7, roll pastry scraps about ⅛ inch thick. With a sharp, small knife, cut pastry into small leaf shapes, about 1 inch long. For leaf veins, using the dull side of the knife blade, make an indentation down the middle of each leaf and smaller indentations branching off from the centers.

Nutrition information per serving: 325 cal., 15 g fat, 59 mg chol., 19 g pro., 28 g carbo., 2 g fiber, 946 mg sodium. RDA: 18% calcium, 10% iron, 43% vit. A, 53% vit. C, 13% thiamine, 18% riboflavin, 28% niacin.

◆ Deep-Dish Tuna Pie

$.87
PER SERVING
Zesty Vegetable Enchiladas

Smother enchiladas with tomato sauce and cheese, just the way you like 'em, and still save money. The bargain is the vegetable-lentil filling. For pennies per serving, lentils add protein, fiber, and flavor.

Zesty Vegetable Enchiladas

TO SAVE TIME, COOK THE LENTILS UP TO 24 HOURS AHEAD AND CHILL, COVERED, IN A STORAGE CONTAINER—

1⅓ cups water
½ cup dry lentils (3½ ounces)
¼ teaspoon salt
8 6-inch flour tortillas
Nonstick spray coating
2 medium carrots, thinly sliced
1½ teaspoon chili powder or ground cumin
1 tablespoon cooking oil
1 medium zucchini, quartered lengthwise and sliced (2 cups)
1 14½-ounce can chunky chili-style stewed tomatoes or Mexican-style stewed tomatoes, cut up
6 ounces Monterey Jack cheese with jalapeño peppers, shredded (1½ cups)

In a medium saucepan combine water, lentils, and salt. Bring to boiling; reduce heat. Cover; simmer for 15 to 20 min-

◆ Zesty Vegetable Enchiladas

utes or till tender. Drain; rinse with cold water. Set aside.

Meanwhile, wrap tortillas in foil; heat in a 350° oven 10 minutes or till warm. Spray a 2-quart rectangular baking dish with nonstick coating.

In a large skillet stir-fry carrots and chili powder or cumin in hot oil for 2 minutes. Add zucchini; stir-fry for 2 to 3 minutes or till crisp-tender. (Add more oil if necessary during cooking.) Remove from heat. Stir in lentils, *half* of the *undrained* stewed tomatoes, and *half* of the cheese.

Spoon vegetable mixture onto the tortillas, dividing it evenly. Roll up tortillas;

place, seam side down, in the prepared baking dish. Cover with foil.

Bake in a 350° oven for 8 minutes. Remove foil; bake for 7 to 12 minutes more or till heated through and tortillas are crisp.

In a small saucepan heat remaining *undrained* tomatoes; spoon over enchiladas. Top with remaining cheese; bake 1 minute or till melted. Serves 4.

Nutrition information per serving: 473 cal., 20 g fat, 38 mg chol., 22 g pro., 53 g carbo., 7 g fiber, 762 mg sodium. RDA: 54% calcium, 34% iron, 117% vit. A, 35% vit. C, 18% thiamine, 29% riboflavin, 20% niacin.

$.64
PER SERVING
Italian Bean Soup

Always-dollar-wise dry beans conjure images of a soothing, cold-weather soup. Use the crusty herb bread to soak up the seasoned tomato broth.

Italian Bean Soup

SIMMER THIS HEARTY, MEATLESS SOUP ON THE RANGE TOP OR IN A CROCKERY COOKER—

1 cup dry great northern beans
1 cup dry red beans or pinto beans
1 28-ounce can tomatoes, cut up
1 medium onion, chopped
2 tablespoons instant beef bouillon granules
or 6 vegetable bouillon cubes
2 cloves garlic, minced
2 teaspoons Italian seasoning, crushed
¼ teaspoon pepper
1 9-ounce package frozen Italian-style
green beans or cut green beans
1 tablespoon margarine
⅛ teaspoon garlic salt
⅛ teaspoon Italian seasoning, crushed
12½-inch-thick slices baguette-style French
bread or six 1-inch-thick slices Italian
bread

Rinse dry beans. In a Dutch oven combine rinsed beans and 5 cups *cold water*. Bring to boiling; reduce heat. Simmer for 2 minutes. Remove from heat. Cover; let stand for 1 hour. (Or, soak beans overnight in a covered pan.) Drain and rinse beans.

◆ Italian Bean Soup

In the same pan combine rinsed beans, 5 cups *fresh water, undrained* tomatoes, onion, bouillon, garlic, the 2 teaspoons Italian seasoning, and pepper. Bring to boiling; reduce heat. Cover; simmer about 1½ hours or till beans are tender. Mash beans slightly with a wooden spoon. Add frozen green beans; simmer for 5 minutes or till green beans are tender.

Meanwhile, stir together margarine, garlic salt, and the ⅛ teaspoon Italian seasoning. Spread atop 1 side of each bread slice. Place bread, margarine side up, on the unheated rack of a broiler pan. Broil 4 to 5 inches from the heat for 45 to 60 seconds or till crisp and light brown.

To serve, ladle soup into bowls. Float 2 small pieces or 1 large piece of herb toast atop each bowl of soup. Serve immediately. Makes 6 servings.

Crockery cooker directions: Soak and rinse beans as directed. In a 3½- or 4-quart crockery cooker combine beans, *4 cups* fresh water (instead of 5 cups), *undrained* tomatoes, onion, bouillon, garlic, the 2 teaspoons Italian seasoning, and pepper. Cook, covered, on high-heat setting 5½ to 6½ hours (low-heat setting: 11 to 13 hours) or till beans are almost tender. Meanwhile, thaw green beans; stir into soup. Cook about 30 minutes more on high setting or till beans are tender. Continue as directed.

Nutrition information per serving: 343 cal., 3 g fat, 0 mg chol., 18 g pro., 62 g carbo., 11 g fiber, 1,304 mg sodium. RDA: 18% calcium, 41% iron, 16% vit. A, 43% vit. C, 43% thiamine, 18% riboflavin, 21% niacin.

Meatball Stew with Winter Vegetables

FOR SMALL FAMILIES COOL LEFTOVER STEW TO ROOM TEMPERATURE, THEN STORE IN A COVERED CONTAINER FOR UP TO 2 DAYS—

2 medium potatoes (unpeeled), cut into 1-inch pieces
2 medium carrots, peeled and cut into ¾-inch pieces
1 large onion, cut into wedges
2 tablespoons instant beef bouillon granules
1 bay leaf
1½ teaspoon dried thyme or oregano, crushed
1 teaspoon dried rosemary or basil, crushed
½ teaspoon pepper
1 recipe Seasoned Meatballs
2 medium sweet potatoes or yams, peeled and cut into 1-inch pieces (about 3 cups)

$.74
PER SERVING
Meatball Stew with Winter Vegetables

This hearty, weeknight stew cuts cost and cooking time while adding flavor. The key: substitute easy-to-make meatballs for more-expensive, long-cooking stew meat.

◆ Meatball Stew with Winter Vegetables

2 medium parsnips, peeled and cut into ¾-inch pieces
1 cup frozen peas
⅓ cup all-purpose flour

In a Dutch oven bring 4½ cups *water* to boiling. Add potatoes, carrots, onion, bouillon granules, bay leaf, thyme or oregano, rosemary or basil, and pepper. Return to boiling; reduce heat. Cover, simmer for 10 minutes.

Meanwhile, prepare Seasoned Meatballs. Add sweet potatoes and parsnips to the hot broth mixture. Add uncooked meatballs, a few at a time, to the hot broth mixture. Return to boiling; reduce heat. Cover and simmer about 15 minutes more or till vegetables are tender and meatballs are fully cooked. Stir in frozen peas.

Stir together ½ cup *cold water* and the flour. Stir flour mixture into hot broth mixture. Cook and stir till thickened and bubbly. Cook and stir for 1 minute more. Ladle into soup bowls and serve. Makes 6 servings.

Seasoned Meatballs: In a medium mixing bowl combine 1 beaten *egg*, ½ cup *fine dry bread crumbs*, 1 teaspoon minced dried onion, 1 teaspoon *Worcestershire sauce*, ¼ teaspoon *garlic salt*, and ⅛ teaspoon *pepper*. Add 1 pound lean *ground beef*; mix well. Shape into thirty 1-inch balls.

Nutrition information per serving: 388 cal., 9 g fat, 83 mg chol., 22 g pro., 56 g carbo., 3 g fiber, 1,111 mg sodium. RDA: 11% calcium, 25% iron, 231% vit. A, 57% vit. C, 31% thiamine, 31% riboflavin, 36% niacin.

30 SUPER-SAVING SHOPPING TIPS

SAVING MONEY WHILE SHOPPING TAKES EXTRA EFFORT, BUT THE RESULTS ARE REWARDING. TRY THESE SHOPPING TIPS AND WATCH YOUR POCKET CHANGE GROW.

MEAT, POULTRY, FISH

1. Check the price per pound on several packages of the same cut. This price can vary, depending on packing date, brand, or sale price.

2. For beef steak cuts, Swiss and round steak are usually less expensive. These meat cuts work best for braising and stir-frying, not broiling or grilling.

3. The leaner the ground meat, the more it costs. When buying higher-fat meat (70% or 80% lean), drain off excess fat after cooking to make it more healthful. Or, extend lean meat with low-fat, low-cost fillers such as bread crumbs or oatmeal.

4. For chicken, whole fryers are a wise choice. Precut whole fryers cost about 20 cents more per pound. Other cheap cuts include drumsticks and hindquarters.

5. Treat your family to seafood's sister, surimi. This fish-based substitute tastes like crab or lobster but costs about three times less.

(Continued on page 13)

$.86
PER SERVING
Sweet-and-Sour Steak Stir-Fry

Steak dinner takes on an affordable Polynesian twist. Stir-fry tender top round steak with tangy-sweet pineapple, juicy orange slices, and fresh green pepper. To cut both cost and fat, use less meat than traditional recipes, and slice it into thin strips.

◆ Zesty Vegetable Enchiladas

Sweet-and-Sour Steak Stir-Fry

THIS STIR-FRY IS QUICK TO FIX, AS WELL AS AFFORDABLE. PLAN ON LESS THAN 30 MINUTES FROM START TO FINISH.

½ pound boneless beef top round steak
1 cup long-grain rice
1 15¼-ounce can pineapple chunks (juice pack)
2 tablespoons vinegar
2 tablespoons soy sauce
1 tablespoon cornstarch
1 tablespoon brown sugar
⅛ teaspoon ground red pepper
1 small orange
1 medium green pepper, cut into 1-inch pieces (1 cup)
1 small onion, cut into thin wedges
1 tablespoon cooking oil

Partially freeze meat. Cook rice according to package directions.

Meanwhile, for sauce, drain pineapple, reserving juice. Add ½ cup of reserved juice to a 1-cup liquid measure. Stir in vinegar, soy sauce, cornstarch, brown sugar, and ground red pepper; set aside.

Thinly slice meat across the grain into bite-size pieces; set aside. Peel and slice orange. Cut slices in half or in quarters; set aside.

In a wok or large skillet stir-fry green pepper and onion in hot oil for 3 to 4 minutes or till crisp-tender. Remove from wok. (Add more oil if necessary.) Add meat to wok. Stir-fry meat for 2 to 3 minutes or till brown. Push meat from center of the pan.

Stir sauce; add to center of wok. Cook and stir till thickened and bubbly. Add vegetables and pineapple chunks. Cook and stir for 2 minutes or till hot. Stir in oranges. Serve immediately over rice. Makes 4 servings.

Nutrition information per serving: 399 cal., 8 g fat, 36 mg chol., 19 g pro., 65 g carbo., 5 g fiber, 548 mg sodium. RDA: 18% iron, 75% vit. C, 35% thiamine, 16% riboflavin, 38% niacin.

Curried Pork and Cabbage

2 tablespoons margarine
2 teaspoons curry powder
½ teaspoon salt
⅛ teaspoon pepper
1 medium head cabbage, cored and coarsely chopped (6 cups)
1 small onion, chopped (⅓ cup)
2 medium cooking apples (such as Jonathan, Rome Beauty, or Winesap), thinly sliced

$.88
PER SERVING

Curried Pork and Cabbage

Gather friends midweek for a tasty pork dinner that won't blow your budget. These chops pair lusciously with winter best-buys: cabbage and apples.

Nonstick spray coating
¼ teaspoon salt
⅛ teaspoon pepper
1 pound boneless pork loin roast,
cut into 6 thin slices or 6 thinly
sliced boneless pork loin chops

In a Dutch oven or large saucepan melt margarine. Stir in curry powder, the ½ teaspoon salt, and ⅛ teaspoon pepper. Add cabbage, onion, and ¼ cup *water*; toss to coat. Cover and cook about 5 minutes or till cabbage is crisp-tender. Add apples. Cover; cook for 3 to 4 minutes more or till cabbage and apples are tender.

Meanwhile, spray a large skillet with nonstick coating. Heat pan for 1 to 2 minutes or till hot. Season pork with the ¼ teaspoon salt and remaining ⅛ teaspoon pepper. Add pork to skillet. Cook over medium-high heat for 2 to 3 minutes or till no longer pink, turning once. Serve pork atop cabbage mixture. Makes 6 servings.

Nutrition information per serving: 205 cal., 11 g fat, 43 mg chol., 15 g pro., 14 g carbo., 4 g fiber, 361 mg sodium. RDA: 73% vit C, 44% thiamine, 13% riboflavin, 20% niacin.

◆ Zesty Vegetable Enchiladas

30 SUPER-SAVING SHOPPING TIPS

(continued from p. 11)

6. Stock your shelves with budget-wise canned fish, such as tuna. Compare prices; canned seafood prices vary with brand and variety.

7. Check the prices on deli meats and the prepackaged brands. Figure the cost per ounce and go with the least expensive option.

FRUITS AND VEGETABLES

8. For fresh produce, winter availability and prices are less than optimum. In winter, choose items that are plentiful, such as citrus fruits, winter squash, and brussels sprouts.

9. Purchase common produce, such as onions, potatoes, and apples in the largest package you can use.

10. Canned or frozen fruits and vegetables offer greater year-round availability than fresh produce, more-consistent prices, and convenience.

DAIRY PRODUCTS

11. Choose common cheese varieties, such as mozzarella, Swiss, American, and cheddar, for the best prices. Specialty cheeses, such as Brie, Havarti, and feta, and cheeses with additional seasonings, usually cost more.

Baked Cavatelli

USE A TWO-QUART CASSEROLE OR SIX
INDIVIDUAL CASSEROLES—

2½ cups wagon wheel macaroni or
corkscrew macaroni
12 ounces fresh Italian sausage links, sliced
½ inch thick
¾ cup chopped green onion
2 cloves garlic, minced
1 15-ounce can tomato sauce
1 14-ounce jar spaghetti sauce with
mushrooms
4 ounces mozzarella cheese, shredded
(1 cup)
1 teaspoon Italian seasoning, crushed
¼ teaspoon pepper

Prepare pasta according to package directions. Drain; set aside.

In a large skillet cook sausage till no pink remains; remove from skillet. Drain off fat, reserving *1 tablespoon*. Cook green onion and garlic in reserved drippings till tender.

In a 2-quart casserole combine cooked pasta, sausage, onion mixture, tomato sauce, spaghetti sauce, *half* of the mozzarella, Italian seasoning, and pepper. Toss gently to combine.

Bake, covered, in a 375° oven for 25 minutes. Uncover; sprinkle with remaining mozzarella. Bake for 5 to 10 minutes more or till heated through. Makes 6 servings.

Note: For individual casseroles, prepare as directed *except* combine ingredients in a large mixing bowl. Spoon into six individual casseroles. Bake, covered, in a 375° oven for 15 minutes. Uncover; sprinkle with remaining mozzarella. Bake for 5 to 10 minutes more or till heated through.

$.91
PER SERVING
Baked Cavatelli

Cavatelli, an old-time Italian dish, combines down-home favorite flavors. With each bite, savor pasta, Italian sausage, tomato sauce, and melted cheese. Whether you use the traditional pasta wheels or slightly cheaper elbow macaroni, the pasta makes this dish a money saver.

Nutrition information per serving:
439 cal., 18 g fat, 43 mg chol., 21 g pro., 49 g carbo., 1 g fiber, 1,312 mg sodium. RDA: 22% calcium, 23% iron, 28% vit. A, 36% vit. C, 53% thiamine, 27% riboflavin, 37% niacin.

◆ Baked Cavatelli

---

30 SUPER-SAVING SHOPPING TIPS

(continued from page 13)

12. Compare block cheese to shredded. Block is usually cheaper, unless shredded is on sale.

13. You'll find coupons regularly for national brand dairy products.

14. Compare brands and sizes for the best deal, looking especially for value or store brands. Margarine, for example, can vary greatly in price.

BAKERY ITEMS

15. Stock up on frozen bread dough. It's considerably less expensive than purchased bread. Baking the dough takes a little more effort, but the cost of firing up your oven is minimal.

16. Purchase day-old bakery items, then freeze or use immediately.

17. If you have the time, bake breads and cookies from scratch.

PASTA, RICE, AND LEGUMES

18. Dry beans cost about three times less than canned, and they are lower in sodium. Choose the more common varieties, such as great northern, pinto, and navy beans.

19. Purchase protein-packed dry lentils for meatless meals.

20. Buy plain long-grain rice and add your own seasonings.

21. Opt for dried pasta over frozen or fresh. Fancy shapes and colored pasta also cost more than simple shapes and plain pasta.

CONDIMENTS

22. Buy herb mixes, such as Italian seasoning or apple-pie spice, instead of several individual containers of pure spices.

(continued on page 19)

$.54
PER SERVING
Baked Spinach and Ham Frittata

Sink your fork into this cheese-topped baked omelet. With flavor this good, it's hard to believe that the main ingredients, eggs, cost just five cents apiece.

Baked Spinach and Ham Frittata

IF YOU'RE CONCERNED ABOUT CHOLESTEROL, USE THE FROZEN EGG PRODUCT OPTION. FOR EACH SERVING, IT INCREASES THE COST BY 49 CENTS AND DECREASES THE CHOLESTEROL BY 425 MILLIGRAMS—

8 eggs or two 8-ounce cartons frozen egg product, thawed
¼ teaspoon dried basil, crushed
⅛ teaspoon pepper
¼ cup chopped onion
1 tablespoon margarine
1 10-ounce package frozen chopped spinach, thawed and well-drained
4 ounces thinly sliced, fully cooked ham or turkey ham, chopped
1 tablespoon grated Parmesan cheese

In a medium mixing bowl combine eggs or egg product, basil, and pepper; beat till combined. Set aside.

In a 10-inch ovenproof skillet cook onion in hot margarine till tender but not brown. Remove from heat. Stir in

◆ Baked Spinach and Ham Frittata

spinach and ham or turkey ham. Add egg mixture.

Bake, uncovered, in a 350° oven about 15 minutes or till a knife inserted near the center comes out clean. Sprinkle with Parmesan cheese. Cover and let stand for 5 minutes before serving. Cut into 8 wedges. Makes 4 servings.

Nutrition information per serving: 241 cal., 15 g fat, 442 mg chol., 21 g pro., 5 g carbo., 0 g fiber, 571 mg sodium. RDA: 18% calcium, 18% iron, 75% vit. A, 21% vit. C, 28% thiamine, 50% riboflavin, 10% niacin.

How we figured the cost per serving:

The costs for these dinners were based on prices in Des Moines, Iowa, supermarkets in May, 1992. Each recipe cost was figured using nationally advertised brands. We did not include the price of these staples: salt, pepper, dried seasonings, and nonstick spray coating. When alternate ingredients are listed, we priced the first choice.

◆ Cheese and Corn Chowder

Cheese and Corn Chowder

3 medium (1 pound) potatoes, peeled
and coarsely chopped
1 cup water
2 teaspoons instant chicken bouillon
granules
⅛ teaspoon ground red pepper
Dash black pepper
3 cups milk
1 10-ounce package frozen whole
kernel corn
2 tablespoons all-purpose flour
6 ounces American cheese,
shredded (1½ cups)
1 tablespoon snipped parsley

In a large saucepan combine chopped potatoes, water, bouillon granules, ground red pepper, and black pepper. Bring to boiling; reduce heat. Cover and simmer about 10 minutes or till potatoes are just tender, stirring occasionally.

Stir in 2½ cups of the milk and the corn. In a small bowl stir together remaining ½ cup milk and flour; stir into potato mixture. Cook and stir over medium heat till slightly thickened and bubbly. Cook and stir for 1 minute more. Add cheese; stir till melted. Spoon into 4 soup bowls. Top each serving with snipped parsley. Makes 4 main-dish servings.

$.80
PER SERVING
Cheese and Corn Chowder
American cheese melts smoothly in the soup, giving it a mild, creamy texture—

Nutrition information per serving:
426 cal., 18 g fat, 54 mg chol., 20 g pro., 50 g carbo., 0 g fiber, 1,142 mg sodium. RDA: 62% calcium, 35% vit. A, 22% vit. C, 31% thiamine, 42% riboflavin, 20% niacin.

$.70
PER SERVING

Parmesan Chicken And Crispy Potato Wedges

For the potato wedges, save even more money by substituting another baking potato for the sweet potato—

Parmesan Chicken and Crispy Potato Wedges

2 medium baking potatoes
1 medium sweet potato or yam
2 tablespoons cooking oil
1 tablespoon grated Parmesan cheese
1 teaspoon paprika
¾ teaspoon garlic salt
½ teaspoon dried thyme, crushed
¼ teaspoon pepper
1 2½- to 3-pound whole broiler fryer chicken, cut up
1 beaten egg
⅓ cup grated Parmesan cheese
3 tablespoons all-purpose flour
¾ teaspoon dried thyme, crushed
Dash pepper
2 tablespoons cooking oil
1 pound broccoli, cut up

Cut potatoes lengthwise into 8 wedges (24 wedges total). On an ungreased 15x10x1-inch baking pan arrange wedges in a single layer, skin side down. Mix the first 2 tablespoons oil, the 1 tablespoon Parmesan cheese, paprika, garlic salt, the ½ teaspoon thyme, and the ¼ teaspoon pepper. Brush Parmesan mixture onto wedges. Set aside.

Skin chicken pieces, if desired. Rinse chicken; pat dry with paper towels. In a shallow bowl combine egg and 2 tablespoons water. In another shallow bowl combine the ⅓ cup Parmesan, flour, the ¾ teaspoon thyme, and dash pepper. Dip chicken into egg mixture; coat with cheese mixture. Arrange, skin side up, in an ungreased 13x9x2-inch baking pan. Drizzle with remaining 2 tablespoons cooking oil.

Bake chicken pieces and potato wedges, uncovered, in a 375° oven for 45 to 55 minutes or till chicken is no longer pink and potatoes are tender.

Meanwhile, cook broccoli, covered, in a small amount of boiling salted water for 8 to 12 minutes or till crisp tender; drain. Serve with chicken and potatoes. Makes 6 servings.

Nutrition information per serving: 394 cal., 22 g fat, 106 mg chol., 26 g pro., 22 g carbo., 1 g fiber, 457 mg sodium. RDA: 15% calcium, 13% iron, 71% vit. A, 24% vit. C, 16% thiamine, 20% riboflavin, 51% niacin.

---

30 SUPER-SAVING SHOPPING TIPS

(continued from page 14)

23. Purchase white or cider vinegar and make your own gourmet versions by adding herbs and flavorings.

24. Dissolve instant bouillon granules or cubes in hot water to make a quick broth.

25. Make your own salad dressings. It takes minutes to shake together salad oil, vinegar, and seasonings.

26. Purchase plain vegetable oils for cooking and salad dressings. If you prefer the flavor of olive oil, check the different brands and grades for the cheapest price. (Virgin and extra-virgin will be the most expensive.)

PANTRY FOODS

27. Look for spaghetti sauces with meat and vegetables included, instead of adding your own. These sauces cost the same as the plain variety.

28. Stock up on simple canned soups, such as chicken noodle, cream of mushroom, and tomato, which cost less than heartier varieties. Add your own leftover vegetables, legumes, and meats to personalize them.

29. Opt for cooked oatmeal or other hot cereals to fill you up in the morning. Plain oatmeal costs just pennies per serving if you buy the large container. You can flavor oatmeal by cooking it with fruit juice or by adding your own spices or dried fruits.

30. Stock up on commonly used pantry items when you find a good sale. Purchase large sizes if the price per unit is less and you know your family will use them. Purchasing larger sizes instead of several small containers helps the environment, too.

Prize Tested Recipes.

Lime and Beer Pork with Chunky Guacamole

TONYA CREATED THIS PORK AND RICE RECIPE OUT OF HER PASSION FOR SOUTHWESTERN FOODS—

1¼ pounds pork tenderloin
1 cup salsa
½ cup lime juice
½ cup beer
2 cloves garlic, minced
1 tablespoon snipped cilantro or parsley
½ teaspoon ground cumin
¼ teaspoon ground red pepper
¼ teaspoon black pepper
1 recipe Chunky Guacamole
12 flour tortillas
1½ cups quick-cooking rice

Partially freeze pork; thinly slice across grain into bite-size strips. Place pork in a plastic bag set into a bowl. Combine salsa, lime juice, beer, garlic, cilantro, cumin, and red and black peppers. Pour over pork; seal bag. Marinate in refrigerator 3 to 4 hours.

Prepare Chunky Guacamole; chill.

Wrap tortillas in foil. Heat in a 350° oven for 10 minutes to soften. For rice, drain pork and set aside; reserve marinade. Add enough water to marinade to equal 1½ cups. In a saucepan bring marinade mixture to boiling. Add rice. Remove from heat. Let stand, covered, 5 minutes.

◆ Lime and Beer Pork with Chunky Guacamole

Meanwhile, spray a 10-inch skillet with *nonstick cooking spray;* preheat over medium heat. Add *half* of the pork to skillet. Stir-fry 4 minutes or till no longer pink. Remove from skillet using a slotted spoon; drain liquid if necessary. Repeat with remaining pork.

To serve, fill tortillas with pork and Chunky Guacamole. Top with *nonfat yogurt* and *sliced green onion*, if desired. Roll up. Serve with hot rice. Makes 6 servings.

Chunky Guacamole: Halve, seed, peel, and cube *2 avocados*. In a bowl combine avocados and 3 tablespoons *each* of *lemon juice* and *salsa.* Cover; chill up to 24 hours.

Nutrition information per serving: 621 cal., 19 g fat, 67 mg chol., 31 g pro., 84 g carbo.

$200 WINNER
Tonya Morrow, Boulder, Colo.

Cheese, Bacon, and Bread Bake

A SAVORY BREAD SHELL HOLDS A HEARTY MIXTURE OF CHEESES AND BACON FOR THIS WINNER—

1½ cups all-purpose flour
1½ teaspoons baking powder
½ teaspoon baking soda
½ teaspoon dried dillweed
½ teaspoon finely shredded lemon peel
1 8-ounce carton dairy sour cream
8 slices bacon
½ cup ricotta cheese
½ cup shredded Swiss cheese
1 3-ounce package cream cheese
3 tablespoons milk
2 teaspoons Dijon-style mustard
1 green onion, finely chopped
1 tablespoon snipped parsley

◆ Cheese Bacon and Bread Bake

In a medium bowl combine flour, baking powder, baking soda, dillweed, and peel. Stir in sour cream. On a floured surface, knead dough till smooth. Cover; set aside.

In a 10-inch oven-safe skillet cook bacon till crisp. Drain and crumble. Set aside.

Cool skillet; wipe with paper towels. Press dough onto the bottom and ½ inch up the sides of skillet; sprinkle with all but *2 tablespoons* crumbled bacon. Combine cheeses, milk, mustard, onion, and parsley; spread into skillet. Bake in a 400° oven 25 minutes or till golden. Cool slightly. Cut into wedges; sprinkle with reserved bacon. Serves 8.

Nutrition information per serving:
266 cal., 16 g fat, 41 mg chol., 10 g pro., 317 mg sodium.
$200 WINNER
Roxanne E. Chan, Albany, Calif.

Baked Eggs with Cheese And Basil Sauce

ANGELA'S RECIPE DRESSES UP BAKED EGGS FOR A SPECIAL BREAKFAST OR BRUNCH—

3 tablespoons margarine or butter
2 tablespoons all-purpose flour
¼ teaspoon salt
⅛ teaspoon pepper
¼ cup snipped fresh basil or
1 teaspoon dried basil, crushed
1 cup milk
Nonstick spray coating
4 eggs
Salt and pepper
¼ cup shredded mozzarella cheese (1 ounce)
Snipped fresh basil (optional)

◆ Baked Eggs with Cheese and Basil Sauce

In a small saucepan melt the margarine or butter. Stir in the flour, ¼ teaspoon salt, ⅛ teaspoon pepper, and dried basil, if using. Add milk all at once. Cook and stir over medium heat till thickened and bubbly. Cook and stir 1 minute more. Remove from heat. Stir

continued on page 22

continued from page 21

in fresh basil, if using. Spray four 8- to 10-ounce round baking dishes or 6-ounce custard cups with nonstick coating. To assemble, spoon about *2 tablespoons* basil sauce into *each* dish. Gently break an egg into the center of each dish; season with salt and pepper. Spoon remaining sauce atop eggs. Bake in a 350° oven for 18 to 20 minutes or till egg is set. Sprinkle with cheese. Let stand till cheese melts. Garnish with snipped basil, if desired. Serves 4.

Nutrition information per serving: 214 cal., 16 g fat, 221 mg chol., 11 g pro., 7 g carbo., 0 g fiber, 493 mg sodium. RDA: 19% calcium, 31% vit. A, 31% riboflavin.

$100 WINNER

Angela Bumbalo, East Amherst, N.Y.

Pollo Relleno (Stuffed Chicken)

EXPECT OOHS AND AAHS WHEN YOU SERVE THESE CHICKEN ROLLS, EACH WITH A CHEESE-STUFFED CHILI PEPPER INSIDE—

◆ Pollo Relleno (Stuffed Chicken)

6 medium skinless, boneless chicken breast halves (about 1½ pounds)
⅓ cup cornmeal
½ of a 1¼-ounce package taco seasoning mix (2 tablespoons)
1 beaten egg
1 4-ounce can whole green chili peppers, rinsed, seeded and cut in half lengthwise (6 pieces total)
2 ounces Monterey Jack cheese, cut into six 2 x ½-inch strips
2 tablespoons snipped cilantro or parsley
¼ teaspoon black pepper
¼ teaspoon crushed red pepper

1 8-ounce bottle green or red taco sauce
2 ounces cheddar or Monterey Jack cheese, shredded

Rinse chicken; pat dry. Place *each* breast half between 2 pieces of plastic wrap. Pound chicken with a meat mallet to ⅛-inch thickness. Remove plastic.

In a bowl combine cornmeal and seasoning mix. Place egg in another bowl. For each roll, place 1 chili pepper on a chicken piece. Place 1 cheese strip atop chili pepper near one edge. Sprinkle with *some* of the cilantro and peppers. Fold in sides of chicken. Roll up, starting from edge with cheese. Repeat to make 6 rolls. Dip rolls into egg, then into cornmeal mixture. Place rolls, seam down, in a shallow baking pan. Bake, uncovered, in a 375° oven for 25 to 30 minutes. Heat taco sauce. Sprinkle chicken with cheese; serve with sauce. Garnish with chopped tomato and cilantro, if desired. Serves 6.

Nutrition information per serving: 261 cal., 12 g fat, 113 mg chol., 29 g pro., 11 g carbo., 493 mg sodium. RDA: 19% calcium, 10% iron, 42% vit. A, 35% vit. C, 10% thiamine.

$100 WINNER

Lynne M. Waldron, Campbell, Calif.

February

A Taste of Romance

Prize Tested Recipes

A Taste of
Romance
From Historic Inns

By Julia Malloy

Pamper yourselves with a little Valentine romance. We've gathered a luscious sampling of dishes from three of the country's most charming historic inns for you to share at home. Savor these delicious recipes for brunch, dinner, or for a sweet, oh-so-sinful splurge. And, should our culinary tour whet your appetite for a more exotic escape, we'll tell you how to find a romantic inn in your area.

St. James Hotel's
Elegant Brunch

Overlooking the winding Mississippi River stands the proud St. James, an Italianate steamboat inn built in 1875. The riverboat era still lingers about the hotel in the form of ships' helms, tin ceilings, and saloon-style friezes. You may catch riverboat fever yourself after hopping aboard a sight-seeing cruise from the dock near the hotel. Later, spend the afternoon scrambling up the bluffs for a sweeping view of the historic Red Wing Valley or gear up for skiing at Welch Village.

Lemon Bread

BAKE ONE LARGE LOAF OR MAKE TWO SMALLER LOAVES SO YOU CAN FREEZE ONE—

½ cup butter
1 cup sugar
2 eggs
1⅔ cups all-purpose flour
¾ cup buttermilk
1½ teaspoons finely shredded lemon peel
½ teaspoon baking soda
¼ teaspoon salt
⅓ cup toasted chopped nuts, such as almonds,
walnuts, or pecans
3 tablespoons lemon juice

1 tablespoon sugar
Lemon slice twist (optional)
Lemon peel curl (optional)
Marigolds or other edible flowers
(optional)

Grease bottom and halfway up the sides of two 7½x3½x2-inch loaf pans or one 8x4x2-inch loaf pan.

In a large mixer bowl beat butter with an electric mixer on medium speed about 30 seconds or till softened. Add the 1 cup sugar; beat about 5 minutes or till light and fluffy. Add eggs, one at a time, beating till combined. Add flour, buttermilk, shredded lemon peel, baking soda, and salt; beat just till moistened. Stir in nuts.

Pour batter into prepared pan(s); spread evenly. Bake in 350° oven till a wooden toothpick inserted near center comes out clean, allowing 40 minutes for 7½x3½x2-inch loaves and 45 minutes for 8x4x2-inch loaf. Cover with foil, if necessary, the last 10 to 15 minutes to prevent overbrowning.

Cool in pan(s) on wire rack 10 minutes. Remove from pan(s). Place wire rack and loaves over waxed paper.

For glaze, in a small bowl combine the lemon juice and the 1 tablespoon sugar; stir till the sugar is dissolved. Spoon glaze over loaves. Cool loaves completely on the wire rack. If desired, garnish with lemon twists, lemon peel curls, and edible flowers. Makes 2 small loaves or 1 large loaf (16 servings).

Nutrition information per slice: 173 cal., 8 g fat, 43 mg chol., 3 g pro., 23 g carbo., 1 g fiber, 139 mg sodium. RDA: 10% thiamine, 10% riboflavin.

◆ Lemon Bread

◆ Ginger Marinated Fruit

◆ Spinach Souffle Quiche

◆ Strudel Sticks

Spinach Soufflé Quiche

THE FILLING PUFFS DURING BAKING SO SHAPE
THE PASTRY EDGES HIGH IN THE PAN—

Pastry for Single-Crust Pie or 1 folded
refrigerated unbaked piecrust
1 medium onion, chopped
6 slices bacon, chopped
8 eggs
½ cup dairy sour cream
½ cup half-and-half, light cream, or milk
¼ teaspoon salt
⅛ teaspoon white pepper
Dash ground nutmeg (optional)
3 cups lightly packed chopped fresh spinach
⅔ cup shredded mozzarella
cheese (2.5 ounces)
½ cup shredded Swiss cheese (2 ounces)
Plum tomato slices (optional)
Fresh oregano (optional)
Cracked black pepper (optional)

Prepare and roll out pastry. (Or, unfold refrigerated pastry and dust with flour according to the package directions.) Loosely wrap rolled pastry around a rolling pin. Unroll onto an ungreased 9-inch pie plate. Ease pastry into pie plate, being careful not to stretch pastry. Trim to ½ inch beyond edge of pie plate; fold under extra pastry. Make a high fluted edge all the way around. To flute, press forefinger of one hand against outside edge of dough, pushing between forefinger and thumb of the other hand pressing from inside of pie plate.

Line unpricked pastry shell with double thickness of foil. Bake in a 450° oven 8 minutes. Remove foil. Bake 4 to 5 minutes more or till pastry is set and dry.

Remove from oven; set on a wire rack. Reduce oven to 300°; allow 10 minutes for heat to adjust.

Meanwhile, in a skillet cook onion and bacon till onion is tender and bacon is crisp. Drain on paper towels.

In a medium mixing bowl beat eggs slightly with a fork. Stir in sour cream; half-and-half, cream, or milk; salt; pepper; and nutmeg, if desired. Stir in onion mixture, spinach, mozzarella cheese, and Swiss cheese. Pour into the baked pastry shell.

Bake in a 300° oven for 45 to 50 minutes or till a knife inserted near the center comes out clean. If necessary, cover edges with foil to prevent over-browning. Let stand for 10 minutes before serving. If desired, garnish with tomato slices, oregano, and pepper. Serves 6 to 8.

Pastry for Single-Crust Pie: In a mixing bowl combine 1¼ cups *all-purpose flour* and ¼ teaspoon *salt*. Cut in ⅓ cup *shortening* till pieces are the size of small peas. Sprinkle 1 tablespoon *cold water* over part of mixture. Gently toss with a fork. Push to the side of bowl. Repeat with 2 to 3 more tablespoons *cold water* till all is moistened. Form dough into a ball. On a lightly floured surface, flatten dough slightly with hands. Roll dough from center to edges, forming a circle about 12 inches in diameter.

Nutrition information per serving:
469 cal., 32 g fat, 321 mg chol, 21 g pro., 23 g carbo., 1 g fiber, 487 mg sodium. RDA: 36% calcium, 20% iron, 54% vit. A, 18% vit. C, 29% thiamine, 51% riboflavin, 15% niacin.

Strudel Sticks

FROZEN PUFF PASTRY MAKES THESE FLAKY
ROLLS SO-O-O EASY. YOU CAN MAKE YOUR
OWN FILLING OR OPT FOR CANNED PIE
FILLING—

1 17¼-ounce package frozen puff pastry
(2 sheets), thawed
1 egg
2 tablespoons water
1 recipe Apple-Almond Filling or Poppy
Seed and Cream Cheese Filling
Sliced almonds, poppy seed, coarse sugar,
or cinnamon sugar (optional)

Unfold puff pastry sheets. Cut into six 5x3-inch rectangles. Stir together egg and water; brush onto edges.

Place *2 teaspoons* apple filling or *1 tablespoon* poppy seed filling in the center of *each* pastry rectangle; spread to ½ inch from edges. Roll up from one of the long edges, jelly-roll style. Pinch edges and seams to seal. Brush with egg mixture. If desired, sprinkle with additional sliced almonds, poppy seed, coarse sugar, or cinnamon sugar.

Arrange sticks, seam side down, on a lightly greased baking sheet. Bake in a 350° oven for 20 to 25 minutes or till light brown. Serve warm or cool. Makes 12.

Apple-Almond Filling: In a saucepan combine 1½ cups peeled, cored, and chopped *cooking apples* (such as Rome Beauty or Granny Smith); ⅓ cup *sugar*; 3 tablespoons *apple juice*; and ⅛ teaspoon *ground cinnamon*. Bring to boiling; reduce heat. Cover; simmer 20 minutes or till apples are very tender and syrup is slightly thickened. Remove from heat; cool. Stir in ¼ cup sliced almonds.

Nutrition information per stick: 232 cal., 15 g fat, 18 mg chol., 3 g pro., 23 g carbo., 1 g fiber, 159 mg sodium.

Poppy Seed and Cream Cheese Filling: In a small mixing bowl stir together two 3-ounce packages softened *cream cheese,* ⅓ cup *sugar,* and 2 teaspoons *poppy seed.*

Nutrition information per stick: 259 cal., 18 g fat, 33 mg chol., 3 g pro., 21 g carbo., 0 g fiber, 201 mg sodium.

Ginger-Marinated Fruit

½ cup water
4 teaspoons finely shredded orange peel
1 tablespoon sugar
1 teaspoon grated gingerroot
½ cup orange liqueur or ½ cup orange juice plus 1 tablespoon sugar
⅓ cup orange juice
¼ cup honey
6 cups cut-up assorted fruit, such as kiwi fruit, apples, oranges, cantaloupe, honeydew melon, pineapple, pears, and red seedless grapes
Fresh mint (optional)

In a small saucepan combine water, peel, sugar, and gingerroot. Bring to boiling; reduce heat. Cover; simmer over low heat 5 minutes. Remove saucepan from heat. Stir in liqueur, orange juice, and honey. Cool thoroughly.

Pour cooled ginger mixture over fruit. Cover and marinate fruit for at least 1 hour or up to 12 hours in the refrigerator. To serve, spoon fruit and marinade into individual dishes. Garnish with fresh mint. Serves 8 to 10.

Nutrition per serving: 158 cal., 0 g fat, 0 mg chol., 1 g pro, 38 g carbo., 5 g fiber, 3 mg sodium. RDA: 158% vit. C, 10% thiamine.

♦ Hershey Bar Terrine

Hotel Hershey's
Fabulous Chocolate Desserts

Hotel Hershey flourishes amid acres of garden paths and golf courses. Built in 1933 by chocolate maven Milton Hershey, the hotel captures a vibrant Spanish flair with fountains, tiled floors, stained glass windows, and stucco walls. Besides golf and other outdoor activities, you can visit nearby Hersheypark, ZooAmerica, and yes, the whimsical chocolate-making exhibit, too. Gettysburg and Amish farm country lie just down the road.

Hershey Bar Terrine

LAYER STRIPS OF CHOCOLATE SHEET CAKE AND MARSHMALLOW FILLING IN HALF-ROUND OR RECTANGULAR LOAF PANS. YOU CAN PURCHASE HALF-ROUND LOAF PANS BY CALLING MAID OF SCANDINAVIA AT 800/328-6722. FOR A SIMPLE FAMILY-STYLE DESSERT, MAKE JUST THE WHIPPED CREAM FILLING. POUR IT INTO A BAKED PIECRUST AND FREEZE. TO SERVE, LET PIE STAND A FEW MINUTES, CUT INTO WEDGES, AND DRIZZLE EACH SERVING WITH CHOCOLATE SAUCE—

⅓ cup milk
2 cups tiny marshmallows
1½ 7-ounce bars milk chocolate (without almonds), broken up (10 ounces total)
1 cup whipping cream
1 recipe Chocolate Sheet Cake
1 recipe Creme de Cacao Syrup
1 recipe Bitter Chocolate Sauce
1 recipe Simple Cream (optional)
Whipped cream (optional)
Edible flowers, such as pansies or violas (optional)
Chocolate twigs* or curls (optional)

For filling, in a saucepan heat and stir milk over low heat till steaming. Add marshmallows; heat and stir over low heat till melted. Add candy bars; heat and stir till melted. Remove from heat. Cover surface with waxed paper; cool to room temperature.

Chill a medium mixing bowl and the beaters of an electric mixer. In the chilled bowl beat whipping cream on medium speed till soft peaks form. Gradually fold cooled chocolate mixture into whipped cream.

Line two 7½x3½x2-inch halfround or rectangular loaf pans with plastic wrap. Cut cake into strips to fit long sides and bottom of pans. Line pans with strips, cutting to fit. Do not line the ends of pans.

Sprinkle about *¼ cup* Creme de Cacao Syrup over the cake in each pan. Fill with cooled chocolate filling. Place additional strips of cake atop filling to cover. Moisten with remaining syrup. Cover and freeze overnight.

To serve, uncover and invert terrine onto a serving platter. Remove plastic wrap. Slice the terrine. Place 2 slices on each dessert plate. Spoon Bitter Chocolate Sauce onto plates. If desired, drizzle Simple Cream in parallel lines onto chocolate sauce; draw a knife through lines, alternating the direction, to create a web effect. Garnish plates with additional whipped cream, edible flowers, and chocolate twigs or curls. Serves 12 to 14.

Creme de Cacao Syrup: In a small saucepan combine ½ cup *water* and ⅓ cup *sugar*. Bring to boiling, stirring just till sugar is dissolved. Remove from heat; stir in ¼ cup *creme de cacao*. Cover and cool. Makes 1 cup.

Bitter Chocolate Sauce: In a small saucepan melt 2 squares (2 ounces) cut-up *unsweetened chocolate* over low heat; remove from heat. Stir in ⅓ to ½ cup *fudge ice-cream topping* to desired sweetness. (The chocolate may become stiff but will thin when cream is added.) Gradually stir in 1 cup *whipping cream*. Heat and stir over medium heat till bubbly. Cool quickly in ice water, stirring constantly. Stir in additional *whipping cream or milk* till sauce reaches drizzling consistency. Makes about 1½ cups.

Simple Cream: Stir enough *whipping cream* (2 to 3 tablespoons) into ½ cup *dairy sour cream* to make of drizzling consistency. Makes ⅔ cup.

Note: You can buy chocolate twigs at specialty food shops.

Nutrition information per serving: 444 cal., 27 g fat, 165 mg chol., 7 g pro., 47 g carbo., 0 g fiber, 78 mg sodium. RDA: 14% calcium, 11% iron, 30% vit. A, 21% riboflavin.

Chocolate Sheet Cake

CUT THIS STURDY CAKE INTO STRIPS FOR HERSHEY BAR TERRINE—

⅓ cup all-purpose flour
¼ cup unsweetened cocoa powder
6 egg yolks
2 tablespoons sugar
5 egg whites
¼ cup sugar

Grease and line a 15x10x1-inch baking pan with waxed paper; grease and flour paper. Set pan aside.

In a small mixing bowl stir together flour and cocoa powder; set aside.

In a medium mixing bowl combine egg yolks and the 2 tablespoons sugar; beat with an electric mixer on high speed about 5 minutes or till thick and light colored. Wash beaters.

In a large mixing bowl beat egg whites on medium speed till soft peaks form (tips curl). Gradually add the ¼ cup sugar, beating on high speed till stiff peaks form (tips stand straight).

Using a spatula, fold beaten whites into yolk mixture. Sprinkle flour mixture over egg mixture; gently fold till combined. Pour batter into prepared pan; spread evenly.

Bake in a 350° oven for 10 to 12 minutes or till cake springs back when touched and a wooden toothpick inserted near center comes out clean.

Cool cake in pan on wire racks for 5 minutes; use a knife to loosen edges and remove from pan. Cool completely on wire racks. Makes 1 sheet cake.

Midnight Chocolate Cake

TOP THIS CAKE WITH MARBLEIZED CHOCOLATE CURLS. OR, OVERLAP WEDGES OF MARZIPAN-CHOCOLATE TRIANGLES—

3 eggs
2¾ cups sugar
1 teaspoon vanilla
¾ cup cooking oil
1¾ cups water
1½ cups European-style cocoa powder or unsweetened cocoa powder
3 cups sifted cake flour*
¾ teaspoon baking powder
¼ teaspoon baking soda
1 recipe Sabayon Filling
1 recipe Chocolate Buttercream Frosting
1 recipe Marbleized Chocolate Curls, Dark Chocolate Curls, or Marzipan-Chocolate Triangles (optional)

Grease and flour a 10-inch springform pan; set aside. In a large mixing bowl combine eggs, sugar, and vanilla. Beat with an electric mixer on high speed 5 minutes or till light and fluffy. While mixer is running, slowly add oil to egg mixture, beating till combined.

Bring water to boiling; gradually add to cocoa powder, stirring till smooth. Beat chocolate mixture into egg mixture. Set aside.

In another mixing bowl stir together flour, baking powder, and baking soda. Add flour mixture to egg mixture, beat-

◆ Midnight Chocolate Cake

ing on low speed just till smooth, and scraping the sides of the bowl occasionally. Turn batter into the prepared pan.

Bake in a 325° oven about 1¾ hours or till a wooden toothpick inserted in the center comes out clean.

Cool in pan for 20 minutes; loosen sides and remove from pan. Cool completely. Clean and reassemble pan.

To assemble cake, use a serrated knife to trim top of cake to make it even and smooth. (Reserve trimmings for another dessert, such as trifle.) Holding the knife level and using a gentle sawing motion, split cake horizontally into thirds. Place first layer in the bottom of the springform pan.

Pour *half* of the Sabayon Filling on top. Place another cake layer over filling.
continued on page 30

continued from page 29

Pour in remaining filling; place the third layer of chocolate cake on top. Cover and chill in the refrigerator for 3 to 4 hours or till firm.

Run a hot knife or narrow metal spatula around the edge of the pan; invert the cake onto a serving platter.

To decorate, frost top and sides with Chocolate Buttercream Frosting. Using a decorating bag and tips, pipe frosting as desired. Decorate cake with Marbleized Chocolate Curls, Dark Chocolate Curls, or overlapping Marzipan-Chocolate Triangles. Chill till serving. Makes 16 servings.

Chocolate Buttercream Frosting: Melt ⅔ cup *semisweet chocolate* pieces; let cool. In a medium mixing bowl combine 2½ cups sifted *powdered sugar* and 1¼ cups softened *butter*; beat with an electric mixer on low to medium speed till creamy. Add ¾ cup *shortening*, beat till smooth. Stir in cooled chocolate and 1 teaspoon *vanilla*. Makes 4 cups.

Marbleized Chocolate Curls: Melt 12 ounces *vanilla-flavored candy coating*. To half the coating, stir in a small amount of *red paste food coloring* till desired shade. (Or, use 6 ounces each of *pink* and *white vanilla-flavored candy coating*, melt in separate pans). Line a baking sheet with plastic wrap. Spoon the 2 colors of coating in alternating mounds; spread ½ inch thick. Use a small spatula or knife to swirl candy slightly. Chill 20 minutes or till firm. When coating is firm, break it into large chunks. Place on a cutting board. Use a vegetable peeler or cheese slicer to scrape

◆ Chocolate Fruit Frangipane Tart

diagonally or straight across the coating to form curls. Chill till needed.

Dark Chocolate Curls: Make Marbleized Chocolate Curls as directed, except use 12 ounces *chocolate-flavored candy coating* instead of the vanilla-flavored candy coating.

Note: To substitute all-purpose flour for cake flour, for each cup of cake flour, substitute 1 cup *minus* 2 tablespoons (⅞ cup) sifted all-purpose flour.

Nutrition information per serving: 775 cal., 50 g fat, 172 mg chol., 7 g pro., 84 g carbo., 0 g fiber, 204 mg sodium.

Sabayon Filling

1 4-ounce package sweet baking chocolate
1 envelope unflavored gelatin
¼ cup cold water
5 egg yolks
½ cup dry sherry
⅓ cup granulated sugar
1⅓ cups whipping cream
1 teaspoon powdered sugar
½ teaspoon vanilla

Melt chocolate; let cool. In a small saucepan combine gelatin and cold water; let stand for 5 minutes.

Meanwhile, in a saucepan combine egg yolks, sherry, and granulated sugar. Cook and stir over medium heat till mixture thickens slightly and bubbles just around edge. Remove from heat. Transfer to a large mixing bowl.

Heat and stir gelatin mixture over low heat till gelatin is dissolved. Add melted chocolate and gelatin mixture to sherry mixture; beat with an electric mixer on low speed till combined. Cover and cool for 30 minutes.

In a medium mixing bowl combine whipping cream, powdered sugar, and vanilla; beat on low speed till soft peaks form. Fold whipped cream into egg mixture. Cover and chill about 1 hour or till mixture mounds when spooned, stirring gently occasionally. Makes 3½ cups.

Marzipan-Chocolate Triangles

½ of an 8-ounce can (scant ½ cup)
almond paste
2 tablespoons butter, softened
1½ to 1¾ cups sifted powdered sugar
1 teaspoon light corn syrup
6 ounces chocolate-flavored candy coating

For marzipan, crumble almond paste into a medium mixing bowl. Add butter; beat with an electric mixer on medium speed till combined. Add ½ cup of the powdered sugar and corn syrup; beat till combined. Shape the mixture into a ball. Knead in enough additional sifted powdered sugar (1 to 1¼ cups) to make a very stiff mixture.

Line a baking sheet with waxed paper; dust with powdered sugar. Place marzipan on waxed paper; flatten slightly. Top marzipan with another sheet of waxed paper. Use a rolling pin to spread marzipan into a 9½-inch round; remove top piece of paper. Trim to a 9-inch round.

Melt candy coating; spread evenly onto marzipan. If desired, use a cake comb to make concentric circles on top of chocolate. Cool till chocolate holds a cut edge. Cut into 16 wedges. Cover; chill till needed. Makes 16 pieces.

Chocolate-Fruit Frangipane Tart

1 recipe Frangipane Tart Pastry
1 8-ounce package semisweet chocolate
1 8-ounce can almond paste
¾ cup sugar
¾ cup butter
5 eggs
1 cup sifted cake flour or ¾ cup plus 2
tablespoons sifted all-purpose flour
⅓ cup apricot preserves
1 16-ounce can pear halves, drained
1 8¾-ounce can unpeeled apricot halves,
drained and sliced
½ cup fresh raspberries
Toasted sliced almonds (optional)
Whipped cream (optional)

On a lightly floured surface, flatten chilled dough with hands. Roll dough from center to edges, forming a 12-inch circle. Loosely wrap around rolling pin. Unroll onto an ungreased 10-inch fluted quiche pan* or springform pan with a removable bottom. Ease into pan, being careful not to stretch pastry. Trim pastry even with rim of quiche pan or 1½ inches up sides of springform pan. Set aside.

For filling, in a saucepan melt chocolate with ½ cup *water* over low heat, stirring constantly; cool.

In a medium mixing bowl combine almond paste and sugar; beat with an electric mixer on medium speed till crumbly. Add butter; beat till very creamy. Add eggs, one at a time, beating till combined. Add flour; beat on low speed just till combined. Add chocolate mixture; beat on low speed just till combined.

Pour filling into prepared pastry. Place on a baking sheet. Bake in a 350° oven 1¼ hours or till toothpick inserted near center comes out clean. Cool in pan on a wire rack. Cover and chill till serving.

For topping, in a saucepan combine apricot preserves and 1 tablespoon *water*; heat and stir till melted. If desired, strain through a sieve.

Place pear halves, flat side down, on a cutting board. Cutting from wide end to narrow end, slice pears lengthwise into ¼-inch thick slices, leaving attached at the narrow end.

Remove tart from pan. Arrange fanned pear halves and apricot slices on top, starting at the outside edge. Place raspberries in the center. Spoon preserves over fruit. Before serving, top with almonds. Serve with whipped cream, if desired. Serves 16.

Frangipane Tart Pastry: In a large mixing bowl beat ⅔ cup *butter* with an electric mixer on medium speed till softened. Add ⅔ cup *sugar*; beat till light and fluffy. Beat in 2 *egg yolks*, Add 2 cups sifted *cake flour* or 1¾ cups sifted *all-purpose flour*. Add ¼ teaspoon *baking powder*; beat till combined. Wrap dough in plastic wrap; chill till firm enough to roll.

Note: To order a 10-inch fluted quiche pan, call SCI Cuisine Internationale at 800/966-5489.

Nutrition information per serving: 475 cal., 26 g fat, 137 mg chol., 7 g pro., 58 g carbo., 1 g fiber, 194 mg sodium. RDA: 19% iron, 26% vit. A.

The Majestic's
Romantic Dinner

Just a two-block walk from the nearest cable-car stop, the Edwardian Majestic reigns over the hills of San Francisco. Built in 1902, the hotel eloquently captures the romance of the turn of the century. Take a moment to relax amid the tapestries, marble columns, antique furnishings, and chandeliers that give the hotel its old-world ambience. Then, catch that cable car to the Bay City's favorite sights: Golden Gate Bridge, Alcatraz, and Chinatown.

Goat Cheese on Shiitake Mushrooms

LOOK FOR FRESH SHIITAKE MUSHROOMS IN ORIENTAL MARKETS OR IN THE SPECIALTY PRODUCE SECTION OF YOUR SUPERMARKET—

2 large (2½- to 3-inch-diameter) fresh shiitake mushrooms
2 ounces log-style semisoft goat cheese (chévre), sliced crosswise into 2 rounds
1 recipe Cilantro Tomato Sauce or tomato sauce
1 tablespoon pesto
Fresh cilantro (optional)

Clean mushrooms; cut off stems and discard. In a lightly greased shallow baking pan arrange mushroom caps, stem

◆ Goat Cheese on Shiitake Mushrooms

sides up. Place a round of cheese on each cap. Bake, uncovered, in a 450° oven for 6 to 8 minutes or till mushrooms are tender and cheese is slightly soft.

To serve, pour warm Cilantro Tomato Sauce onto 2 appetizer plates; top with stuffed mushrooms. Top *each* cheese round with *1 teaspoon* pesto. If desired, garnish with cilantro. Makes 2 appetizer servings.

Nutrition information per serving: 160 cal., 10 g fat, 14 mg chol., 7 g pro., 12 g carbo., 1 g fiber, and 219 mg sodium. RDA: 10% vit. A, 39% vit. C, and 15% riboflavin.

Cilantro Tomato Sauce

SERVE WITH THE MUSHROOM APPETIZER OR SUBSTITUTE A PURCHASED TOMATO SAUCE—

½ pound Roma or regular tomatoes
3 sprigs fresh cilantro
1 shallot or green onion
1 clove garlic
1 teaspoon cornstarch
Dash salt
Dash pepper
Dash ground red pepper

In a blender container or food processor bowl combine tomatoes, cilantro, shallot or green onion, garlic, and cornstarch. Cover and blend or process till nearly smooth.

Place a sieve over a small saucepan; pour tomato mixture into sieve, pressing with the back of a spoon if necessary. Discard seeds, skin, and pulp left in sieve. In the saucepan cook and stir the tomato mixture till thickened and bubbly. Cook and stir for 2 minutes more. Season to taste with salt, pepper, and ground red pepper. Makes about ¾ cup.

To make ahead: Cook tomato sauce as directed; cover, cool, and chill. In a small saucepan cook and stir sauce over medium-low heat till heated through. (Or, micro-cook in 2-cup glass measure, uncovered, on 100% power or high about 2 minutes or till heated through, stirring once.) Continue as directed.

Nutrition information per ⅛ cup: 31 cal., 0 g fat, 0 mg chol., 1 g pro., 7 g carbo., 74 mg sodium, 1 g fiber. RDA: 30% vit. C

◆ Red Pepper Soup

Red Pepper Soup

THIS CREAMY ANISE-FLAVORED SOUP MAKES ENOUGH FOR FOUR SERVINGS. AFTER YOUR DINNER FOR TWO, COVER AND CHILL THE REMAINING SOUP FOR ANOTHER MEAL—

1 large red onion, coarsely chopped (1 cup)
3 cloves garlic
1 tablespoon butter or margarine
2 small red or green sweet peppers, coarsely chopped (1½ cups)
1 large tomato, chopped (¾ cup)
1 tablespoon ouzo or anise liqueur or ⅛ teaspoon aniseed, crushed
½ teaspoon dried herbes de Provence or fines herbes, crushed
½ teaspoon paprika
1½ cups chicken broth
¼ cup dairy sour cream
1 recipe Lemon Sour Cream
Lavender or other edible flowers (optional)

In a medium saucepan cook onion and garlic in hot butter or margarine till tender but not brown. Add peppers; cover and cook over medium heat for 8 to 10 minutes or till peppers are soft, stirring occasionally.

Add tomato, liqueur or aniseed, herbes de Provence or fines herbes, and paprika. Add broth. Bring to boiling; remove from heat. Cool slightly.

Pour the soup into a blender container or a food processor bowl (half at a time if necessary). Cover and blend or process till smooth; return to saucepan. Stir in the ¼ cup sour cream; heat through, but *do not boil.*

To serve, spoon into soup bowls. Top each serving with about *1 tablespoon* of Lemon Sour Cream; draw a knife through to swirl. If desired, garnish with lavender or other edible flowers. Makes 4 appetizer servings.

Lemon Sour Cream: In a small mixing bowl stir together ¼ cup *dairy sour cream,* ½ teaspoon finely shredded *lemon peel,* 1 teaspoon *lemon juice,* and a few drops *bottled hot pepper sauce.*

To make ahead: Prepare and blend soup, but do not add the sour cream. Transfer soup to a storage container. Cover, cool, and chill. Before serving, transfer soup to a saucepan; bring to boiling. Remove from heat; stir in the sour cream. Serve as directed.

Nutrition information per serving: 150 cal., 10 g fat, 20 mg chol., 4 g pro., 11 g carbo., 1 g fiber, 343 mg sodium. RDA: 53% vit. A, 127% vit. C, 13% niacin.

Salmon with Peppers and Black Bean Sauce

*½ of a medium yellow or green
sweet pepper*
*½ of a medium red sweet pepper or ⅓ cup
chopped, seeded tomato*
*2 6-ounce salmon fillets (about
1-inch thick)*
1 cup fresh spinach leaves
1 recipe Black Bean Sauce

Bake peppers, skin side up, on a foil-lined baking sheet in a 425° oven for 25 minutes or till charred. Place charred peppers in a paper bag. Close the bag; let stand for 20 to 30 minutes or till cool enough to handle.

Remove skin from salmon fillets, if present. Cut each salmon fillet into two 1½- to 2-inch-long strips. For each portion, roll up 1 strip jelly-roll style, rolling a second strip around first. Secure with string or a skewer. Sprinkle with salt and pepper.

Cook salmon rolls, covered, in a steamer basket over boiling water 10 minutes or till salmon flakes easily when tested with a fork. (Or, bake in a lightly greased shallow baking pan in a 450° oven for 12 to 15 minutes.)

When peppers are cool enough to handle, peel skin away from flesh. With a knife, cut off stems and scrape away seeds and ribs. Cut lengthwise into ¼-inch-wide strips.

Place spinach in a small mixing bowl; add enough *boiling water* to cover. Let stand for 1 minute; drain.

To serve, spoon about *½ cup* warm Black Bean Sauce onto each dinner plate. Remove string or skewer from salmon rolls; place a roll on each plate. Top salmon with spinach, yellow pepper, and red pepper or tomato. Makes 2 main-dish servings.

Nutrition information per serving with ½ cup saute: 351 cal., 7 g fat, 30 mg chol., 37 g pro., 36 g carbo., 3 g fiber, 273 mg sodium. RDA: 12% calcium, 36% iron, 46% vit. A, 125% vit. C, 22% thiamine, 19% riboflavin, 47% niacin.

Black Bean Sauce

TO TURN ANY LEFTOVER SAUCE INTO A SOUP, STIR IN A LITTLE MILK AND REHEAT—

*1 cup dry black beans or one 16-ounce
can black beans*
*½ of a medium onion, sliced and
separated into rings*
2 cloves garlic, minced
1 bay leaf
1 teaspoon ground cumin
1 teaspoon dried thyme, crushed
¼ teaspoon salt
Dash ground red pepper
*Whipping cream, fish stock, or water
(optional)*

Rinse dry black beans. (Or, drain and rinse canned black beans). For dry black beans, in medium saucepan combine beans and enough water to cover. Bring to boiling; reduce heat. Simmer for 2 minutes. Remove from heat. Cover; let stand 1 hour. (Or, soak beans in water overnight in a covered pan.) Drain beans and rinse. In same pan combine beans and enough water to cover. Bring to boiling; reduce heat. Cover and simmer 2½ to 3 hours or till tender; drain and rinse.

Return cooked or canned beans to saucepan. Add onion rings, garlic, bay leaf, cumin, thyme, salt, red pepper, and 1 cup *water*. Bring to boiling; reduce heat. Cover and simmer till onion is tender. Remove bay leaf.

Pour bean mixture into a blender container or food processor bowl. Cover; blend or process till smooth. If needed, blend in a little whipping cream, fish stock, or water till the sauce reaches desired consistency. Season to taste with *salt* and *pepper*. If necessary, return to saucepan to heat through. Makes about 3½ cups.

Nutrition information per ½ cup: 180 cal., 1 g fat, 0 mg chol., 12 g pro., 33 g carbo., 170 mg sodium, 2 g fiber. RDA: 23% iron, 15% thiamine.

◆ Salmon with Peppers and Black Bean Sauce
◆ Walnut Bread

Walnut Bread

YOU'LL LOVE THIS CHEWY BREAD FOR DINNER OR TOASTED FOR BREAKFAST—

1½ cups warm water (115° to 120°)
¼ cup honey
3 tablespoons walnut oil or olive oil
1 package active dry yeast
1½ teaspoons salt
3¼ to 3¾ cups bread flour or all-purpose flour
1¼ cups all-purpose flour
1½ cups toasted chopped walnuts

In a large mixing bowl stir together water, honey, oil, yeast, and salt. Let stand for 10 minutes.

Add *1 cup* of the bread flour or all-purpose flour and the 1¼ cups all-purpose flour. Beat with an electric mixer on low speed 30 seconds, scraping sides of bowl constantly. Beat on high speed 3 minutes more. Using a spoon, stir in walnuts. Stir in as much of the remaining bread flour or all-purpose flour as you can.

Turn the dough out onto a lightly floured surface. Knead in enough remaining bread flour or all-purpose flour to make a moderately stiff dough that is smooth and elastic (8 to 10 minutes total). Shape into a ball. Place dough in a lightly greased bowl; turn once to grease surface. Cover and let rise in a warm place till double (about 1½ hours).

Punch dough down. Turn out onto a lightly floured surface. Divide in half. Let rest 10 minutes. Shape each portion into a round loaf. Arrange loaves, 4 inches apart, on a lightly greased baking sheet; flatten slightly to 8-inch rounds. With a sharp knife, make crisscross slashes in tops of loaves. Cover; let rise in a warm place till nearly double (about 1 hour).

Bake in a 400° oven for 30 to 35 minutes or till bread sounds hollow when tapped, covering with foil after 15 minutes, if necessary, to prevent overbrowning. Remove from baking sheet. Cool on a wire rack. Makes 2 loaves (32 servings).

To make ahead: Wrap bread in freezer wrap; seal, label, and freeze for up to 6 months. Thaw overnight in the refrigerator.

Nutrition information per slice: 123 cal., 5 g fat, 0 mg chol., 3 g pro., 17 g carbo., 1 g fiber, 101 mg sodium. RDA: 16% thiamine, 10% niacin.

Passion Fruit Meringue Tarts

PASSION FRUIT ARE HARD-SHELLED PURPLE OR PINK FRUIT WITH YELLOWISH-GREEN PULP AND EDIBLE SEEDS INSIDE. FOR THE TART FILLING, YOU CAN PUREE THE PULP AND SEEDS IN YOUR BLENDER OR BUY FROZEN PUREE FROM A SPECIALTY FOOD SHOP. OR, YOU CAN USE PUREED FRESH OR CANNED MANGO, OR PASSION FRUIT JUICE OR MANGO JUICE—

1 recipe Rich Tart Pastry
½ cup sugar
½ cup fresh or frozen passion fruit puree or mango puree, or ½ cup passion fruit juice or mango juice
⅓ cup unsalted butter
3 eggs
2 egg whites
½ teaspoon vanilla
⅛ teaspoon cream of tartar
¼ cup sugar

The Majestic's
Romantic Desserts

Put a little passion in your Valentine's dessert with Passion Fruit Meringue Tarts. Or, bake another sparkling idea—Génoise Cake in Strawberry Champagne Sauce.

Divide the chilled tart pastry into 4 portions. On a lightly floured surface, roll each portion to ⅛-inch thickness. Cut each portion into a 5-inch round. Fit the pastry rounds into 4 ungreased 4-inch tart pans with removable bottoms. Line pastry in tart pans with a double thickness of foil to prevent over browning. Place pans on a baking sheet.

Bake pastry in a 350° oven for 15 minutes; remove foil. Bake for 8 to 10 minutes more or till golden. Cool in pans on a wire rack.

For filling, in a saucepan combine the ½ cup sugar, fruit puree or juice, and butter. Bring just to boiling over medium heat, stirring occasionally.

In a medium mixing bowl beat the whole eggs slightly with a fork. Slowly add fruit mixture, beating continuously. Return to saucepan; heat and stir over medium heat about 5 minutes or until slightly thickened, but do not boil. Strain, if using puree; transfer to a nonmetal bowl. Cover and chill till mixture is cool.

continued on page 39

◆ Passion Fruit Meringue Tarts

continued from page 36

For meringue, let the egg whites stand at room temperature for 30 minutes. In a large mixing bowl beat the egg whites with an electric mixer on high speed till foamy. Add the vanilla and the cream of tartar, beat till soft peaks form (tips curl). Gradually add the ¼ cup sugar, beating on high speed till stiff peaks form (tips should stand straight).

To assemble, remove pastry shells from pans. Place shells on a baking sheet. Spoon passion fruit filling into shells. Spoon meringue into a pastry bag fitted with a large star tip. Pipe meringue onto the top of each tart in a woven pattern. (Or, spoon meringue atop each tart.) Bake in a 350° oven for 10 to 12 minutes or till meringue edges are golden. Makes 4 tarts.

Rich Tart Pastry (food processor): In a food processor bowl combine ⅓ cup cut-up *unsalted or regular butter*, 1¼ cups *all-purpose flour or cake flour*, ¼ cup *sugar*, and a dash *salt*. Cover and process till mixture resembles coarse cornmeal. Add 1 *egg yolk* and 1 tablespoon *milk*; process just till mixture begins to form a ball. If dough seems dry, add another tablespoon *milk*. Form dough into a ball. Wrap the dough in plastic wrap and chill about 1 hour.

Rich Tart Pastry (hand mix): In a medium mixing bowl stir together 1¼ cups *all-purpose flour* or *cake flour*, ¼ cup *sugar*, and a dash *salt*. Cut in ⅓ cup cut-up *unsalted* or *regular butter* till pieces are the size of small peas. Combine 1 *egg yolk* and 1 tablespoon *milk*; stir into flour mixture. If necessary, add another tablespoon *milk* if dough seems dry. Form dough into a ball. Wrap in plastic wrap and chill for 1 hour.

Nutrition information per tart: 684 cal., 36 g fat, 297 mg chol., 12 g pro., 81 g carbo., 1 g fiber, 118 mg sodium. RDA: 17% iron, 57% vit. A, 29% thiamine, 40% riboflavin, 19% niacin.

Génoise Cake in Strawberry Champagne Sauce

OLIVE OIL IS THE SECRET TO THIS DELICATELY FLAVORED SPONGE CAKE—

6 eggs
Granulated sugar
Cake flour or all-purpose flour
¾ cup granulated sugar
⅓ cup extra light or pure olive oil (not extra-virgin olive oil)
1⅓ cups sifted cake flour or 1¼ cups sifted all-purpose flour
Powdered sugar
Strawberry Champagne Sauce
Fresh strawberries (optional)
Fresh mint (optional)

Let eggs stand at room temperature for 30 minutes. Grease bottom and sides of a 9-inch springform pan. Line bottom with parchment paper; grease paper. Sprinkle with sugar; dust with flour. Set pan aside.

In a large mixer bowl combine eggs and the ¾ cup granulated sugar. Beat with an electric mixer on high speed for 15 minutes. After 15 minutes, with mixer running, gradually add oil in a thin, steady stream (this will take 1½ to 2 minutes). Turn off mixer immediately after all of the oil has been added.

Sift flour over egg mixture; fold till no lumps remain. Pour into the prepared pan; place on a baking sheet.

Bake in a 350° oven about 35 minutes or till cake springs back when touched. Cool cake completely in the pan on a wire rack.

To assemble, remove cake from pan; remove and discard parchment paper. Sift powdered sugar atop cake. Cut cake into wedges. Place wedges on plates or in shallow bowls; sprinkle rims with powdered sugar, if desired. Pour sauce around the cake wedges. Garnish with strawberries and mint, if desired. Makes 10 to 12 servings.

Strawberry Champagne Sauce: In a blender container combine 5 cups *strawberries*, ¾ cup *champagne* or *sparkling white wine*, and ¼ cup *sugar*. (Or, for food processor, combine half of the ingredients at a time.) Cover and blend or process till smooth. Cover and chill for several hours or overnight. Makes 4 cups.

Nutrition information per serving: 271 cal., 11 g fat, 128 mg chol., 6 g pro., 37 g carbo., 3 g fiber, 39 mg sodium. RDA: 10% iron, 84% vit. C, 14% thiamine, 22% riboflavin.

◆ Génoise Cake in Strawberry Champagne Sauce

Prize Tested Recipes

Cumin Chicken with Hot-Citrus Salsa

IN A HURRY? THIS SPECIAL CHICKEN ENTRÉE, WITH AN ORANGE-AND-JALAPEÑO-PEPPER SALSA, COOKS IN ABOUT 6 MINUTES—

4 dried tomato halves
½ cup boiling water
1 medium orange
2 teaspoon snipped fresh cilantro or parsley
1 teaspoon grated gingerroot
½ teaspoon finely chopped jalapeño pepper
2 skinless, boneless chicken breast halves
(about ½ pound)
¾ teaspoon ground cumin
⅛ teaspoon salt
⅛ teaspoon pepper
1 tablespoon cooking oil
Hot cooked rice

For salsa, in a small bowl combine tomatoes and boiling water. Let stand 10 minutes. Drain; chop tomatoes. Peel and chop orange, reserving about *2 teaspoons* of the juice.

In a medium bowl combine tomatoes, chopped orange, reserved juice, cilantro or parsley, gingerroot, and jalapeño pepper. Set aside.

Rinse chicken; pat dry with paper towels. Place each breast half between 2 pieces of plastic wrap. Pound chicken with a meat mallet to ¼-inch thickness. Remove plastic. Combine cumin, salt, and pepper; rub on both sides of chicken.

◆ Cumin Chicken with Hot Citrus Salsa

In a skillet cook chicken in hot oil over medium heat about 3 minutes per side or till chicken is no longer pink. To serve, spoon salsa atop chicken. Serve with hot cooked rice. Makes 2 servings.

Nutrition information per serving: 351 cal., 11 g fat, 59 mg chol., 26 g pro., 37 g carbo., 2 g fiber, 210 mg sodium. RDA: 19% iron, 48% vit. A, 39% vit. C.

$200 WINNER

Anne Fredrick, New Hartford, N.Y.

Raspberry Truffle Cake

DON'T WORRY IF THIS NEARLY FLOURLESS CAKE SEEMS SOFT AFTER BAKING—IT FIRMS UPON CHILLING—

16 ounces (16 squares) semisweet chocolate, cut up
½ cup butter
1 tablespoon sugar
1½ teaspoon all-purpose flour
1 teaspoon raspberry liqueur (optional)
4 eggs, separated
1½-ounce jar seedless raspberry jam (1 cup)
Whipped cream
Fresh raspberries (optional)

In a large heavy saucepan combine chocolate and butter. Cook and stir over low heat till chocolate melts. Remove from heat. Stir in sugar, flour, and liqueur. Using a spoon, beat in egg yolks, one at a time, till combined. Set aside.

In a bowl beat egg whites with an electric mixer on high speed till stiff peaks form. Fold into chocolate mixture. Pour into a greased 8-inch springform pan. Bake in a 350° oven 25 to 30 minutes or till edges puff. Cool on a rack for 30 minutes. Remove sides of pan; cool completely. Chill, covered, for 4 to 24 hours.

◆ Peanut-Butter-Chocolate Shortbread

◆ Raspberry Truffle Cake

Heat jam just till melted. To serve, drizzle jam on each dessert plate; top with cake slice, whipped cream, and fresh raspberries, if desired. Serves 12.

Nutrition information per serving: 459 cal., 29 g fat, 119 mg chol., 53 g carbo.

$200 WINNER

Melissa Luebkemann, Tallahassee, Fla.

Peanut-Butter-Chocolate Shortbread

A CREAMY PEANUT BUTTER FILLING HIDES INSIDE TWO RICH CHOCOLATE SHORTBREAD LAYERS—

1½ cups margarine or butter
1½ cups sifted powdered sugar
1½ teaspoon vanilla
2 cups all-purpose flour
⅔ cup unsweetened cocoa powder
2 tablespoons cornstarch
¼ teaspoon salt
1 cup finely chopped unsalted peanuts
1 cup creamy peanut butter
1 cup sifted powdered sugar
½ cup semisweet chocolate pieces
16 milk chocolate kisses
16 whole unsalted peanuts

continued on page 42

February

◆ Spicy Beef and Cabbage Roll-ups

continued from page 41

In a large mixer bowl beat margarine or butter till softened; beat in the 1½ cups powdered sugar and the vanilla. Add flour, cocoa powder, cornstarch, and salt; beat till smooth. Stir in chopped peanuts. Reserve 1⅓ cups of cocoa mixture. Spread remaining cocoa mixture in the bottom and up the sides of an ungreased 10-inch tart pan with a removable bottom, or in the bottom and one inch up the sides of a 10-inch springform pan.

In a bowl stir together peanut butter and the 1 cup powdered sugar; stir in chocolate pieces. Carefully spread peanut butter mixture over crust. Spoon remaining cocoa mixture over peanut butter mixture; carefully spread to cover. Using the tines of a fork, score shortbread into 16 wedges. Bake in 325° oven about 50 minutes or till surface looks slightly dry. Cool slightly. While warm,

place a chocolate kiss on each wedge.

When kiss softens (about 10 minutes), top with a peanut. Score wedges again. Cool completely. Remove sides of pan; cut into wedges. Makes 16 servings.

Nutrition information per serving: 494 cal., 35 g fat, 48 mg chol., 10 g pro., 41 g carbo., 1 g fiber, 117 mg sodium. RDA: 11% iron, 21% vit A, 13% thiamine, 11% riboflavin.

$100 WINNER

Anne Evans, Southborough, Mass

Spicy Beef and Cabbage Roll-ups

THESE BUNDLES OF BEEF, RICE, AND VEGETABLES SHOWCASE FLAVORS FROM THE ORIENT—

6 ounce boneless beef sirloin steak
2 teaspoons cornstarch
2 teaspoon soy sauce
1½ teaspoons sugar

4 large Chinese cabbage leaves
or cabbage leaves
4 teaspoons hoisin sauce or catsup
1½ teaspoons bean sauce or
bean paste (optional)
1 teaspoon ground ginger
1 teaspoon rice wine or dry sherry
1 teaspoon sesame oil
¼ to ½ teaspoon ground red pepper clove
garlic, minced
2 tablespoons cooking oil
1 large carrot, shredded
½ of a medium red or green sweet pepper,
cut into julienne strips
3 green onions, thinly sliced
¾ cup quick-cooking rice, cooked

Trim fat from beef; partially freeze. Thinly slice into julienne strips. In a bowl combine beef, cornstarch, soy sauce, and ½ *teaspoon* of the sugar; set aside. Place cabbage leaves in boiling water for 1 minute; drain. In a small bowl combine remaining sugar, hoisin sauce, bean sauce, ginger, wine, sesame oil, and ground red pepper.

In a wok or large skillet, stir-fry garlic in hot oil over medium-high heat for 15 seconds. Add beef mixture; stir-fry for 2 to 3 minutes or till done. Stir in hoisin mixture, carrot, sweet pepper, and onions. Cook and stir 1 minute more. To serve, place *one-fourth* of the cooked rice on each cabbage leaf; top with *one-fourth* of the beef mixture. Fold in sides of leaves; roll up. Serve at once. Makes 2 servings.

Nutrition information per serving: 494 cal., 24 g fat, 57 mg chol., 24 g pro., 44 g carbo., 3 g fiber, 580 mg sodium. RDA: 10% calcium, 27% iron, 163% vit. A, 85% vit. C.

$100 WINNER

Katherine St. Pierre, Dumfries, Va.

March

Feel Good Food

Prize Tested Recipes

Feel Good Food

By Kristi Fuller R.D.

A Burger to Smile About

Bring a smile to your heart with this low-fat meal. Serve it in less time than it takes to go out for fast food.

Cajun Chicken Burgers

Use just a portion of the garbanzo beans (also called chick-peas) for these mildly spiced burgers. Use the remaining beans in Quick Potato-Bean Salad—

¼ cup garbanzo beans,
drained and mashed
1 beaten egg
2 tablespoons fine dry bread crumbs
1 to 1½ teaspoons Cajun seasoning*
¼ teaspoon salt
1 pound ground raw chicken
4 kaiser rolls or hamburger buns, split
Lettuce leaves (optional)
Tomato slices (optional)
Chili sauce, taco sauce, or catsup

In a medium mixing bowl combine mashed garbanzo beans, egg, bread crumbs, Cajun seasoning, and salt. Add ground chicken and mix well. Shape into four ¾-inch-thick patties.

Preheat oven broiler. Place patties on an ungreased, unheated rack of a broiler pan. Broil 3 to 4 inches from heat for 6 minutes. Turn patties; broil 6 to 8 minutes more or till patties are no longer pink in centers. Toast rolls under broiler, if desired.

Serve patties in buns with lettuce leaves and tomato slices, if desired. Serve with chili sauce, taco sauce, or catsup. Makes 4 servings.

*Note: To make your own Cajun seasoning, in a container with a tight fitting lid combine 2 tablespoons *salt*, 1 tablespoon *ground red pepper*, 1 teaspoon *ground white pepper*, 1 teaspoon *garlic powder*, and 1 teaspoon *ground black pepper*. Store, covered, at room temperature. Makes about ¼ cup.

Nutrition information per serving: 303 cal., 10 g fat, 108 mg chol., 23 g pro., 30 g carbo., 2 g fiber, 696 mg sodium. RDA: 11% calcium, 20% iron, 11% vit. A, 16% vit. C, 27% thiamine, 29% riboflavin, 40% niacin.

◆ Cajun Chicken Burger
◆ Quick Potato-Bean Salad

20 Lighthearted Ways to Lighten Up and Feel Good

EATING RIGHT ISN'T THE ONLY KEY TO FEELING GOOD. THERE ARE LOTS OF THINGS YOU CAN DO TO IMPROVE YOUR HEALTH AND YOUR FEELING OF SELF-ESTEEM. FOR STARTERS, HERE ARE TWENTY EASY IDEAS. DON'T TRY THEM ALL AT ONCE. INSTEAD, MAKE ONE CHANGE AT A TIME AND LET IT BECOME A HABIT. THEN TRY ANOTHER ONE.

1. Put yourself in an upbeat mood. Begin your day by saying, "This will be a great day," and it probably will be.

2. Read the comic strips in your newspaper every day and laugh along with characters such as **Cathy** as she ponders yet another new diet.

3. Find the happy medium. Whether it's food, alcohol, exercise, or work, too much of a good thing, even vitamins, can compromise your health.

4. Play softball, ride the teeter-totter, or hop on a swing alongside your kids. Relive your childhood to recapture that lively spirit. (You'll burn some calories, too.)

5. Take a vigorous hike—or at least a walk—with your family. The exercise will do your heart good, but you'll also gain special time together.

6. Enjoy life's pleasures in little bites. If you love ice cream, have a small scoop on occasion.

7. Reach a healthy weight—one that's realistic and right for you. Super-thin is out.

8. Think and eat slowly. When you feel full, stop eating. You may be surprised at how small amounts can fill you up.

9. Take a low-fat cooking class, or buy and use a cookbook with healthful recipes.

10. Go meatless once in a while. Vegetables are cholesterol free and low in fat and calories.

11. Ban the word DIET from your vocabulary. Focus on eating healthfully and improving your eating habits.

12. Forgive yourself. If you splurged on several chocolate bars today, forget it. Do better tomorrow.

13. Celebrate your accomplishments. Have you lost weight or finished a big project? Buy yourself a small gift that you've wanted (but don't let it be food).

14. Enjoy life. Whether it's a favorite food, something you like to do, or time spent with friends, enjoy!

15. De-stress your life. Get organized, confront your problems and don't worry about the things you can't change. Continual stress takes its toll mentally and physically.

16. Begin a hobby. (For instance, learn to cook a fabulous low-fat dinner.) Creating something with your hands gives you a feeling of pride and accomplishment.

17. Make a list of all the nice things people have said about you or things you've done that make you proud. Refer to that list when you're feeling blue.

18. Smile.

19. Laugh. Laughter and fun have been linked to prolonging life and fighting illness. A philosopher once said, "Laughter is the sun that drives winter from the human face." So, let it shine.

20. Slow down. Take time to smell the roses, hug your kids, or take a vacation.

♦ Baked Sole and Corn Salsa
♦ Southwest Couscous

Quick Potato-Bean Salad

A BOTTLED DRESSING AND CANNED SLICED POTATOES MAKE THIS COLORFUL SALAD A CINCH TO PREPARE—

1 16-ounce can sliced potatoes, rinsed
and drained
1¼ cups garbanzo beans, rinsed
and drained (about ¾ of a 15-ounce can)
½ cup sliced celery
¼ cup sliced pitted ripe olives
2 tablespoons sliced green onion
¼ cup reduced-calorie Italian
salad dressing
• • •
½ cup cherry tomatoes, quartered
2 yellow or green sweet peppers, halved
and seeded, or lettuce leaves (optional)

In a large bowl combine the potatoes, garbanzo beans, celery, olives, and onion. Add the salad dressing; toss gently to coat the vegetables. Cover and chill at least 2 hours.

At serving time, stir in cherry tomatoes. Spoon salad mixture into the sweet pepper halves or serve on lettuce leaves, if desired. Makes 4 side dish servings.

Nutrition information per serving: 164 cal., 4 g fat, 1 mg chol., 5 g pro., 30 g carbo., 6 g fiber, 677 mg sodium. RDA: 21% iron, 174% vit. C, 10% thiamine, 11% niacin.

Good for Your Heart and Sole

Just what the doctor ordered— quick cooking, heart-friendly fish with a two-ingredient salsa. Faster yet, the zippy pasta-like side dish cooks in only five minutes.

Baked Sole and Corn Salsa

FOR AN EASY DESSERT, BAKE THE CHOCOLATE CHIP PEARS (SEE RECIPE, PAGE 54) ALONGSIDE THE FISH, IF YOU LIKE—

1 pound fresh or frozen fish fillets
(such as sole, flounder, or haddock),
cut ½ inch thick
Nonstick spray coating
1½ cups salsa
½ cup frozen whole kernel corn
Fresh cilantro or parsley sprigs (optional)

Thaw fish, if frozen. Spray a 2-quart rectangular baking dish with nonstick coating. Arrange fish in baking dish, turning under any thin edges.

In a small bowl combine salsa and the frozen corn. Spoon over fish. Bake, uncovered, in a 375° oven about 20 to 25 minutes or till fish flakes easily with a fork.

Using a slotted spatula, transfer fish and salsa topping to dinner plates. Garnish with cilantro, if desired. Makes 4 servings.

Microwave directions: Arrange fish in a microwave-safe 2-quart rectangular baking dish, turning under any thin edges. Combine salsa and corn; spoon mixture over fish. Cover dish with heavy clear plastic wrap, venting one corner. Micro-cook on 100% power (high) for 6 to 9 minutes or till fish flakes easily with a fork, rotating dish a half-turn after 3 minutes. Serve as directed. This recipe is not recommended for low-wattage ovens.

Nutrition information per serving: 130 cal., 3 g fat, 45 mg chol., 20 g pro., 9 g carbo., 0 g fiber, 398 mg sodium. RDA: 17% vit. A, 49% vit. C, 13% thiamine, and 21% niacin.

Southwest Couscous

COUSCOUS, A TINY GRAIN-LIKE PASTA, COOKS UP FAST. TO SERVE THIS SIDE DISH WITH THE SOLE, START IT ABOUT 10 MINUTES BEFORE THE FISH IS DONE—

1 cup lower-sodium chicken broth
¼ cup sliced green onion
1 4-ounce can diced green chili peppers
¼ teaspoon ground turmeric
⅛ teaspoon pepper
⅔ cup Couscous

High-Fiber Breakfast Choices

A FEEL-GOOD DAY BEGINS WITH BREAKFAST. CEREALS, WHOLE-GRAIN BREADS, AND FRUITS PLAY STARRING ROLES AT BREAKFAST TIME AND ARE ONE OF THE EASIEST WAYS TO GET MORE FIBER INTO YOUR DIET. THIS CHART WILL HELP YOU MAKE HIGH-FIBER BREAKFAST CHOICES TO GET YOUR DAY STARTED OFF RIGHT.

FOODS   Grams of fiber (approx.)

Cereals (about 1 ounce)
Whole bran cereal (⅓ cup) 8.5
100% bran cereal (½ cup) 8.4
Bite-size bran squares
   cereal (½ cup) 4.6
Sweetened oat and bran
   cereal (½ cup) 4.3
40% bran flakes (¾ cup) 4.0
Granola, homemade (¼ cup) 3.0
Raisin bran (½ cup) 3.0
Oatmeal (¾ cup cooked) 3.0
Shredded wheat (1 biscuit) 2.2
Wheat flakes (1 cup) 2.0
Corn grits (1 cup) 0.6

Bread Items
Oat-bran and raisin muffin 5.2
Whole wheat bread
   (1 slice, toasted) 2.7
Bran muffin, homemade 2.5
Oat-bran English muffin (1 whole) ... 2.0
Plain English muffin,
   toasted (1 whole) 1.5

Plain bagel (1 whole) 1.2
Waffles, frozen (1 4-inch square) 0.9
White bread (1 slice, toasted) 0.6

Fruit
Figs (3) 6.0
Dried prunes (½ cup) 5.5
Dried apricots (½ cup) 5.1
Pear (1 medium) 3.9
Raisins (½ cup) 3.8
Orange (1 medium) 3.1
Dates (5) 3.0
Apple (1 medium, with skin) 3.0
Raspberries (½ cup) 2.8
Peach (1 medium) 2.4
Strawberries (½ cup) 1.9
Banana (1 medium) 1.8
Cantaloupe, cubed (1 cup) 1.3
Orange juice (½ cup) 1.0
Grapefruit (½ of a medium) 1.0

Sources include USDA handbook and other government sources.

In a small saucepan combine broth, green onion, undrained chili peppers, turmeric, and pepper. Bring to boiling; remove from heat.

Stir in couscous. Let stand, covered, for 5 minutes. Fluff with a fork before serving. Makes 4 side-dish servings.

Nutrition information per serving: 128 cal., 1 g fat, 0 mg chol., 5 g pro., 25 g carbo, 5 g fiber, 98 mg sodium. RDA: 17% vit. C.

Curry Up! Soup's On!

Abracadabra! Magically turn a package of lentil pilaf mix into a quick and hearty vegetable soup. A whole grain bread and a salad complete your magic act.

Lentil and Bean Curry Soup

KEEP THESE INGREDIENTS ON HAND SO WHEN YOU'RE SHORT ON TIME, YOU CAN STIR THIS SOUP TOGETHER FAST. LOOK FOR LENTIL PILAF MIX NEXT TO RICE IN YOUR SUPERMARKET—

1 14½-ounce can lower-sodium chicken broth (about 1¾ cups)
1 6.75-ounce package lentil pilaf mix
1 tablespoon curry powder
½ cup frozen peas
1 6-ounce can lower-sodium tomatoes, cut up
1 5-ounce can great northern beans, rinsed and drained

In a 4-quart Dutch oven combine the broth, dry lentil mix and seasonings from packet, curry powder, and 3 cups *water*. Bring mixture to boiling; reduce heat. Simmer, covered, for 30 minutes.

◆ Lentil and Bean Curry Soup
◆ Peppered Whole Wheat Loaf
◆ Red Leaf Salad with Honey Vinaigrette

Add peas; cook, uncovered, 5 to 10 minutes more or till lentils are tender. Stir in undrained tomatoes and beans; heat through. Makes 4 main-dish servings.

Nutrition information per serving: 388 cal., 2 g fat, 0 mg chol., 19 g pro., 68 g carbo., 1 g fiber, 1,157 mg sodium. RDA: 13% calcium, 32% iron, 31% vit. C, 32% thiamine, 35% niacin.

Peppered Whole Wheat Loaf

WHILE THE LENTIL SOUP IS SIMMERING, PREPARE THIS BUBBLE-SHAPED BREAD LOAF TO SERVE WITH IT—

1 tablespoon milk
1 teaspoon butter-flavored sprinkles
¼ teaspoon seasoned pepper or herb pepper
Nonstick spray coating
1 9-ounce package (8) refrigerated multigrain biscuits

For topping, in a small bowl combine milk and butter-flavored sprinkles. Stir till dissolved. Stir in the seasoned pepper.

Spray a 7½x3½x2-inch loaf pan or an 8x1½-inch round baking pan with nonstick coating. Cut each biscuit in half crosswise (do not cut biscuits in half if using a round baking pan). Place the biscuit halves randomly into the prepared loaf pan, pressing the biscuits together slightly (If using a round baking pan, place one whole biscuit in the center and the remaining biscuits around the outside edge of the pan. Do not press together.) Brush biscuits with the pepper-and-milk mixture.

Bake biscuits in a 350° oven for 20 to 25 minutes or till brown. Serve warm. Makes 1 loaf (6 servings).

Nutrition information per serving: 109 cal., 3 g fat, 0 mg chol., 3 g pro., 20 g carbo., 0 g fiber, 309 mg sodium.

With kitchen shears or a knife, cut refrigerated biscuits in half crosswise, then randomly place them in the loaf pan, pressing the pieces together slightly.

Red Leaf Salad with Honey Vinaigrette

FIX THIS SIMPLE SALAD WHILE LENTIL AND BEAN CURRY SOUP SIMMERS—

4 cups torn red leaf lettuce
1 orange, peeled, sliced crosswise, and halved
1 apple, cut into bite-size pieces
½ of a small cucumber, thinly diced
2 tablespoons toasted chopped walnuts or dry roasted peanuts
1 recipe Honey Vinaigrette

Divide lettuce among 4 salad plates. Top *each* serving with the orange slices, apple, cucumber, and nuts. Serve with vinaigrette. Makes 4 side-dish servings.

Honey Vinaigrette: In a screw-top jar combine ¼ cup *white wine vinegar*, 3 tablespoons *honey*, and 2 teaspoons *stone-ground mustard*. Cover; shake to mix well. Makes about ½ cup.

Nutrition information per serving: 124 cal., 3 g fat, 0 mg chol., 2 g pro., 26 g carbo., 3 g fiber, 41 mg sodium. RDA: 14% vit. A, 51% vit. C.

● Ham and Asparagus Pasta

Pasta for Losers

Weight whittlers won't spin their diet wheels with this dinner. Topped with a low-fat tomato sauce and oodles of veggies, the pasta is just right for any weight-loss plan. Add your favorite tossed salad for a quick meal.

Ham and Asparagus Pasta

SERVE THIS NUTRITION GOLD MINE WITH A MIXED SALAD AND HONEY AND SPICE FRUIT COMPOTE—

¾ pound fresh asparagus spears or one 10-ounce package frozen cut asparagus
2 14½-ounce cans lower-sodium stewed tomatoes, cut up
1 tablespoon dried parsley flakes
½ teaspoon dried basil, crushed
½ teaspoon dried oregano, crushed
⅛ teaspoon ground red pepper (optional)
1 cup evaporated skim milk
10 ounces multicolored pasta, such as wagon wheel or cork crew
6 ounces lean fully cooked ham, cut into bite-size strips
1 small red or green sweet pepper, cut into thin strips
Grated Parmesan cheese (optional)

Snap off and discard the woody bases from the fresh asparagus, if using. Bias-slice asparagus into 1-inch pieces. (Or, thaw and drain the frozen cut asparagus.) Set aside.

For sauce, in a medium saucepan combine stewed tomatoes, parsley, basil, oregano, and ground red pepper, if desired. Bring to boiling. Simmer the sauce, uncovered, about 15 minutes or till reduced to 2½ cups, stirring occasionally. Add the evaporated milk all at once, stirring constantly. Heat mixture through; do not boil.

Meanwhile, prepare pasta according to package directions except add the asparagus, ham, and sweet pepper to the boiling water during the last 4 minutes of cooking time. Drain pasta and vegetables.

To serve, place pasta mixture on a serving platter. Spoon the sauce over the pasta. Serve with Parmesan cheese, if desired. Serve at once. Makes 4 or 5 main-dish servings.

Nutrition information per serving: 465 cal., 4 g fat, 15 mg chol., 27 g pro., 81 g carbo., 0 g fiber, 643 mg sodium. RDA: 32% calcium, 31% iron, 47% vit. A, 113% vit. C, 89% thiamine, 44% riboflavin, 45% niacin.

◆ Tangy Baked Chicken
◆ Lemon Pepper Potatoes

sides of chicken breasts with some of the dressing mixture.

Place chicken in a shallow baking dish or pan. Bake, uncovered, in a 375° oven for 20 to 25 minutes or till chicken is no longer pink. In a small saucepan heat any remaining dressing mixture just to boiling; serve with chicken. Makes 4 servings.

Nutrition information per serving: 145 cal., 4 g fat, 59 mg chol., 22 g pro., 4 g carbo., 0 g fiber, 280 mg sodium. RDA: 58% niacin.

Lemon-Pepper Potatoes

TO SERVE THIS SIDE DISH WITH TANGY BAKED CHICKEN, START BAKING THE POTATOES ABOUT 20 MINUTES BEFORE ADDING THE CHICKEN TO THE OVEN—

1½-ounce envelope butter-flavored mix
1 tablespoon snipped fresh chives or sliced green onion tops
½ teaspoon lemon-pepper seasoning
¼ cup water
1 pound small red potatoes (6 to 8), cut into 1-inch pieces

In an 11x7x1½-inch baking pan combine the butter-flavored mix, chives, and lemon-pepper seasoning. Stir in the water. Add the potatoes; toss to coat well.

Bake, uncovered, in 375° oven for 45 to 50 minutes or till potatoes are tender and beginning to brown, stirring twice. Makes 4 side-dish servings.

Nutrition information per serving: 125 cal., 0 g fat, 0 mg chol., 2 g pro., 28 g carbo., 2 g fiber, and 314 mg sodium RDA: 29% vit. C, 13% thiamine, and 12% niacin.

The Right Stuff

For a healthful entrée, super chicken saves the day. Baked in a 1-2-3 sauce and served with vegetables and "buttery" (but low-in-fat) potatoes, this chicken dinner won't blow your fat or food budget.

Tangy Baked Chicken

FOR A TASTY BRUSH-ON SAUCE, MIX TOGETHER A BOTTLED SALAD DRESSING AND A FEW ON-HAND INGREDIENTS—

4 4-ounce boneless, skinless chicken breast halves
⅛ teaspoon ground red pepper
¼ teaspoon black pepper
¼ cup reduced-calorie Catalina salad dressing
1 tablespoon Dijon-style mustard
1 teaspoon Worcestershire sauce

Rinse chicken; pat dry with paper towels. Combine the red and black peppers; rub over chicken breasts. Combine the salad dressing, mustard, and Worcestershire sauce. Lightly brush both

◆ Hot Turkey Salad
◆ Mustard French Bread

Salad Smart

Give this salad an A in nutrition. Broiled lean turkey joins fresh fruits and vegetables to make the grade. Drizzle with a honey-orange dressing and serve with toasty, cheesy bread.

Hot Turkey Salad

SAVE SOME OF THE HONEY-ORANGE DRESSING—A MIXTURE OF MAYONNAISE, ORANGE JUICE, AND HONEY—TO BRUSH ONTO THE TURKEY WHILE IT BROILS—

½ cup reduced-calorie mayonnaise or
salad dressing
¼ cup orange juice
1 tablespoon honey
½ teaspoon dry mustard
Nonstick spray coating

2 turkey breast tenderloin steaks
(½ pound total)
4 cups purchased mixed salad greens
(available in supermarket produce
departments or salad bars)
1 cup seedless red grapes
6 to 8 large strawberries
1 kiwi fruit, peeled and sliced
1 yellow summer squash or small
cucumber, sliced and halved

For dressing, in a small bowl stir together mayonnaise or salad dressing, orange juice, honey, and mustard till combined. Remove *1 tablespoon* of the dressing. Cover and chill the remaining dressing.

Preheat broiler. Spray an unheated rack of a broiler pan with nonstick coating. Place the turkey on the rack; brush the 1 tablespoon dressing over the turkey. Broil 4 inches from heat about 10 minutes or till no longer pink, turning once.

Meanwhile, arrange greens on 2 dinner plates. Arrange grapes, strawberries, kiwi fruit, and squash or cucumber atop greens. Slice each turkey tenderloin crosswise into 5 or 6 pieces; place atop greens. Serve salad with the remaining chilled dressing. Store any leftover dressing in refrigerator for up to 1 week. Makes 2 servings.

Nutrition information per serving with 3 tablespoons dressing: 364 cal., 14 g fat, 50 mg chol., 25 g pro., 36 g carbo., 5 g fiber, 281 mg sodium. RDA: 16% calcium, 22% iron, 29% vit. A.

Don't Desert Desserts

These feel-good desserts bring pure pleasure, not pangs of guilt. All are under 250 calories and have less than 5 grams of fat per serving—so you can have your cake and eat it too!

Mustard French Bread

BROIL THIS BREAD ALONGSIDE THE TURKEY FOR HOT TURKEY SALAD. JUST POP IT IN THE OVEN DURING THE LAST HALF OF THE TURKEY'S BROILING TIME—

1 tablespoon reduced-calorie mayonnaise
or salad dressing
1 teaspoon Dijon-style mustard
2 slices French bread
1 tablespoon snipped parsley
2 teaspoons grated Parmesan cheese

In a small mixing bowl combine the mayonnaise or salad dressing and the mustard. Spread onto one side of the bread slices. Sprinkle tops with parsley and Parmesan cheese.

Arrange bread slices, coated side up, on the unheated rack of a broiler pan. Broil about 5 inches from heat for 3 to 4 minutes or till golden. Serve warm. Makes 2 servings.

Nutrition information per serving: 136 cal., 5 g fat, 2 mg chol., 4 g pro., 18 g carbo., 1 g fiber, 350 mg sodium.

◆ Peppermint Angel Cake with Chocolate Sauce

Peppermint Angel Cake with Fat-Free Chocolate Sauce

OUR TASTE PANEL THOUGHT THIS MINTY DESSERT WENT WELL WITH ZESTY CAJUN CHICKEN BURGERS—

1 16-ounce package angel cake mix
10 striped, round peppermint candies,
finely crushed (1/3 cup)
1 recipe Fat-Free Chocolate Sauce
Striped round peppermint candies, crushed
(optional)

Prepare cake mix batter according to package directions. Gently fold in the crushed candies. Pour batter evenly into an *ungreased* 10-inch tube pan. Gently cut through cake batter with a knife or narrow metal spatula (to remove any air pockets).

Bake cake according to package directions. Immediately invert baked cake in the pan and cool completely. Using a narrow spatula, loosen the sides of the cake from the pan. Remove the cake from pan.

continued on page 54

continued from page 53

To serve, slice the cake and spoon warm chocolate sauce over each serving. Sprinkle with additional crushed peppermint candies, if desired. Chill any remaining sauce; rewarm before serving on leftover cake. Serves 12.

Fat-Free Chocolate Sauce: In a small saucepan stir together ¾ cup *sugar*, ⅓ cup *unsweetened cocoa powder*, and 4 teaspoons *cornstarch*. Add ½ cup *evaporated skim milk*. Cook and stir constantly over medium heat till sauce is thickened and bubbly. Cook and stir for 2 minutes more. Remove from heat. Stir in 1 teaspoon *vanilla*. Cool sauce slightly.

Nutrition information per serving: 228 cal., 0 g fat, 0 mg chol., 6 g pro., 51 g carbo., 0 g fiber, 156 mg sodium. RDA: 14% calcium, 13% riboflavin.

Honey and Spice Fruit Compote

SERVED WARM OR COLD, THIS FRUIT DESSERT IS DELICIOUS. BUT DON'T FORGET THE TOPPING—IT'S WONDERFUL TOO!

1 8-ounce package mixed dried fruit
½ cup light or dark raisins
2 cups water
3 tablespoons orange juice or apple juice
1 tablespoon honey
1 teaspoon cornstarch
½ teaspoon apple-pie spice
1 recipe Sour Cream Topping
Ground nutmeg (optional)
Lemon peel curl (optional)

Cut up any large pieces of dried fruit. In a medium saucepan combine dried fruit, raisins, and water. Heat to boiling; reduce heat. Cook, covered, about 12 minutes or till fruit is just tender, stirring once or twice.

Stir together the juice, honey, cornstarch, and apple-pie spice. Stir into fruit mixture. Cook and stir till thickened and bubbly. Cook and stir for 1 minute more. Serve immediately or chill till serving time.

To serve, top each serving with Sour Cream Topping. Sprinkle with nutmeg and garnish with lemon peel curl, if desired. Makes 6 servings.

Sour Cream Topping: In a small bowl combine ⅔ cup *lower-fat dairy sour cream*, ¼ cup packed *brown sugar*, and 1 teaspoon *vanilla*. Cover; chill till serving time.

Microwave directions: In a 1½-quart microwave-safe round casserole combine the mixed dried fruit, raisins, and water. Micro-cook fruit mixture, covered, on 100% power (high) for 4 to 6 minutes (low-wattage ovens: 8 to 10 minutes) or till fruit is just tender, stirring once or twice. Stir together the juice, honey, cornstarch, and apple-pie spice. Stir into fruit mixture. Micro-cook, uncovered, on high for 4 to 6 minutes (low-wattage ovens: 6 to 8 minutes) or till thickened and bubbly, stirring every 30 seconds. Cook for 1 minute more. Serve immediately or chill till serving time. Serve as directed.

Nutrition information per serving: 204 cal., 1 g fat, 2 mg chol., 2 g pro., 50 g carbo., 1 g fiber, 29 mg sodium. RDA: 14% vit. A, 12% iron.

Chocolate Chip Pears

THIS IS A FUN WAY TO ENJOY A CLASSIC COMBINATION—BAKED PEARS WITH CHOCOLATE. SIMPLY SPRINKLE THE WARM PEARS WITH MINI CHOCOLATE CHIPS—

4 medium pears
2 tablespoons lemon or lime juice
2 teaspoons vanilla
½ teaspoon ground cinnamon
¼ cup miniature semisweet chocolate pieces

Core pears from bottom end, leaving stem intact. Using a vegetable peeler, peel strips at ½-inch intervals, starting at the top. If necessary, cut a thin slice from bottoms to help pears stand upright.

Place pears on sides in a 2-quart square baking dish. Stir together lemon or lime juice, vanilla, and cinnamon. Brush onto pears. Pour any extra lemon juice mixture over pears.

Bake, covered, in a 375° oven for 30 to 35 minutes or till pears are tender. Uncover; spoon any extra liquid over pears.

To serve, place warm pears upright on dessert plates. Holding each pear by the stem and tipping slightly, sprinkle the sides of each pear with 1 tablespoon chocolate pieces, turning the pear as you sprinkle. Serve warm. Makes 4 servings.

Microwave directions: Prepare pears and juice mixture as directed. Brush pears with juice mixture. Place pears in a microwave-safe baking dish. Pour extra juice mixture over pears. Cover with waxed paper. Micro-cook, covered, on 100% power (high) for 4 to 6 minutes (low-wattage ovens: 8 to 10 minutes) or till tender, turning pears over halfway through cooking. Serve as directed.

Nutrition information per serving: 157 cal., 4 g fat, 0 mg chol., 1 g pro., 34 g carbo., 4 g fiber, 2 mg sodium.

Hold the pear in one hand and use a vegetable peeler to peel off pear skin in long vertical strips at about ½-inch intervals.

◆ Honey and Spice Fruit Compote
◆ Chocolate Chip Pears
◆ Gingerbread with Luscious Lemon Cream

Gingerbread with Luscious Lemon Cream

ADD CRYSTALLIZED GINGER, FOUND WITH THE SPICES IN MOST SUPERMARKETS, TO A GINGERBREAD MIX FOR DOUBLE-GINGER ZIP. IF YOU LIKE, TRY THE BLUEBERRY SAUCE, TOO—

1 15-ounce package whole wheat or
regular gingerbread mix
1⅓ cups skim milk
2 egg whites or ¼ cup frozen egg product,
thawed
2 tablespoons finely chopped crystallized
ginger
Nonstick spray coating
12 bear-shaped graham snack cookies
(optional)

In a bowl combine gingerbread mix, milk, and egg whites or egg product. Beat with an electric mixer on low to medium speed till combined. Beat on high speed for 3 minutes more. Stir in *1 tablespoon* of the crystallized ginger.

Spray a 9x9x2-inch baking pan with nonstick coating. Pour batter into pan, spreading evenly. Bake according to package directions. Cool slightly on a rack. To serve, cut cake into squares. Top each serving with some of the lemon cream mixture or blueberry sauce, remaining crystallized ginger, and a cookie, if desired. Makes 12 servings.

Luscious Lemon Cream: In a small bowl stir together ⅓ cup *lower-fat lemon yogurt* and ⅓ cup *lower-fat dairy sour cream*. Cover and chill till serving time. Makes ⅔ cup.

Blueberry Sauce: In a small saucepan stir together 3 tablespoons *sugar* and 1½ teaspoons *cornstarch*. Stir in 3 tablespoons *water* till well mixed. Add 1 cup fresh or frozen *blueberries*. Cook and stir blueberry mixture till thickened and bubbly. Cook and stir for 2 minutes more. Remove sauce from heat. Slightly crush some of the blueberries with the back of a spoon. Serve sauce warm. Makes ¾ cup.

Nutrition information per serving with lemon cream: 150 cal., 4 g fat, 2 mg chol., 4 g pro., 26 g carbo., 2 g fiber, 34 mg sodium. RDA: 10% calcium.

Orange-Spice Pot Roast

LONG, SLOW COOKING TENDERIZES TOUGHER CUTS OF MEAT. BEEF CHUCK IS A GOOD CHOICE HERE BECAUSE IT'S LEANER AND CHEAPER THAN SOME OTHER POT ROASTS—

1 2- to 2½-pound boneless beef chuck
arm pot roast
Nonstick spray coating
3 inches stick cinnamon, broken
6 whole cloves
3 medium sweet potatoes (about 1 pound)
or one 18-ounce can vacuum-packed sweet
potatoes, drained
1 pound turnips or rutabagas, peeled and
cut into 1-inch pieces
1 medium onion, sliced and separated
into rings
3 tablespoons quick-cooking tapioca
⅓ cup frozen orange juice concentrate,
thawed
¼ cup light corn syrup
½ teaspoon salt

Trim as much fat as possible from the pot roast. If necessary, cut the roast to fit into a 3½- or 4-quart electric slow crockery cooker. Spray a cold large skillet with nonstick coating. Heat skillet over medium-high heat. Brown roast on all sides in the hot skillet.

Place cinnamon and cloves on a double thickness of 100%-cotton cheesecloth. Gather up the edges and tie with a string. Place the spices in the crockery cooker.

If using fresh sweet potatoes, wash, peel, and cut off woody portions and ends. Cut sweet potatoes into quarters. Place fresh sweet potatoes, turnips, and onion in crockery cooker. (If using canned sweet potatoes, do not add them to cooker at this point.) Sprinkle tapioca over vegetables.

In a small bowl stir together orange juice concentrate, corn syrup, and salt; pour over vegetables in cooker. Place roast atop vegetables. (If using canned sweet potatoes, place them atop roast.) Cover; cook on the low-heat setting for 10 to 12 hours or on the high-heat setting for 5 to 6 hours.

Transfer roast and vegetables to a serving platter. Skim fat from cooking juices (if necessary). Discard spice bag. Pass the cooking juices with the meat. Makes 6 servings.

Nutrition information per serving: 336 cal., 9 g fat, 96 mg chol., 33 g pro., 31 g carbo., 285 mg sodium. RDA: 29% iron, 161% vit. A, 72% vit. C.

◆ Orange-Spice Pot Roast

Beef and Spice——It's Nice!

Fix and forget this meal—well, almost. The savory aroma won't let you forget about

the slow-simmering, citrus-flavored roast while it cooks in your crockery cooker.

Prize Tested Recipes

Make-Ahead Chimichangas

USE LEFTOVER BEEF POT ROAST, PORK ROAST, OR CHICKEN IN THIS MEXICAN FAVORITE—

1 pound cooked beef, pork, or chicken
1 16-ounce jar salsa
1 16-ounce can refried beans
1 4-ounce can diced green chili peppers
1 1½-ounce envelope burrito or taco seasoning mix
16 8-inch flour tortillas
16 ounces Monterey Jack or cheddar cheese, cut into sixteen 5x½-inch sticks
Cooking oil (optional)

Using two forks, shred cooked meat or chicken (should have about 3 cups). In a large skillet combine meat or chicken, salsa, beans, *undrained* chili peppers, and seasoning mix. Cook and stir over medium heat till heated through.

In another skillet heat tortillas, one at a time, over medium-low heat about 30 seconds per side. For each chimichanga, place ⅓ cup meat mixture atop a tortilla, near one edge. Top with a cheese stick. Fold in sides; roll up, starting with cheese side. Place in freezer containers. Seal, label, and freeze for up to 6 months.

To prepare, wrap frozen chimichangas individually in foil. Bake in a 350° oven about 50 minutes or till heated through. (Or, thaw chimichangas in refrigerator overnight. Bake about 30 minutes.) Remove foil. Bake 10 minutes more or

◆ Make-Ahead Chimichangas

till tortilla is crisp and brown. Or, heat about ¼-inch depth of oil in a skillet. Cook desired number of frozen chimichangas, uncovered, in hot oil about 25 minutes (about 18 minutes if thawed) over medium-low heat or till golden, turning often. Serve with *salsa*, *dairy sour cream*, and hot cooked *rice*, if desired. Makes 16 servings.

Nutrition information per baked chimichanga: 372 cal., 22 g fat, 51 mg chol., 19 g pro., 27 g carbo., 2 g fiber, 730 mg sodium. RDA. 36% calcium, 20% iron, 19% vit. A, 33% vit. C.
$200 WINNER
Chloe Ellenburg, Kapoa, Hawaii

Carrot and Spice Bran Muffins

START YOUR MORNING OFF RIGHT WITH THESE DELICIOUS BRAN MUFFINS—

2 cups whole bran cereal
1¼ cups milk
⅓ cup cooking oil
2 beaten eggs
1½ cups shredded carrot
½ cup coconut
½ cup raisins
1¼ cups all-purpose flour
½ cup packed brown sugar
¼ cup granulated sugar
2 teaspoons baking powder
1 teaspoon baking soda
1½ teaspoons ground cinnamon
½ teaspoon salt

In a large mixing bowl combine cereal, milk, oil, and eggs. Let stand 10 minutes. Stir in carrot, coconut, and raisins.

In another bowl combine flour, sugars, baking powder, baking soda, cinnamon, and salt. Add cereal mixture to flour mixture. Stir just till combined. Grease muffin cups or line with paper bake cups; fill each ⅔ full. Bake in a 375° oven for 15 to 20 minutes or till toothpick inserted near center comes out clean. Serve warm. Makes 18 muffins.

Nutrition information per muffin: 166 cal., 6 g fat, 25 mg chol., 4 g pro., 28 g carbo., 4 g fiber, 270 mg sodium. RDA: 16% iron, 50% vit A, 10% vit. C.

$200 WINNER

Debora MacNeil, Indian Wells, Calif.

◆ Carrot and Spice Bran Muffins

Pear, Ginger, and Walnut Muffins

GRATED FRESH GINGERROOT COMBINED WITH PEARS MAKES THIS MUFFIN A WINNER—

2 cups all-purpose flour
¾ cup sugar
2 teaspoons baking soda
½ teaspoon salt
¼ teaspoon ground cardamom or
1 teaspoon ground cinnamon
2 beaten eggs
½ cup cooking oil
2 tablespoons milk
1 teaspoon grated gingerroot
2 medium pears, peeled, cored, and finely chopped (1½ cups)
¾ cup chopped walnuts
½ cup raisins

continued on page 60

◆ Pear, Ginger, and Walnut Muffins

◆Great Greek Pitas

continued from page 59
In a large mixing bowl combine flour, sugar, baking soda, salt, and cardamom or cinnamon. Make a well in the center. Combine eggs, oil, milk, and gingerroot; add all at once to flour mixture. Stir just till moistened (batter will be thick). Fold in pears, walnuts, and raisins. Lightly grease muffin cups or line with paper bake cups; fill each ¾ full. Bake in a 350° oven for 20 to 25 minutes or till toothpick inserted near center comes out clean. Remove from cups; serve warm. Makes 18 muffins.

Nutrition information per muffin: 194 cal., 10 g fat, 24 mg chol., 3 g pro., 25 g carbo., 1 g fiber, 160 mg sodium. RDA: 12% thiamine.

$100 WINNER

Linda McPhee, Newport, Oreg.

Great Greek Pitas

MAKE THE SAUCE AND MARINATE THE PORK A DAY AHEAD. TO SERVE THIS QUICK MEAL, STIR-FRY THE FLAVORFUL MEAT, SPOON INTO PITA ROUNDS, AND TOP WITH THE CUCUMBER-YOGURT SAUCE—

1¼ pound lean boneless pork
¼ cup olive oil or cooking oil
¼ cup lemon juice
2 tablespoons prepared mustard
2 cloves garlic, minced

1½ teaspoons dried oregano, crushed
1 teaspoon dried thyme, crushed
1 8-ounce carton plain yogurt
1 small cucumber, peeled and chopped
(about 1 cup)
1 teaspoon dried dillweed
¼ teaspoon seasoned salt
3 pita bread rounds, halved
Thinly sliced onion (optional)
Thinly sliced tomato (optional)

Trim fat from pork. Partially freeze pork. Thinly slice into bite-size strips. Place pork in a plastic bag set into a deep bowl.

For marinade, combine oil, lemon juice, mustard, garlic, oregano, and thyme; mix well. Pour over pork in bag. Seal bag. Marinate in the refrigerator 6 to 24 hours, turning bag occasionally. For sauce, in a small mixing bowl stir together yogurt, cucumber, dillweed, and seasoned salt. Cover and chill for 6 to 24 hours.

At serving time, drain pork. Discard marinade. In a large skillet, stir-fry pork, *half* at a time, over medium-high heat about 3 minutes or till pork is no longer pink. Using a slotted spoon, remove pork from skillet; spoon into pita halves. Stir cucumber sauce; spoon atop meat. If desired, garnish with onion and tomato. Makes 6 servings.

Nutrition information per serving: 241 cal., 12 g fat, 45 mg chol., 18 g pro., 15 g carbo., 1 g fiber, 286 mg sodium. RDA: 13% calcium, 10% iron, 49% thiamine, 19% riboflavin.

$100 WINNER

Tracie Ann Cork, Elgin, Ill.

April

The New
American Classics

Prize Tested Recipes

The New American Classics

BY LISA HOLDERNESS

Move over meatloaf. Step aside apple pie.

Our food tastes have changed, so it's time to make room on our dinner plates for the "must have" recipes of the '90s. Today, we want bigger, better flavors, which often come from the ethnic ingredients now found in our markets. We want lighter, more healthful foods, too, but won't give up an occasional splurge. Yes, we want it all—and it's all here in our collection of New American Classics.

California Pizzas

THESE MINI PIZZAS BURST WITH COLOR AND FLAVOR. CHOOSE FROM EITHER A ROASTED SWEET PEPPER AND CHÈVRE TOPPING OR A SHRIMP-PESTO TOPPING—

1 16-ounce loaf frozen whole wheat or white bread dough
2 tablespoons yellow cornmeal
3 tablespoons olive oil or cooking oil
¼ teaspoon crushed red pepper or ⅛ teaspoon ground red pepper
3 medium red, yellow, and/or green sweet peppers, roasted* and cut into 1-inch-wide strips, or one 12-ounce jar roasted sweet peppers, drained and cut into 1-inch-wide strips
1 large tomato, chopped

1 medium onion, cut into very thin wedges and separated into strips
6 ounces semi-soft goat cheese (chèvre) or feta cheese, crumbled or cut up (1½ cups)
10 black olives, such as kalamata or ripe olives, pitted and quartered lengthwise
3 to 4 tablespoons fresh oregano leaves or snipped fresh basil**
1½ cups shredded mozzarella

Thaw bread dough. On a lightly floured surface, divide dough into 8 pieces. Cover; let dough rest for 10 minutes. Roll each piece into a 6-inch circle. Grease 2 extra-large baking sheets; sprinkle with cornmeal. Transfer dough circles to baking sheets. Bake in a 450° oven for 5 minutes. Remove baking sheets from the oven; place on wire racks to cool.

Meanwhile, stir together olive oil or cooking oil and crushed or ground red pepper. Brush the mixture onto the crusts. Top with roasted peppers, tomato, onion, goat cheese or feta cheese, and olives. Sprinkle pizzas with the shredded mozzarella cheese.

Bake in a 450° oven for 5 to 7 minutes more or till mozzarella is golden brown and crusts are crisp. Before serving, sprinkle with fresh oregano or basil. Makes 8 main-dish servings.

*To roast peppers: Halve peppers; remove stems, membranes, and seeds. Place peppers, cut side down, on a foil-lined baking sheet. Bake in a 425° oven for 20 to 25 minutes or till skin is bubbly and brown. Place in a clean brown paper bag; seal and let stand for 20 to 30 minutes or till cool enough to handle. Pull off skin gently and slowly, using a paring knife.

**Note: You can substitute 1 tablespoon dried oregano or basil, crushed, for the fresh options. Instead of sprinkling it atop the pizzas, stir the dried herb into the olive oil mixture before brushing it onto the crusts.

California Pizzas

Thanks to California chef Wolfgang Puck, small, crisp pizzas with inventive toppings are the rage nationwide. To fix your own mini pizzas, start with frozen bread dough. Forget the tomato sauce, and use a vegetable or shrimp topping.

Nutrition information per serving: 323 cal., 16 g fat, 22 mg chol., 15 g pro., 32 g carbo., 7 g fiber, 462 mg sodium. RDA: 27% calcium, 19% iron, 33% vit. A, 86% vit. C, 24% thiamine, 23% riboflavin, 18% niacin.

Shrimp and Pesto Pizzas: Roll out and prebake the crusts on baking sheets as directed for California Pizzas. For the topping, omit olive oil, crushed red pepper, roasted peppers, goat cheese or feta cheese, chopped tomato, and olives. Instead, peel and devein 1½ pounds fresh medium *shrimp.* Cook shrimp in boiling water for 1 to 3 minutes or till pink. Drain; halve shrimp lengthwise. Spread each crust with 1 tablespoon *pesto.* Thinly slice 8 *Italian-style (plum) tomatoes.* Top crusts with tomato slices, cooked shrimp, and onions. Sprinkle each with mozzarella cheese. Bake as directed. Before serving, sprinkle with fresh oregano leaves.

Nutrition information per serving: 369 cal., 17 g fat, 101 mg chol., 23 g pro., 34 g carbo., 7 g fiber, 554 mg sodium. RDA: 25% calcium, 25% iron, 10% vit. A, 20% vit. C, 24% thiamine, 18% riboflavin, 26% niacin.

◆ California Pizzas

Vegetable Lasagna

SERVE A MEATLESS PASTA MEAL, FEATUR-
ING LOWER-FAT CHEESES FOR YOUR NEXT
GATHERING. THIS FOUR-CHEESE LASAGNA
CAN BE PREPARED UP TO 2 DAYS IN
ADVANCE—

*8 ounces lasagna noodles
(10 or 11 noodles)
2 beaten eggs
2 cups lower-fat cream-style cottage cheese
2 cups lower-fat ricotta cheese
1½ teaspoon dried Italian seasoning,
crushed
2 cups sliced fresh mushrooms
1 small onion, chopped (⅓ cup)
1 clove garlic, minced
2 tablespoons margarine or butter
2 tablespoons all-purpose flour
½ to 1 teaspoon pepper
1¼ cups milk
2 10-ounce frozen chopped spinach or
chopped broccoli, thawed and thoroughly
drained
1 medium carrot, shredded (½ cup)
¾ cup shredded Parmesan cheese
(3 ounces)
1 8-ounce package shredded part-skim
mozzarella cheese (2 cups)*

Cook lasagna noodles according to
package directions; drain. Set aside.

In a medium mixing bowl combine
eggs, cottage cheese, ricotta, and Italian
seasoning. Set aside.

In a large skillet cook mushrooms,
onion, and garlic in hot margarine or
butter till tender. Stir in the flour and
pepper; add milk all at once. Cook and
stir till thickened and bubbly; cook and
stir for 1 minute more. Remove from
heat. Stir in the spinach or broccoli, carrot, and ½ *cup* of the Parmesan cheese.

◆ Vegetable Lasagna

To assemble, in a greased 3-quart rectangular baking dish, layer a *third* of the
noodles, folding or cutting to fit, if necessary. Spread with a *third* of the cottage
cheese mixture, then a *third* of the
spinach mixture. Sprinkle with a *third* of
the mozzarella. Repeat the layers 2 more
times. Sprinkle with the remaining ¼
cup Parmesan cheese. Bake lasagna
immediately or chill for up to 48 hours.

To serve immediately, bake, uncovered, in a 350° oven for 35 minutes or
till heated through. Let stand for 10
minutes before cutting.

To make ahead, cover the lasagna with
foil and chill. Bake, covered, in a 350°
oven for 30 minutes. Uncover and bake
30 to 35 minutes more or till heated
through. Let stand for 10 minutes before
cutting. Makes 12 main-dish servings.

Nutrition information per serving:
275 cal., 10 g fat, 61 mg chol., 22 g pro.,
24 g carbo., 1 g fiber, 471 mg sodium.
RDA: 48% calcium, 14% iron, 78% vit.
A, 12% vit. C, 17% thiamine, 40%
riboflavin, 12% niacin.

Fruit Sorbet

FROZEN JUICE CONCENTRATES MAKE
THESE THREE FRUIT ICES A BREEZE TO
MAKE. FOR A COLORFUL DESSERT, SERVE
MINI SCOOPS OF ALL THREE ICES LAYERED
IN A GOBLET WITH FRESH FRUIT—

*2¾ cups water
¼ cup sugar
½ of a 12-ounce can frozen orange-
banana-pineapple juice concentrate or
orange juice concentrate (¾ cup)
1 teaspoon finely shredded orange peel*

In a small saucepan combine the water and sugar. Heat and stir mixture till sugar is dissolved. Cool to room temperature.

Add the frozen concentrate and the orange peel; stir till the concentrate is dissolved. Freeze in a 1- or 2-quart ice-cream freezer according to the manufacturer's directions. Makes about 1 quart or 8 (½-cup) servings.

Nutrition information per ½-cup serving: 63 cal., 0 g fat, 0 mg chol., 1 g pro., 15 g carbo., 0 g fiber, 3 mg sodium. RDA: 35% vit. C.

Cranberry-Raspberry Sorbet: Prepare the Fruit Sorbet as directed, except increase the sugar to *½ cup*, substitute *half* of a 12-ounce can frozen *cranberry-raspberry juice concentrate* for the frozen orange-banana-pineapple juice concentrate, and omit the finely shredded orange peel.

Nutrition information per ½-cup Cranberry-Raspberry Sorbet: 86 cal., 0 g fat, 0 mg chol., 0 g pro., 22 g carbo., 0 g fiber, 6 mg sodium. RDA: 38% vit. C.

Lemon-Mint Sorbet: Prepare Fruit Sorbet as directed, *except* add 1 cup *fresh mint leaves*, crushed, to the dissolved sugar-water mixture. Cover and simmer for 10 minutes more. Strain into a large mixing bowl; discard mint. Continue as directed, except substitute one 6-ounce can frozen *lemonade concentrate* for the orange-banana-pineapple juice concentrate and finely shredded lemon peel for the finely shredded orange peel.

Nutrition information per ½-cup Lemon-Mint Sorbet: 78 cal., 0 g fat, 0 mg chol., 0 g pro., 20 g carbo., 1 g fiber, and 4 mg sodium. RDA: 13% iron, 25% vit. C.

◆ Fruit Sorbet

Lighten up— it's a way of life

This meal-in-a-bun has everything you love: lean, juicy chicken that's easy to grill, plus zesty Southwestern flavors.

Grilled Chicken Sandwiches

GRILLING CHICKEN BREASTS WITH MESQUITE WOOD ADDS A WONDERFUL SMOKY AROMA AND FLAVOR—

Mesquite wood chunks or chips
¼ cup nonfat mayonnaise or salad dressing
1 teaspoon white wine Worcestershire sauce
½ teaspoon finely shredded lime peel or lemon peel
4 skinless, boneless chicken breast halves (1 pound)
2 tablespoons white wine Worcestershire sauce
¼ to ½ teaspoon garlic pepper
⅛ teaspoon salt
½ cup shredded part-skim mozzarella cheese (2 ounces)
4 whole wheat hamburger buns or hard rolls, split and toasted
4 tomato slices
½ of a large avocado, halved, seeded, peeled, and thinly sliced

Cover mesquite wood chunks or chips with water and soak for at least 1 hour before grilling.

Meanwhile, for lime mayonnaise, in a small mixing bowl combine mayonnaise or salad dressing, the 1 teaspoon Worcestershire sauce, and lime or lemon peel. Cover; chill till needed.

◆ Grilled Chicken Sandwiches

Rinse chicken; pat dry with paper towels. Place each chicken piece between 2 sheets of plastic wrap; pound with flat side of a meat mallet to flatten slightly (about ½ inch thick). Brush both sides of chicken with the 2 tablespoons Worcestershire sauce; sprinkle with garlic pepper and salt.

Drain wood chips or chunks. Sprinkle wet chunks or chips over preheated coals. Grill chicken on an uncovered grill directly over medium coals for 5 to 7 minutes or till no longer pink, turning once. Sprinkle each piece of chicken with cheese; grill just till cheese is melted.

(Or, to broil chicken, omit wood chips or chunks. Place chicken on the unheated rack of a broiler pan. Place under the broiler, 4 to 5 inches from the heat. Broil for 5 to 7 minutes or till no longer pink, turning once. Remove from the oven. Sprinkle each piece of chicken with cheese. Return to oven; broil just till cheese is melted.)

To serve, spread the cut side of bottom halves of buns with mayonnaise mixture. Place cooked chicken atop. Top each with more mayonnaise mixture, a tomato slice, 1 to 2 avocado slices, and top halves of buns. Makes 4 main-dish servings.

Nutrition information per serving: 330 cal., 11 g fat, 67 mg chol., 29 g pro., 28 g carbo., 2 g fiber, 695 mg sodium. RDA: 21% calcium, 16% iron, 25% thiamine, 23% riboflavin, 72% niacin.

◆ Rice Pilaf

◆ Polenta

◆ Oven-Roasted Vegetables

Rice Pilaf

¾ cup sliced fresh morel mushrooms; sliced, rehydrated dried morel mushrooms*; or sliced fresh button mushrooms
1 tablespoon cooking oil
1 cup basmati, Texmati, or long grain rice
2 teaspoons instant chicken bouillon granules
⅛ teaspoon pepper
2 cups water
1 tablespoon snipped fresh thyme, sage, or oregano or 1 teaspoon dried thyme, sage, or oregano, crushed
1 cup sliced green onions
1 medium carrot, shredded (½ cup)
Fresh thyme sprigs (optional)

In a large saucepan cook mushrooms in hot oil over medium heat for 3 to 5 minutes or till tender. Stir in rice, bouillon granules, and pepper. Carefully add water. Stir in thyme, sage, or oregano.

Bring to boiling; reduce heat to medium-low. Simmer, covered, for 15 minutes or till water is absorbed and the rice is tender. Stir in green onion and carrot. Cover and cook for 5 minutes more. Spoon into a serving dish and sprinkle with thyme sprigs, if desired. Makes 6 side-dish servings.

*Note: To rehydrate dried mushrooms, cover with warm water; let soak about 30 minutes. Rinse well; squeeze to drain thoroughly. You'll need about ⅓ cup dried morel mushrooms to end up with ¾ cup rehydrated mushrooms.

Nutrition information per serving: 143 cal., 3 g fat, 0 mg chol., 3 g pro., 27 g carbo., 1 g fiber, 296 mg sodium. RDA: 12% iron, 36% vit. A, 19% thiamine, 12% niacin.

Oven-Roasted Vegetables

SAVE TIME BY PURCHASING THE BABY CARROTS PEELED, TRIMMED, AND PACKAGED—

10 unpeeled whole tiny new potatoes, quartered
1 cup peeled and trimmed baby carrots (5 ounces)
1 small onion, cut into wedges
¼ cup olive oil
3 tablespoons lemon juice
3 cloves garlic, minced
1 tablespoon snipped fresh rosemary or oregano, or 1 teaspoon dried rosemary or oregano, crushed
1 teaspoon salt
½ teaspoon pepper
½ of a small eggplant, quartered lengthwise and cut into ½-inch-thick slices (2 cups)
1 medium red or green sweet pepper, cut into ½-inch-wide strips

In a 13x9x2-inch baking pan combine potatoes, carrots, and onion.

In a small mixing bowl combine olive oil, lemon juice, garlic, rosemary or oregano, salt, and pepper. Drizzle over vegetables in baking pan; toss to coat. Roast, uncovered, in a 450° oven for 30 minutes, stirring occasionally.

Remove from oven. Add eggplant and sweet pepper; toss to combine. Return to oven; roast 15 minutes more or till vegetables are tender and brown on the edges, stirring occasionally. Makes 6 to 8 side-dish servings.

Nutrition information per serving: 178 cal., 9 g fat, 0 mg chol., 2 g pro., 23 g carbo., 3 g fiber, 373 mg sodium. RDA: 45% vit. A, 61% vit. C, 12% thiamine, 10% niacin.

Polenta

POLENTA (POH LEN TUH) IS AN ITALIAN-STYLE, BOILED CORNMEAL MIXTURE THAT IS EATEN AS A HOT CEREAL OR AS A SIDE DISH. FOR THE LATTER, SLICE, BAKE, AND SAUCE THE POLENTA, AS BELOW—

3 cups water
1 cup yellow cornmeal
1 cup cold water
1 teaspoon salt
1 recipe Basil-Tomato Sauce or one 27- or 30-ounce jar purchased spaghetti sauce
¼ cup shaved* or grated Parmesan cheese
Fresh basil sprig (optional)

In a 2-quart saucepan bring the 3 cups water to boiling.

In a small bowl combine the cornmeal, the 1 cup cold water, and salt. Slowly add the cornmeal mixture to the boiling water, stirring constantly. Cook and stir till mixture returns to boiling. Reduce heat to very low. Cover and simmer for 15 minutes, stirring occasionally.

Pour the hot mixture into a greased 8x4x2-inch loaf pan. Cool 1 hour. Cover and chill several hours or till firm.

At serving time, remove polenta from pan; cut into ½ inch-thick slices. Place slices in single layer on a greased baking sheet. Bake, covered, in a 400° oven for 10 to 12 minutes or till heated through.

To serve, transfer hot polenta to a serving platter. Ladle Basil-Tomato Sauce atop; sprinkle with Parmesan cheese. Garnish with basil, if desired. Makes 8 side-dish servings (16 slices).

*Note: To make Parmesan cheese shavings, start with a block of Parmesan cheese. Use a potato peeler to shave off chips or shavings of the cheese.

Nutrition information per serving with Basil-Tomato Sauce: 125 cal., 3 g fat, 2 mg chol., 4 g pro., 21 g carbo., 2 g fiber, 649 mg sodium. RDA: 10% calcium, 10% iron, 13% vit. A, 39% vit. C, 17% thiamine, 10% riboflavin, 13% niacin.

Basil-Tomato Sauce

ALTHOUGH FRESH BASIL OFFERS THE FULLEST FLAVOR, YOU CAN SUBSTITUTE DRIED BASIL. USE 1 TABLESPOON DRIED BASIL, CRUSHED, AND ADD IT ALONG WITH THE TOMATOES—

1 small onion, chopped
2 cloves garlic, minced
1 tablespoon olive oil or cooking oil
1 28-ounce can crushed Italian-style (plum) tomatoes or two 14½-ounce cans Italian-style tomatoes, cut up
½ teaspoon sugar
¼ to ½ teaspoon crushed red pepper
3 tablespoons snipped fresh basil

In a large saucepan cook onion and garlic in hot oil over medium heat till tender. Carefully add *undrained* tomatoes, sugar, crushed red pepper, and ¼ teaspoon *salt*. Bring to boiling; reduce heat.

Simmer, uncovered, for 10 to 15 minutes or till of desired consistency. Stir in the fresh basil. Cook for 1 minute more. Serve immediately or transfer to a covered storage container and chill for up to 24 hours. Reheat before serving. Makes 3 cups.

◆ Chocolate Hazelnut Cheesecake

Some days we deserve a splurge

Even with today's trend toward lighter eating, we all yearn for an occasional treat. This creamy rich cheesecake sends us searching for a fork. Choose from three versions: chocolate hazelnut, triple chocoholic, or white chocolate.

Chocolate Cheesecake

1¾ cups finely crushed chocolate wafers (30 cookies)
⅓ cup margarine or butter, melted
4 ounces semisweet chocolate, chopped
1 ounce unsweetened chocolate or semisweet chocolate, chopped
3 8-ounce packages cream cheese, softened
1¼ cups sugar
2 tablespoons all-purpose flour
1 teaspoon vanilla
4 eggs
¼ cup milk

For crust, in a mixing bowl combine crushed wafers and margarine. Press mixture evenly onto the bottom and 1¾ inches up the sides of an ungreased 9-inch springform pan. Place the pan on a baking sheet. Chill till needed.

In a small heavy saucepan combine the chocolates; melt over low heat, stirring occasionally. Cool slightly.

In a large mixer bowl beat cream cheese, sugar, flour, and vanilla with an electric mixer on medium speed till smooth. With mixer running, slowly add melted chocolate, beating till combined. Add eggs all at once, stirring just till mixed. Do not overbeat. Stir in milk. Pour filling into crust.

Bake in a 350° oven for 45 to 50 minutes or till the center appears nearly set when gently shaken. (Do not overbake.) Cool on a wire rack for 10 minutes. Loosen the sides of the cheesecake from the pan. Cool for 30 minutes. Remove sides of pan. Cover and chill for 4 to 24 hours. Makes 12 servings.

Nutrition information per serving: 479 cal., 33 g fat, 136 mg chol., 9 g pro., 40 g carbo., 0 g fiber, and 363 mg sodium. RDA: 12% iron, 43% vit. A.

Chocolate Hazelnut Cheesecake: Prepare Chocolate Cheesecake as directed *except*, for the hazelnut crust, omit the chocolate wafers and melted margarine or butter. Using 2 teaspoons *margarine* or *butter*, grease the bottom and 1¾ inches up the sides of a 9-inch springform pan. Press 1 cup toasted, finely ground *hazelnuts* or *almonds* onto the bottom and 1¾ inches up the sides of the greased springform pan. Cover and chill crust.

For filling, prepare as directed, except substitute 3 tablespoons *hazelnut liqueur* for 3 tablespoons of the milk. If desired, top the cooled cheesecake with whole and/or halved small *fresh strawberries*.

Nutrition information per serving: 441 cal., 33 g fat, 134 mg chol., 9 g pro., 32 g carbo., 1 g fiber, 200 mg sodium. RDA: 10% calcium, 12% iron, 36% vit. A, 9% vit. C, 18% riboflavin.

White Chocolate Cheesecake: Prepare Chocolate Cheesecake as directed, *except* substitute one 6-ounce *white baking bar* or three 2-ounce *white baking bars*, melted, for all of the semisweet and unsweetened chocolate squares. (To melt white baking bars, heat and stir constantly over very low heat.)

Nutrition information per serving: 498 cal., 33 g fat, 136 mg chol., 9 g pro., 43 g carbo., 0 g fiber, 375 mg sodium.

A Classic-to-Be for the 21st Century

Here's your chance to taste tomorrow's classic today. Recipes such as Mexican Catfish with Quinoa will grow in popularity, based on America's changing taste buds and food trends such as:

—Our growing wish for quality fish and seafood, which will boost demand for farm-raised fish such as catfish.

—Our desire for healthful foods, which we'll satisfy with a variety of grains, such as quick-cooking quinoa.

—Greater availability of Mexican imports in the U.S., including tomatillos and mangoes, due to the North-American Free Trade Agreement.

Mexican Catfish with Quinoa

1 pound fresh or frozen catfish or other white fish fillets
1 to 2 jalapeño or serrano peppers
½ cup chopped onion
1 tablespoon cooking oil
5 or 6 fresh tomatillos, with husks removed, chopped (1 cup), or one 13-ounce can tomatillos, drained, rinsed, and chopped
¼ cup dry white wine or chicken broth
1 tablespoon snipped fresh cilantro or parsley
1 teaspoon sugar
½ teaspoon ground cumin
¼ teaspoon salt
1 large tomato, seeded and chopped (1 cup)
1 tablespoon lime juice

◆ Mexican Catfish with Quinoa

2 tablespoons toasted pumpkin seeds (optional)
Sliced jalapeño or serrano pepper (optional)
2 cups hot cooked quinoa or rice
1 tablespoon snipped fresh cilantro or parsley
Mango slices (optional)
Lime slices (optional)

Thaw fish if frozen. Separate fillets or cut into 4 serving-size portions. Rinse; pat dry with paper towels.

Wearing plastic gloves or working under cold running water, cut the 1 or 2 jalapeño or serrano peppers in half hori-zontally; remove seeds and stems. Finely chop peppers.

For salsa, in a medium saucepan cook onion in hot oil till tender but not brown. Stir in chopped peppers, tomatillos, wine or broth, the first 1 tablespoon snipped cilantro or parsley, sugar, cumin, and salt. Bring to boiling. Reduce heat; boil gently, uncovered, for 8 to 10 minutes or till sauce is thickened. Stir in tomato. Remove from heat.

Meanwhile, place fish in a greased 2-quart rectangular baking dish. Sprinkle with lime juice and 1/8 teaspoon *pepper*. Spoon salsa over fish. Bake, uncovered, in a 450° oven for 9 to 11 minutes or till fish flakes easily with a fork.

Transfer fish to a platter. Spoon salsa atop fish; sprinkle with pumpkin seeds and sliced pepper, if desired. Stir remaining cilantro or parsley into quinoa or rice. Serve fish with quinoa or rice mixture, mango slices, and lime slices, if desired. Makes 4 main-dish servings.

Nutrition information per serving: 270 cal., 8 g fat, 35 mg chol. , 21 g pro., 28 g carbo., 2 g fiber, 271 mg sodium. RDA: 24% iron, 12% vit. A, 30% vit. C, 11% thiamine, 12% riboflavin.

Note: When handling hot chili peppers, it is important to wear gloves or to work with hands under running water to protect skin from the oils in the peppers. Avoid direct contact with your eyes. When finished handling the peppers, wash hands thoroughly.

Greek Salad

KALAMATA OLIVES ARE SOLD CURED OR IN BRINE; EITHER IS FINE FOR THIS SALAD. IF DESIRED, REMOVE THE PITS BEFORE SERVING WITH AN OLIVE/CHERRY PITTER OR A KNIFE—

5 cups torn mixed greens, such as red and green leaf lettuce, curly endive, romaine, and mesclun
1 medium tomato, coarsely chopped
½ of a small seedless or regular cucumber, sliced
½ of a medium red onion, halved lengthwise and thinly sliced
1 cup kalamata olives or ripe olives
1 cup crumbled feta cheese (4 ounces)
½ cup thinly sliced radishes
1 recipe Greek Vinaigrette
Fresh oregano sprigs (optional)
Chive blossoms (optional)

◆ Greek Salad

In a large salad bowl toss together the torn mixed greens, tomato, cucumber, onion, olives, feta cheese, and radishes. Cover and chill till serving time, up to 2 hours.

Just before serving, shake Greek Vinaigrette to mix. Pour vinaigrette over salad; toss gently to coat. Sprinkle with oregano and chive blossoms. Makes 6 to 8 side-dish servings.

Greek Vinaigrette: In a screw-top jar combine ⅓ cup *olive oil;* 3 tablespoons *wine vinegar;* 2 tablespoons *lemon juice;* 1½ teaspoons snipped *fresh oregano* or ½ teaspoon *dried oregano,* crushed; 1 teaspoon *sugar;* 1 small clove *garlic,* minced; and ¼ teaspoon *pepper.* Cover; shake well to mix. Store, covered, in the refrigerator for up to 2 weeks.

Nutrition information per serving: 185 cal., 17 g fat, 17 mg chol., 4 g pro., 6 g carbo., 2 g fiber, 257 mg sodium. RDA: 17% calcium, 29% vit. A, 34% vit. C, 18% riboflavin.

Scones

TRY ALL THREE FLAVORS OF SCONES, INCLUDING THE DRIED CHERRY AND ROSEMARY VARIATIONS—

2 cups all-purpose flour
3 tablespoons brown sugar
2 teaspoons baking powder
½ teaspoon baking soda
¼ cup margarine or butter
1 8-ounce carton dairy sour cream
1 beaten egg yolk
1 slightly beaten egg white

In a large mixing bowl stir together flour, brown sugar, baking powder, baking soda, and ½ teaspoon *salt*. Using a pastry blender, cut in margarine or butter till mixture resembles coarse crumbs. Make a well in the center.

In a small mixing bowl stir together sour cream and egg yolk; add all at once to flour mixture. With a fork, stir till combined (mixture may seem dry).

Turn dough onto a lightly floured surface. Quickly knead dough, by gently folding and pressing, for 10 to 12 strokes or till nearly smooth. Pat or lightly roll dough into a 7-inch circle. Cut into 12 wedges.

Arrange wedges on an ungreased baking sheet about 1 inch apart. Brush with egg white.

Bake in a 400° oven for 10 to 12 minutes or till light brown. Cool on a wire rack for 10 minutes. Serve warm. Makes 12 scones.

Nutrition information per scone: 165 cal., 8 g fat, 26 mg chol., 3 g pro., 19 g carbo., 1 g fiber, and 233 mg sodium. RDA: 13% vit. A, 15% thiamine.

Dried Cherry Scones: In a small bowl pour enough boiling water over ½ cup snipped *dried sweet cherries or raisins*

◆ Scones

to cover. Let stand for 5 minutes; drain well. Prepare Scones as directed, *except* toss drained cherries and 1 teaspoon finely shredded *orange peel* into the margarine-flour mixture before adding the sour cream mixture. Continue as directed, *except* omit the egg white for brushing.

To glaze the baked scones, in a small mixing bowl stir together 1 cup sifted *powdered sugar*, 1 tablespoon *orange juice*, and ¼ teaspoon *vanilla*. Stir in more orange juice, *1 teaspoon* at a time, till of drizzling consistency. Drizzle atop warm scones.

Nutrition information per serving: 213 cal., 8 g fat, 26 mg chol., 3 g pro.,

31 g carbo., 1 g fiber, and 228 mg sodium. RDA: 16% vit. A, 15% thiamine.

Savory Rosemary Scones: Prepare Scones as directed, *except* substitute 1 tablespoon *granulated sugar* for the 3 tablespoons brown sugar. Stir in 1 tablespoon snipped *fresh rosemary* or 1 teaspoon *dried rosemary*, crushed, and ⅛ teaspoon *pepper* with the dry ingredients. After brushing scones with egg white, sprinkle with additional snipped rosemary, if desired.

Nutrition information per serving: 156 cal., 8 g fat, 26 mg chol., 3 g pro., 17 g carbo., 1 g fiber, and 232 mg sodium. RDA: 13% vit. A, 15% thiamine.

Crème Brûlée

FOR OUR VERSION OF THIS FAMOUS DESSERT, CARAMELIZE THE SUGAR TOPPING IN A SKILLET AND SPOON IT ATOP THE CREAMY CUSTARD—

2 cups half-and-half or light cream
5 slightly beaten egg yolks
⅓ cup sugar
1 teaspoon vanilla
⅓ cup sugar

In a small heavy saucepan heat half-and-half or light cream over medium-low heat just till bubbly. Remove from heat; set aside.

In a medium mixing bowl combine egg yolks, the first ⅓ cup sugar, vanilla, and ¼ teaspoon *salt*. Beat with a wire whisk or rotary beater just till combined. Slowly whisk or stir the hot cream into the egg mixture.

Place four 4-inch quiche dishes or oval or round tart pans without removable bottoms into a 13x9x2-inch baking pan. Set the baking pan on oven rack in a 325° oven. Pour the custard mixture evenly into the 4 dishes. Pour *very* hot water into the baking pan around the 4 dishes, about *halfway* up the sides of the dishes.

Bake in 325° oven for 18 to 24 minutes or till a knife inserted near the center of each dish comes out clean. Remove dishes from the water bath; let cool on a wire rack. Cover and chill for at least 1 hour or for up to 8 hours.

Before serving, remove custards from the refrigerator; let stand at room temperature for 20 minutes.

Place remaining ⅓ cup sugar in a heavy 10-inch skillet. Heat skillet over medium-high heat till sugar begins to melt, shaking skillet occasionally to heat

◆ Crème Brûlée

sugar evenly. *Do not stir.* Once sugar starts to melt, reduce heat to low; cook till sugar is completely melted and golden (3 to 5 minutes more), stirring as needed.

Spoon melted sugar quickly over custards in a lacy pattern or in a solid piece. If melted sugar starts to harden in pan, return to heat, stirring till it melts. If it starts to form clumps, carefully stir in 1

to 2 teaspoons water. Serve immediately. Makes 4 servings.

Nutrition information per serving: 376 cal., 20 g fat, 311 mg chol., 7 g pro., 40 g carbo., 0 g fiber, 191 mg sodium. RDA: 20% calcium, 35% vit. A, and 24% riboflavin.

Amaretto Crème Brûlée: Prepare Crème Brûlée as directed, *except* substitute 2 tablespoons *amaretto* for all of the vanilla.

Quesadillas

6 6-inch flour tortillas
1 8-ounce package shredded cheddar or
Monterey Jack cheese, or Monterey Jack
cheese with jalapeño peppers
1 4-ounce can diced green chili peppers,
drained, or ¼ cup chopped, seeded fresh
jalapeño peppers
1 teaspoon cooking oil
Red and/or green salsa (optional)
Slivered or sliced, pitted ripe olives
(optional)
Dairy sour cream (optional)

To pan-fry tortillas, sprinkle 3 of the tortillas with cheese and peppers. Top with remaining 3 tortillas. Brush a large skillet or griddle with the oil. Heat skillet or griddle till a drop of water sizzles when dropped onto it. Cook quesadillas, one at a time, over medium heat about 4 minutes (total) or till cheese is melted and tortillas are light brown, turning once.

(Or, to bake the quesadillas, brush one side of 3 tortillas with some of the oil. Place tortillas, oiled side down, on a baking sheet. Top with the cheese, peppers, and remaining tortillas. Brush tops with remaining oil. Bake in 450° oven about 6 minutes or till light brown.)

To serve, cut each quesadilla into 4 wedges. Top with sour cream, salsa, and olives, if desired. Makes 16 appetizer servings.

Nutrition information per serving: 84 cal., 5 g fat, 15 mg chol., 4 g pro., 5 g carbo., 0 g fiber, 121 mg sodium. RDA: 14% calcium, 10% vit. A.

Vegetable Quesadillas: For filling, in a l-quart microwave-safe casserole combine ¾ cup finely chopped *broccoli*, ¼ cup shredded *carrot*, ¼ cup sliced *green*

◆ Quesadillas

onion, and 2 tablespoons *water*. Cover; micro-cook on 100% power (high) for 2 to 4 minutes or till the vegetables are crisp-tender. Drain. Prepare Quesadillas as directed, *except* substitute vegetable mixture for peppers. Cook and serve as directed.

Nutrition information per serving: 86 cal., 5 g fat, 15 mg chol., 4 g pro., 5 g carbo., 0 g fiber, 90 mg sodium. RDA: 15% calcium, 13% vit. A.

Chicken-Jicama Quesadillas: Prepare Quesadillas as directed, *except* substitute

½ cup rinsed and drained canned *black beans* for the peppers. Lightly mash beans; stir into the cheese. Spread the bean mixture onto 3 of the tortillas. Top with ½ cup finely chopped, cooked *chicken*; ½ cup finely chopped, peeled *jicama*, and 2 tablespoons sliced *green onion*. Top with the remaining tortillas. Cook and serve as directed.

Nutrition information per serving: 101 cal., 6 g fat, 19 mg chol., 6 g pro., 6 g carbo., 1 g fiber, 147 mg sodium. RDA: 15% calcium, 10% vit. A.

Szechwan Beef Stir-Fry

1 pound boneless beef sirloin steak
6 dried mushrooms (1 cup), such as
shiitake or wood ear mushrooms
¼ cup hot bean sauce or hot bean paste
¼ cup dry sherry
2 tablespoons soy sauce
¾ teaspoon whole Szechwan pepper,
crushed, or whole black peppers, crushed
½ teaspoon cornstarch
½ to 1 teaspoon chili oil
2 to 3 tablespoons cooking oil
2 medium carrots, bias sliced
1 clove garlic, minced
1½ cups broccoli flowerets or one 10-ounce
package frozen cut broccoli, thawed
1 8½-ounce can bamboo shoots, drained
and cut into narrow strips
3 cups hot cooked rice
Sliced green onion (optional)

Trim fat from beef. Partially freeze beef. Thinly slice across the grain into bite-size strips. Set aside.

In a small mixing bowl cover mushrooms with warm water; let soak for 30 minutes. Rinse; squeeze to drain thoroughly. Slice thinly, discarding stems. Set aside.

For sauce, in a small bowl combine bean sauce, sherry, soy sauce, crushed Szechwan pepper or black pepper, cornstarch, and chili oil. Set aside.

Pour *1 tablespoon* of the cooking oil into a wok or large skillet. (Add more cooking oil as necessary during cooking.) Preheat oven medium-high heat. Stir-fry carrots and garlic in hot oil for 2 minutes. Add broccoli; stir-fry for 2 minutes. Add the mushrooms and bamboo shoots; stir-fry for 1 to 2 minutes more or till vegetables are crisp-tender.

◆ Szechwan Beef Stir-Fry

Remove the vegetables from the wok or skillet.

Add *half* of the beef to the hot wok or skillet. Stir-fry for 2 to 3 minutes or to desired doneness. Remove beef from wok or skillet. Repeat with the remaining beef. Return all beef to the wok or skillet, pushing it from the center of wok or skillet.

Stir sauce. Add the sauce to the center of wok or skillet. Cook and stir till thickened and bubbly.

Return the cooked vegetables to the wok or skillet. Stir all ingredients togeth-er to coat with sauce. Cook and stir about 1 minute more or till heated through. Serve immediately over hot cooked rice. Sprinkle with green onions, if desired. Makes 4 servings.

*Make-ahead tip:** The night before, rehydrate the mushrooms, stir together the sauce, and cut up the vegetables. Chill the sauce and vegetables in separate covered containers.

Nutrition information per serving:
579 cal., 19 g fat, 76 mg chol., 36 g pro., 62 g carbo., 3 g fiber, 705 mg sodium.

Prize Tested Recipes®

Springtime Rice and Asparagus Salad

THE FLAVOR COMBINATION OF ASPARA-GUS, CITRUS, NUTS, AND RICE EXCELS—

1 14½-ounce can chicken broth
1 cup long-grain rice
10 ounces asparagus, cut into 2-inch pieces (about 2 cups)
¾ cup shelled peas or frozen peas
⅓ cup pecan halves or slivered almonds, toasted
¼ cup snipped cilantro or parsley
3 green onions, sliced
4 tablespoons olive oil or salad oil
½ teaspoon finely shredded lemon peel
3 tablespoons lemon juice
3 tablespoons dairy sour cream or plain yogurt
¼ teaspoon ground white pepper
Fresh spinach leaves
3 cups torn fresh spinach
Twisted lemon slices (optional)

Add enough *water* (about ¼ cup) to broth to make 2 cups. In a saucepan bring broth to boiling. Add rice. Return to boiling; reduce heat. Cover; simmer about 15 minutes or till tender.

Meanwhile, cook asparagus, covered, in a small amount of boiling water for 2 minutes. Add peas; cook 2 to 3 minutes more or till crisp-tender. Drain. In a large bowl combine cooled rice, aspara-gus and peas, nuts, cilantro or parsley, and onions. In a small bowl combine oil, lemon peel, lemon juice, sour cream or

◆ Spicy Lamb and Spaghetti Squash

yogurt, pepper, and ¼ teaspoon *salt*. Pour over rice mixture; toss to coat. Cover; chill thoroughly. To serve, line a large platter with spinach leaves. Top with torn spinach, then rice mixture. Garnish with lemon, if desired. Makes 6 side-dish servings.

Nutrition information per serving: 280 cal., 13 g fat, 3 mg chol., 8 g pro., 33 g carbo., 3 g fiber, 379 mg sodium. RDA: 11% calcium, 23% iron, 42% vit. A, 53% vit. C, 30% thiamine.

$100 WINNER
Sally Vog, Springfield, Oreg.

East Indian Roasted Leg of Lamb

AN INTRIGUING BLEND OF HOT PEPPERS, GARLIC, LIME, HONEY, AND GINGER COM-PLEMENTS LAMB IN THIS WINNING RECIPE—

1 large onion, cut up
4 fresh or canned jalapeño peppers, seeded and cut up
3 cloves garlic, halved
3 tablespoons lime juice
1 tablespoon honey
1 teaspoon Dijon-style mustard
1 teaspoon grated gingerroot or ¼ teaspoon ground ginger

◆ Oriental Vegetable and Pasta Salad   ◆ Springtime Rice and Asparagus

1 teaspoon salt
½ teaspoon pepper
1 3½- to 4-pound leg of lamb
2 tablespoons margarine or butter, melted

In a blender container or food processor bowl combine onion, peppers, garlic, lime juice, honey, mustard, gingerroot, salt, and pepper. Cover and blend or process till nearly smooth, stopping to scrape sides if necessary. Set aside.

Trim fat from meat. Cut ½-inch slits all over into meat at 1-inch intervals. Line a shallow roasting pan with a double thickness of heavy foil. Place meat, fat side up, on a rack in the lined pan. Spoon pureed mixture over meat, rubbing the mixture into the meat with your fingers. Drizzle with melted margarine or butter. Roast, uncovered, in a 325° oven for 2 hours or till of desired doneness. Cover loosely; let stand for

15 minutes before carving. Makes 10 to 12 servings.

Nutrition information per serving:
273 cal., 12 g fat, 109 mg chol., 35 g pro., 4 g carbo., 0 g fiber, 437 mg sodium. RDA: 19% iron, 13% thiamine, 28% riboflavin, 52% niacin.

$100 WINNER

Mrs. Aloma Moore, East Point, Ga.

Spicy Lamb and Spaghetti Squash

FOND FOOD MEMORIES OF LIVING IN SINGAPORE INSPIRED LINDA TO CREATE THIS LAMB DISH—

1 pound boneless lamb shoulder roast or boneless lamb sirloin roast trimmed of fat
1 tablespoon margarine or butter
1 cup chopped onion
1 cup chopped celery

2 cloves garlic minced
½ cup tomato sauce
⅓ cup water
1½ teaspoons curry powder
1½ teaspoons grated gingerroot or
½ teaspoon ground ginger
¼ teaspoon ground cumin
¼ cup plain yogurt
2 teaspoons all-purpose flour
1 2½- to 3-pound spaghetti squash, halved lengthwise and seeded
Snipped fresh cilantro or parsley (optional)
Cilantro or parsley sprigs (optional)

Cut lamb into 1-inch cubes. In a large saucepan brown *half* of the meat in hot margarine or butter. Remove meat. Brown remaining meat with onion, celery, and garlic till vegetables are tender. Drain fat. Return all meat to pan. Stir in tomato sauce, water, curry powder,

continued on page 78

April
77

continued from page 77

ginger, cumin, ½ teaspoon *salt,* and ⅛ teaspoon *pepper.* Bring to boiling; reduce heat. Cover; simmer for 1 hour or till lamb is tender. Combine yogurt and flour; add to meat mixture. Cook and stir till bubbly; cook 1 minute more.

Meanwhile, place squash, cut side down, in a shallow baking dish. Bake, uncovered, in a 350° oven for 30 to 40 minutes or till tender. Using a fork, separate the squash pulp into strands. To serve, spoon lamb mixture over squash. If desired, sprinkle with chopped cilantro or parsley. Garnish with cilantro or parsley sprig, if desired. Serves 4.

Nutrition information per serving: 257 cal., 12 g fat, 67 mg chol., 22 g pro., 16 g carbo., 3 g fiber, 591 mg sodium. RDA: 12% calcium, 19% iron, 10% vit. A, 20% vit. C.

$200 WINNER

Linda Morten, Katy, Tex.

◆ East Indian Roasted Leg of Lamb

Oriental Vegetable and Pasta Salad

PLUM SAUCE, SOY SAUCE, AND SESAME OIL DRESS THIS SENSATIONAL SIDE-DISH SALAD—

> *8 ounces fine noodles or spaghetti*
> *4 ounces asparagus spears, cut into 1-inch pieces (about 1 cup)*
> *⅓ cup plum sauce*
> *1 to 2 tablespoons soy sauce*
> *½ teaspoon toasted sesame oil*
> *⅛ teaspoon crushed red pepper*
> *1 medium red or green sweet pepper, cut into strips*
> *1 11-ounce can mandarin orange sections, drained*
> *1 cup fresh or frozen sugar snap peas, halved crosswise*
> *⅓ cup sliced green onion*
> *⅓ cup toasted slivered almonds*

Cook pasta according to package directions. Drain. Cover and chill. In a saucepan cook asparagus, covered, in a small amount of boiling water 4 to 6 minutes or till crisp-tender. Drain. For dressing, stir together plum sauce, soy sauce, oil, and red pepper. In a bowl combine pasta, asparagus, sweet pepper, oranges, peas, onion, and almonds. Add dressing; toss to coat. Serve immediately. Makes 8 to 10 side-dish servings.

Nutrition information per serving: 189 cal., 4 g fat, 0 mg chol., 7 g pro., 34 g carbo., 1 g fiber, 141 mg sodium. RDA: 12% iron, 21% vit. A, 58% vit. C, 19% thiamine.

$200 WINNER

John Guinivere, Las Vegas, Nev.

May

Viva la Greens, Grains
& Beans

Prize Tested Recipes

Viva la
Greens, Grains & Beans

BY JUILIA MALLOY

Welcome to the fresh, new tastes of vegetarian cooking. Across the country, restaurant chefs are proving that greens, grains, and beans (and timeless tofu, too) can be just as delicious as meat and potatoes. Let your family in on these healthful ideas by sampling the best from five innovative restaurants.

What better place to start than at the beginning of it all? Try a popular dish from Moosewood Restaurant, the mother of creative vegetarian invention.

Herbed Linguine with Snap Peas

TOO BUSY TO MAKE FRESH PASTA? NO PROBLEM. BUY SOME FROM THE REFRIGERATED SECTION OF YOUR SUPERMARKET. IT'LL TAKE LESS TIME TO COOK THAN DRIED PASTA—

2 9-ounce packages fresh linguine or fettuccine or 9 ounces dried linguine or fettuccine
⅓ cup vegetable broth* or water
⅔ cup chopped green onions
1½ cups sugar snap peas cut in half crosswise or 12 ounces torn fresh spinach (9 cups)
⅓ cup snipped fresh parsley
⅓ cup snipped fresh dill, basil, or chervil, or 2 teaspoons dried dillweed, basil, or chervil, crushed
¼ teaspoon salt
¼ teaspoon pepper
12 ounces semisoft goat cheese (chèvre)
¾ cup milk
2 tablespoons margarine or butter, cut into small pieces
1 large tomato, chopped
¼ cup toasted chopped hazelnuts
6 small artichokes, steamed and halved (optional)

In a 4½-quart Dutch oven cook pasta according to package directions.

Meanwhile, in a large saucepan bring broth or water to boiling. Add green onions and peas or spinach. Cook and stir for 2 to 4 minutes or till peas are crisp-tender or spinach is wilted. Add parsley, herb, salt, and pepper; toss gently to mix. Remove from heat; cover and set aside.

Drain pasta; keep warm. In the same Dutch oven combine goat cheese, milk, and margarine or butter. Cook and stir till cheese is melted. Return pasta to Dutch oven; toss to coat. Remove from heat.

Add vegetable mixture and *half* of the tomato to the pasta mixture; toss gently to mix. Transfer to a warm serving platter. Garnish with remaining tomato and nuts. Serve immediately, with artichokes, if desired. Makes 6 main-dish servings.

*Note: You can purchase canned vegetable broth or make your own from instant bouillon granules.

Nutrition facts per serving: 546 cal., 22 g total fat (10 g sat. fat), 102 mg chol., 478 mg sodium, 63 g carbo., 2 g fiber, 25 g pro. Daily Value: 18% vit. A, 54% vit. C, 21% calcium, 33% iron.

Reprinted with permission from The *Moosewood Restaurant Kitchen Garden*, copyright 1992 by Vegetable Kingdom, Inc. Published by arrangement with Simon & Schuster.

◆ Herbed Linguine with Snap Peas

"My first experience with
Moosewood was exchanging
herbs from my garden for
free meals. Now I cook with
them there."

—DAVID HIRSCH, CHEF
MOOSEWOOD RESTAURANT
ITHACA, N.Y.

◆ Japanese Noodle Salad

"Many of our guests have a more relaxed approach to vegetarian eating, one that includes fish and seafood. They're thrilled to see it as an alternative on our menu."
—BRENDA LANGTON
OWNER-CHEF
CAFE BRENDA
MINNEAPOLIS, MINN.

◆ Salmon with Lentil Pilaf

◆ Couscous Croquettes with Orange Saute

Salmon with Lentil Pilaf

CHEF BRENDA LANGTON FROM CAFE BRENDA SUGGESTS COOKING THE LENTIL PILAF BEFORE YOU BROIL THE FISH—

2 pounds fresh or frozen salmon fillets, cut
½ to ¾ inch thick
Lentil Pilaf (see recipe, right)
Olive oil or cooking oil
1 8-ounce carton plain low-fat yogurt
1 tablespoon lemon juice
2 teaspoons prepared horseradish
Dash pepper
Fresh fennel leaves (optional)
Lime slices, halved (optional)

Thaw fish, if frozen. Prepare Lentil Pilaf; keep warm. Cut fish into 8 equal pieces; measure the thickness. Brush the unheated rack of a broiler pan with oil; arrange fish on the rack. Broil 4 inches from the heat till fish flakes easily when tested with a fork, allowing 4 to 6 minutes for each ½ inch of thickness.

For sauce, in a small mixing bowl stir together yogurt, lemon juice, horseradish, and pepper. To serve, place salmon on Lentil Pilaf. Serve with sauce. If desired, garnish with fennel and lime. Makes 8 servings.

Nutrition facts per serving: 298 cal., 9 g total fat (2 g sat. fat), 22 mg chol., 260 mg sodium, 27 g carbo., 5 g fiber, 27 g pro. Daily Value: 66% vit. A, 39% vit. C, 14% calcium, 28% iron.

Lentil Pilaf

THIS RECIPE CALLS FOR FRENCH LENTILS, WHICH ARE SMALLER AND DARKER THAN MOST AMERICAN LENTILS, BUT YOU CAN USE ANY GREEN OR BROWN LENTIL—

1¼ cups French lentils or other dry lentils
2 bay leaves
1 large onion or 3 leeks, chopped (1 cup)
8 cloves garlic, minced (2 teaspoons)
2 tablespoons olive oil or cooking oil
1 fennel bulb, chopped (1 cup)
2 medium carrots, chopped (1 cup)
1 medium red or green sweet pepper,
chopped (1 cup)
½ cup dry white wine
¼ cup snipped fresh parsley
2 tablespoons snipped fresh basil, thyme, or
marjoram, or 1 teaspoon dried basil,
thyme, or marjoram, crushed
2 tablespoons Pernod, Anisette, or other
anise-flavored liqueur (optional)
½ teaspoon salt

In a medium saucepan combine lentils, bay leaves, and 3 cups *water*. Bring to boiling; reduce heat. Cover and simmer about 30 minutes or till tender.

In a large saucepan cook onion or leeks and garlic in hot oil about 3 minutes or till tender. Add fennel and carrots; cook for 3 minutes more. Add sweet pepper, wine, parsley, herb, liqueur (if desired), and salt. Cover and simmer about 5 minutes or till carrots are tender.

Drain lentils, discarding bay leaves; stir into fennel mixture. Makes 8 sidedish servings.

Nutrition facts per serving: 170 cal., 4 g total fat (1 g sat. fat), 0 mg chol., 92 mg sodium, 25 g carbo., 5 g fiber, 9 g pro. Daily Value: 63% vit. A, 37% vit. C, 6% calcium, 23% iron.

Cousous Croquettes with Orange Sauce

CHILLING HELPS THE CROQUETTES OR PATTIES KEEP THEIR SHAPE DURING COOKING. SHAPE AND CHILL THEM UP TO 24 HOURS BEFORE BROWNING—

¾ cup couscous
1½ cups water or vegetable broth
¼ cup currants or raisins
½ teaspoon salt
½ teaspoon aniseed, crushed
¼ cup finely chopped onion
2 cloves garlic, minced
1 tablespoon olive oil or cooking oil
1 medium carrot, shredded (½ cup)
¼ cup finely chopped celery
• • •
2 eggs
1¼ cups soft bread crumbs (about 1½ slices bread)
½ cup toasted sliced almonds
1 tablespoon snipped fresh parsley or
1½ teaspoons snipped fresh mint
⅛ teaspoon ground red pepper
2 tablespoons cooking oil
Orange Sauce
Assorted fresh fruits (optional)

In a 10-inch skillet cook the couscous over medium-high heat for 5 to 8 minutes or till golden brown, stirring constantly. Cool slightly.

Carefully add water or broth, currants or raisins, salt, and aniseed. Bring to boiling; remove from heat. Let stand, covered, for 5 to 10 minutes or till water is absorbed.

In a small skillet cook onion and garlic in the 1 tablespoon oil for 1 minute. Add carrot and celery; cook for 2 to 3 minutes more or just till tender.

To shape the couscous mixture, pack it firmly into a ⅓-cup measure and unmold it onto a baking sheet. Repeat to make 8 mounds total. Flatten with fingers into ½-inch-thick patties.

In a large bowl beat eggs slightly with a fork. Stir in couscous mixture, carrot mixture, bread crumbs, almonds, parsley or mint, and red pepper.

To shape, pack ⅛ of the couscous mixture firmly into a ⅓-cup measure; unmold onto a baking sheet. Repeat to make 8 mounds total. With moistened fingers, flatten into ½-inch-thick patties. Cover and chill for at least 1 hour or up to 24 hours.

In the large skillet cook patties, *half* at a time, in the 2 tablespoons oil over medium-low heat till crispy and light brown on both sides (5 to 7 minutes total). Serve the couscous patties warm with Orange Sauce and cut-up fresh fruits, if desired. Makes 4 main-dish servings.

Note: Couscous is a tiny round pasta about the size of sesame seed. You'll find it in the pasta section of your supermarket.

Nutrition facts per serving with ¼ cup sauce: 496 cal., 25 g total fat (5 g sat. fat), 114 mg chol., 556 mg sodium, 55 g carbo., 8 g fiber, 13 g pro. Daily Value: 60% vit. A, 33% vit. C, 15% calcium, 19% iron.

Orange Sauce

SERVE THIS FRAGRANT SAUCE OVER THE COUSCOUS CROQUETTES, COOKED RICE, OR STEAMED VEGETABLES—

¼ cup finely chopped shallots or onion
1 tablespoon margarine or butter
⅔ cup orange juice
¼ cup dry white wine or orange juice
1 bay leaf
¼ teaspoon salt
1 tablespoon cold water
2 teaspoons cornstarch
1 tablespoon snipped fresh chives
¼ teaspoon finely shredded orange peel

In a small saucepan cook shallots or onion in hot margarine or butter about 3 minutes or till tender but not brown. Add orange juice, wine or orange juice, bay leaf, and salt. Bring to boiling; reduce heat. Cover and simmer for 10 minutes.

In a small bowl mix the cold water and cornstarch; stir into the orange mixture. Cook and stir till thickened and bubbly. Cook and stir for 2 minutes more. Remove bay leaf. Stir in chives and orange peel. Makes about 1 cup.

Nutrition facts per tablespoon: 16 cal., 1 g total fat (0 g sat. fat), 2 mg chol., 41 mg sodium, 2 g carbo., 0 g fiber, 0 g pro.a Daily Value: 1% vit. A, 7% vit. C, 0% calcium, 1% iron.

Japanese Noodle Salad

THE TANGY VINAIGRETTE ON THE GREENS BLENDS WELL WITH THE CREAMY GINGER DRESSING ON THE NOODLES. ALTHOUGH THEY'RE DELICIOUS TOGETHER, YOU CAN SERVE EITHER ON A TOSSED SALAD. THEY'LL KEEP IN YOUR REFRIGERATOR FOR UP TO TWO WEEKS—

1 8½-ounce package soba (buckwheat noodles) or spaghetti
1 cup pea pods or green beans, halved lengthwise (4 ounces)
2 medium carrots cut into julienne strips (1 cup)
10 cups mixed greens or 1 medium head lettuce, torn
1 recipe Toasted Sesame Vinaigrette
1 recipe Spicy Tahini-Ginger Dressing
1 medium cucumber, thinly sliced
2 medium tomatoes, cut into wedges
⅔ cup bias-sliced green onions

Cook noodles according to package directions. Rinse and drain. Cover and chill till ready to serve.

In a medium saucepan cook green beans (if using) and carrots, covered, in a small amount of boiling water for 2 to 3 minutes or till crisp-tender (add pea pods the last 30 seconds, if using). Drain; transfer to a storage container. Cover and chill till ready to serve.

To assemble, in a large bowl toss greens with Toasted Sesame Vinaigrette; set aside. In another large bowl toss soba noodles with Spicy Tahini-Ginger Dressing.

On individual plates arrange greens. Top with soba noodles. Arrange cucumber, tomatoes, pea pods or green beans, and carrots on noodles. Top with green onions. Serves 6.

Toasted Sesame Vinaigrette: In a screw-top jar combine ¼ cup *rice vinegar* or *white wine vinegar*; 2 tablespoons *salad oil*; 2 teaspoons toasted *sesame seed*; 1 teaspoon *honey*; 1 teaspoon *tamari* or *soy sauce*; ½ teaspoon *toasted sesame oil*; and a dash *ground red pepper*. Cover and shake well to mix. Makes about ⅓ cup.

Spicy Tahini-Ginger Dressing: In a blender container combine ⅓ cup *tahini paste (sesame seed paste)*; ⅓ cup *water*; 3 tablespoons *rice vinegar*; 3 tablespoons *tamari* or *soy sauce*; 2 tablespoons thinly sliced, peeled *gingerroot*; 2 to 3 cloves *garlic*, peeled; 1 tablespoon *honey*; and ½ to 1 teaspoon *chili paste* or *chili sauce*. Cover; blend till smooth. Strain through a sieve to remove the gingerroot fibers. Makes about 1 cup.

Nutrition facts per serving: 354 cal., 14 g total fat (2 g sat. fat), 0 mg chol., 933 mg sodium, 52 g carbo., 7 g fiber, 12 g pro. Daily Value: 101% vit. A, 55% vit. C, 29% calcium, 37% iron.

Reprinted with permission from *The Cafe Brenda Cookbook: Redefining Seafood and Vegetarian Cuisine*, copyright 1992 by Brenda Langton and Margaret Stuart. Published by Voyageur Press, 123 North Second Street, Stillwater, MN 55082.

Timesaving Ideas for Vegetarian Cooking

Because of all the grains, beans, and flavors in vegetarian dishes, they can take time to prepare. To cut your time in the kitchen, try some of these helpful hints:

• Use your food processor to cut up vegetables such as onions, carrots, potatoes, and sweet peppers.

• Shred cheese ahead of time. Freeze or chill it in ½-cup portions so it's ready to use.

• Cook beans, grains, and rice in large quantities, then freeze in smaller portions to add to recipes as needed.

• Make salad dressings ahead. Oil and vinegar based dressings can stay in the refrigerator for several weeks.

• Cook a double batch of pasta; serve half, and refrigerate the rest for another meal. Use the extra pasta for chilled salads, or warm it in the microwave with extra sauce.

• Bake any serve-alongs, such as the grits triangles for Hoppin' John with Grits Polenta, the day before serving. Then broil them before mealtime.

Curried Vegetables

Tofu Fajita Pita

Greek Spinach Pie

Curried Vegetables

FORGET THE HEAVY, CREAMY SAUCE THAT "CURRY" CALLS TO MIND. THIS LIGHT AND SPICY VERSION REALLY ACCENTS THE VEGETABLES. SERVE IT WITH CHUTNEY—

1 large red onion, cut into strips (1½ cups)
1 teaspoon minced garlic (2 to 3 cloves)
1 tablespoon cooking oil
¾ cup water
½ cup apple juice
2 medium potatoes, cut into ½-inch chunks (2½ cups)
1 medium carrot, cut into ½-inch chunks (½ cup)
2 tablespoons tamari or soy sauce
1 tablespoon curry powder
1 teaspoon grated gingerroot
¼ teaspoon ground cardamom
¼ teaspoon ground cinnamon
2 cups cauliflower flowerets
1 medium zucchini, cut into ½-inch chunks (1½ cups)
1 cup frozen peas
1 medium red or green sweet pepper, cut into short ½-inch-wide strips (1 cup)
½ cup raisins
Hot cooked brown rice
Chutney (optional)

In a 4½-quart Dutch oven cook onion and garlic in hot oil over medium heat

"Tofu stretches my imagination. It absorbs the flavors of other ingredients, so I use it in our most popular Mexican, Oriental, and Caribbean dishes."

—Mark Parsons, Chef
Kung Food Restaurant
San Diego, Calif.

about 10 minutes or till tender, stirring occasionally. Add water, apple juice, potatoes, carrot, tamari or soy sauce, curry powder, gingerroot, cardamom, and cinnamon. Bring to boiling; reduce heat. Cover; simmer for 10 minutes.

Add cauliflower, zucchini, peas, pepper strips, and raisins. Cover and simmer for 3 to 5 minutes more or till zucchini is tender. Serve over hot cooked rice. If desired, serve with chutney. Makes 4 main-dish servings.

Nutrition facts per serving: 401 cal., 5 g total fat (1 g sat. fat), 0 mg chol., 568 mg sodium, 81 g carbo., 9 g fiber, 11 g pro. Daily Value: 70% vit. A, 133% vit. C, 11% calcium, 22% iron.

Tofu Fajita Pita

BE SURE THE TOFU YOU BUY IS LABELED "FIRM." IT'S BETTER FOR STIR-FRYING THAN SOFT TOFU—

1 10½-ounce package firm tofu (fresh bean curd), chopped
1 medium green pepper, cut into strips (1 cup)
1 small red onion, cut into strips
2 tablespoons snipped fresh cilantro
2 teaspoons chili powder
¾ teaspoon salt
½ teaspoon ground cumin
¼ teaspoon garlic powder
¼ teaspoon pepper
1 tablespoon olive oil or cooking oil
1 tablespoon lime juice
5 large whole wheat pita bread rounds or 8-inch whole wheat tortillas
¾ cup alfalfa sprouts
1 tomato, seeded and chopped
Salsa (optional)

continued on page 88

continued from page 87

For filling, in a medium mixing bowl combine tofu, green pepper, onion, cilantro, chili powder, salt, cumin, garlic powder, and pepper. In a 10-inch skillet cook filling, uncovered, in hot oil about 4 minutes or till vegetables are crisp tender. Stir in lime juice.

Spoon filling atop one side of each pita round or tortilla. Top with alfalfa sprouts and tomato. Fold opposite sides of pita or tortilla over filling; skewer closed with toothpicks. If desired, serve with salsa. Makes 5 main-dish servings.

Nutrition facts per serving: 239 cal., 9 g total fat (1 g sat. fat), 0 mg chol., 558 mg sodium, 28 g carbo., 3 g fiber, 14 g pro. Daily Value: 9% vit. A., 31% vit C, 21% calcium, 53% iron.

Greek Spinach Pie

THE CHEFS AT KUNG FOOD MAKE THEIR OWN WHOLE WHEAT DOUGH FOR THIS LAYERED CASSEROLE, BUT YOU CAN USE REGULAR PHYLLO DOUGH—

1¼ cups chopped onion
¼ cup snipped fresh parsley
½ teaspoon ground nutmeg
½ teaspoon pepper
2 tablespoons olive oil or cooking oil
2 tablespoons snipped fresh dill or
1½ teaspoons dried dillweed
5 eggs
½ cup milk
2 10-ounce packages frozen chopped spinach, thawed and well drained
1 pound feta cheese, crumbled
⅓ cup unsalted butter, melted

½ of a 16-ounce package frozen phyllo dough (10 to 12 sheets)
Dairy sour cream (optional)
Snipped fresh dill (optional)

For filling, in a medium saucepan cook chopped onion, snipped parsley, nutmeg, and pepper in hot oil, covered, over low heat about 20 minutes or till onions are very tender, stirring occasionally. Stir in fresh or dried dill. Set mixture aside.

In a medium mixing bowl combine eggs and milk; beat with a rotary beater or a wire whisk till smooth. Stir in onion mixture, spinach, and feta.

Brush the bottom of a 3-quart rectangular baking dish with *some* of the melted butter. Unfold phyllo sheets; cut in half crosswise to fit into the dish. (To prevent drying, keep phyllo sheets covered with clear plastic wrap till ready to use.) Place *one* phyllo sheet half in the bottom of the dish. Brush with melted butter. Repeat with 9 to 11 more half-sheets of phyllo and melted butter.

Spread spinach filling over the layers of buttered phyllo in the baking dish. Layer remaining phyllo sheets over filling, brushing each with melted butter. If desired, use a sharp knife to score the top of the phyllo dough into 9 rectangles.

Bake, uncovered, in a 375° oven about 30 minutes or till golden. Let stand for 10 minutes. To serve, cut into rectangles along scored lines. If desired, top each serving with sour cream and fresh dill. Makes 9 main-dish servings.

Nutrition facts per serving: 371 cal., 24 g total fat (13 g sat. fat), 182 mg chol., 753 mg sodium, 26 g carbo., 2 g fiber, 16 g pro. Daily Value: 91% vit. A, 18% vit. C, 48% calcium, and 18% iron.

Hoppin' John with Grits Polenta

COOK THE DRY BLACK-EYED PEAS AHEAD OF TIME OR USE FROZEN OR CANNED VERSIONS—

½ cup dry black-eyed peas, one 10-ounce package frozen black-eyed peas (2 cups), or one 15-ounce can black-eyed peas, drained
¾ cup long-grain rice
1½ cups chopped red, yellow, and/or green sweet pepper
2 medium carrots, thinly bias sliced (1 cup)
1 cup frozen or canned whole kernel corn
1 tablespoon finely chopped shallots or onion
1½ teaspoons minced garlic (4 cloves)
1 tablespoon margarine or butter
1 cup chopped, seeded tomatoes
2 tablespoons snipped fresh parsley
1 tablespoon snipped fresh thyme or 1 teaspoon dried thyme, crushed
½ teaspoon salt
¼ to ½ teaspoon red pepper flakes
⅛ teaspoon pepper
Purple kale (optional)
1 recipe Grits Polenta (see recipe, page 90)
Chili peppers (optional)

Rinse dry black-eyed peas. In a medium saucepan combine peas and enough water to cover. Bring to boiling; reduce heat. Cover and simmer for 45 to 60 minutes or till tender. (Or, cook frozen black-eyed peas according to package directions). Drain peas.

Cook rice according to package directions. Drain and set aside.

In a 12-inch skillet cook peppers, carrots, corn, shallots or onion, and garlic in margarine, covered, for 6 to 8 minutes or till crisp-tender, stirring once or twice.

continued on page 90

Three Grain Salad with
Roasted Garlic Vinaigrette

Hoppin' John with Grits Polenta

"Two or three grains are
more interesting than
one. We cook up big
batches to mix and
match in our specialties."
—Jim Watkins, Chef
Cafe Flora
Seattle, Wash.

continued from page 88

Add black-eyed peas, cooked rice, and tomatoes; stir gently to mix. Cook, covered, over low heat about 5 minutes or till heated through, stirring occasionally. Add parsley, thyme, salt, red pepper flakes, and pepper.

To serve, line 4 to 6 dinner plates with kale, if desired. Spoon pea mixture onto plates. Arrange Grits Polenta triangles alongside. If desired, garnish with peppers. Makes 4 to 6 main-dish servings.

Nutrition facts per serving: 551 cal., 14 g total fat (10 g sat. fat), 16 mg chol., 669 mg sodium, 89 g carbo, 11 g fiber, and 18 g pro. Daily Value: 178% vit. A, 134% vit. C, 44% calcium, and 29% iron.

Grits Polenta

SMOKED CHEESE IS THE FLAVOR SECRET TO THESE SOUTHERN-STYLE GRITS TRIANGLES. CAFE FLORA USES MOZZARELLA, BUT YOU MAY FIND OTHER SMOKED CHEESES IN YOUR AREA. ASK THE DELI CLERK IF YOU CAN TASTE A SAMPLE BEFORE BUYING—

2 cups water
1 cup milk, half-and-half, or light cream
¼ teaspoon salt
¾ cup quick-cooking hominy grits
¾ cup shredded smoked mozzarella, provolone, Swiss, or cheddar cheese (3 ounces)
2 tablespoons margarine or butter

In a large saucepan combine the water; milk, half-and-half, or cream; and salt. Bring to boiling; reduce heat. Slowly add

Cut the cooled 8-inch square of grits into four equal squares. Then cut each small square diagonally into 4 triangles.

grits, stirring with a whisk. Cook and stir for 5 to 7 minutes or till very thick. Remove from heat.

Add cheese and margarine; stir till melted. Pour onto a greased cookie sheet; spread into an 8-inch square (about ½ to ¾ inch thick). Cover; let stand at room temperature till cool and firm. (Or, chill overnight.)

Cut firm grits into 16 triangles. Arrange triangles on the rack of an unheated broiler pan. Broil 4 to 5 inches from the heat for 4 to 5 minutes or till the surface is slightly crisp and beginning to brown. Makes 16 triangles.

Nutrition facts per triangle: 41 cal., 3 g total fat (1 g sat. fat), 4 mg chol., 82 mg sodium, 2 g carbo., 0 g fiber, 2 g pro. Daily Value: 5% vit. A, 0% vit. C, 7% calcium, 1% iron.

Three-Grain Salad with Roasted Garlic Vinaigrette

ROASTING GIVES THE GARLIC A MELLOW, TOASTY FLAVOR. DEPENDING ON HOW MUCH GARLIC FLAVOR YOU WANT, USE BETWEEN 3 AND 8 CLOVES—

4 cups water
½ cup wheat berries
½ cup quinoa
¼ cup millet
1 recipe Roasted Garlic Vinaigrette
1 10-ounce package frozen lima beans
1 cup chopped red, yellow, and/or green sweet pepper
1 cup finely chopped celery
½ cup currants or raisins
¼ cup snipped fresh parsley
1 tablespoon snipped fresh thyme or
½ teaspoon dried thyme, crushed
1 tablespoon snipped fresh dill or
½ teaspoon dried dillweed
½ teaspoon salt
¼ teaspoon pepper
Flowering kale or mixed greens (optional)
Cut-up fresh fruits or vegetables, such as red grapes or sliced pear, or cucumber (optional)

In a medium saucepan heat the water to boiling. Add wheat berries; reduce heat. Cover and simmer for 40 minutes. Add quinoa and millet; cover and simmer about 15 minutes more or till tender. Drain.

In a large mixing bowl stir together the cooked grains and Roasted Garlic Vinaigrette; toss to coat. Cover and chill for several hours or overnight.

Cook lima beans according to package directions; drain and chill.

To serve, add lima beans, chopped peppers, celery, currants or raisins, parsley, thyme, dill, salt, and pepper to the chilled grain mixture. If desired, line 6 salad plates with kale or greens; set aside. Press the grain mixture into six 1-ounce custard cups; unmold onto the lined salad plates. (Or, spoon the loose mixture onto salad plates.) If desired, garnish each salad with fruits or vegetables. Makes 6 main-dish servings.

Roasted Garlic Vinaigrette: Peel 3 to 8 cloves *garlic;* place the peeled garlic in a shallow baking pan. Bake, uncovered, in a 350° oven for 15 to 20 minutes or till golden brown and soft in the centers. In a blender container combine roasted garlic, ⅓ cup *balsamic vinegar,* 2 tablespoons *chopped shallots or onion,* 1 tablespoon *Dijon-style mustard,* and 1 teaspoon sugar. Cover and blend for 5 seconds. With the blender running, slowly add 3 tablespoons *olive oil or salad oil* in a thin, steady stream. Makes ⅔ cup.

Nutrition facts per serving: 312 cal., 9 g total fat (1 g sat. fat), 0 mg chol., 296 mg sodium, 53 g carbo., 5 g fiber, 9 g pro. Daily Value: 3% vit. A, 41% vit. C, 7% calcium, 28% iron.

Three Grains to Try

You can find the grains for Three-Grain Salad in the rice section of your supermarket or in a health food store.

Quinoa: a grain with complete protein. (It provides the same protein components as meat.) Cook, covered, in twice the amount of water for 15 minutes to serve in salads, pilafs, soups, casseroles, and breakfast cereals.

Wheat berries: unpolished whole wheat kernels. Cook, covered, in three times the amount of water for 1 hour to add to salads, soups, breads, and side dishes.

Millet: unpolished yellow whole kernels from the millet plant. Cook, covered, in three times the amount of water for 15 to 20 minutes to use in cereals and side dishes.

"We emphasize low-fat protein sources in teaching vegetarian cooking to our culinary students. Beans and grains are cheap, nutritious, and very versatile."

—Robert H. Briggs, Chef
The Culinary Institute of America
Hyde Park, N.Y.

Black Bean Burritos
So spicy and satisfying, this burrito tastes as if it came from your favorite Mexican eatery. The difference? It's low in fat. For ideas on reducing fat in vegetarian cooking, see Chef Briggs' cooking tips, below.

Tips for low-fat vegetarian cooking

Vegetarian eating can be high in fat, especially if you rely heavily on nuts and cheese for protein. To keep the fat low in vegetarian cooking, follow Chef Briggs' tips:

• Reduce the amount of butter or oil needed in cooking. Use nonstick pans and spray them with nonstick cooking spray before heating.

• Rely on combinations of beans and grains for your primary protein. Low-fat fish is a good source too, if it fits your definition of vegetarian eating.

• If your vegetarian diet includes dairy products, look for lower-fat versions of yogurt, sour cream, and cheeses. Use evaporated skim milk in place of cream or whipping cream. (It can even be whipped.)

• Use nuts and cheeses sparingly, just to add flavor and complement other sources of protein.

• Bake, grill, simmer, broil, and steam when possible. Keep frying, sautéing, and stir-frying to a minimum.

• Thicken sauces by adding pureed fruits, vegetables, or rice, rather than starting with a butter-flour base.

• To replace the rich flavor of fat, turn to citrus peel and juices, fresh herbs, and flavored vinegars. Or, use a small amount of an intensely flavored oil, such as sesame, to add flavor without adding much fat.

• Chef Briggs' interest in low-fat cooking stems from his involvement as a food professional with Project LEAN (*Low-fat Eating for America Now*). Sponsored by the National Center for Nutrition and Dietetics (NCND), of The American Dietetic Association, this national nutrition education campaign promotes low-fat shopping, cooking, and dining. For more information on low-fat cooking and a free copy of Project LEAN's *New LEAN Toward Health* booklet, call the NCND's Consumer Nutrition Hotline: 800/366-1655.

Black Bean Burritos

JALAPEÑO PEPPERS CONTAIN OILS THAT MAY BURN YOUR EYES, LIPS, AND SKIN. FOR THAT REASON, WEAR PLASTIC GLOVES WHEN WORKING WITH HOT PEPPERS. AND, WASH YOUR HANDS AFTERWARDS—

8 ounces dry black beans* or two 15-ounce cans black beans
1 medium onion, finely chopped
2 cloves garlic, minced
1 to 2 jalapeño peppers, seeded and finely chopped
1 tablespoon chili powder
1 teaspoon ground cumin
1 tablespoon olive oil or cooking oil
1 16-ounce can tomatoes, cut up
1 ¼-inch-thick lemon slice
1 teaspoon dried oregano, crushed
Dash bottled hot pepper sauce (optional)
6 6-inch flour tortillas
Salsa
Guacamole or low-fat dairy sour cream
Chopped tomato (optional)
Snipped cilantro (optional)

Cook dry beans.* Rinse and drain cooked or canned beans. Set aside.

In a 4½-quart Dutch oven cook onion, garlic, peppers, chili powder, and cumin in hot oil till tender, stirring occasionally. Stir in drained beans, *undrained* tomatoes, lemon, oregano, pepper sauce (if desired), and ¼ teaspoon *salt*. (Omit salt if using canned beans.) Bring to boiling; reduce heat. Simmer, uncovered, about 15 minutes or till thick.

Remove lemon. In a blender container or food processor bowl place *one-third* of the bean mixture. Cover; blend till smooth. Repeat with remaining mixture. Return to pan; heat through.

Meanwhile, wrap tortillas in foil; warm in a 350° oven for 10 minutes.

Place about ½ cup of the bean mixture onto *each* tortilla; fold edges over to cover. Serve with salsa and guacamole or sour cream. If desired, top with chopped tomato and snipped cilantro. Makes 3 main-dish servings.

*Note: To cook dry beans, in a 4½-quart Dutch oven, combine beans and enough *water* to cover. Bring to boiling; reduce heat. Simmer, uncovered, 2 minutes. Remove from heat. Cover; let stand for 1 hour. (Or, without cooking, soak beans overnight.) Drain beans and rinse. In the same Dutch oven combine beans and 5 cups *water or vegetable broth*. Bring to boiling; reduce heat. Cover; simmer 1 to 1½ hours or till tender.

Nutrition facts per serving: 503 cal., 13 total g fat (1 g sat. fat), 0 mg chol., 576 mg sodium, 81 g carbo., 7 g fiber, 22 g pro. Daily Value: 37% vit. A, 80% vit. C, 24% calcium, 51% iron.

Vegetarian Eating for Your Family

The recipes in this story contain no red meat, following one definition of vegetarian eating. But, your family may embrace a stricter definition and exclude fish, poultry, eggs, and dairy products. No matter which approach you take for vegetarian dining, your family wins by eating more fruits, vegetables, and whole grains—foods that should make up the bulk of your diet. Even so, vegetarian eating isn't always low in fat. To keep fat at a reasonable level in vegetarian meals, follow Chef Briggs' cooking tips on page 92.

When you eliminate all animal-based products from your diet, you must plan carefully to ensure a nutritional balance of necessary protein, vitamins, and minerals. For strict vegetarians, intake of such nutrients as iron, calcium, zinc, vitamin B12, and vitamin D can be lower than recommended. Because strict vegetarianism may lack the necessary nutrients needed for growth, this diet is not recommended for children, unless closely supervised by a registered dietician or someone with a master's degree or doctorate in nutrition and some clinical nutrition expertise.

Children's special needs

Johanna Dwyer, D.Sc., R.D., Director of Frances Stern Nutrition Center at New England Medical Cenmter Hospital in Boston, and Professor at Tufts University Schools of Medicine and Nutrition, has researched children's vegetarian diets for over 20 years. She (along with other experts in the field) recommends that children who don't eat meat adopt a less stringent form of vegetarianism, one that includes dairy products.

Just by consuming dairy products, kids are more likely to get the nutrients their bodies need. It is especially important that children aged 2 and younger eat regular, not low-fat, dairy products, because they need the fat for calories.

Prize Tested Recipes.

Chicken Kabobs with Lime and Chutney Sauce

NORMA JAZZED UP A JAR OF CHUTNEY TO MAKE A KABOB MARINADE WITH WINNING FLAVOR—

¾ pound skinless, boneless chicken breast halves
1 8½- to 9-ounce jar chutney (about ¾ cup), snipped
2 tablespoons lime juice
4 teaspoons olive oil or cooking oil
2 teaspoons curry powder
1 large mango or papaya, seeded, peeled, and cut into 1-inch pieces (about 2 cups) or one 15-ounce jar mango slices, cut into 1-inch pieces
2 medium red and/or green sweet peppers, cut into 1-inch pieces
Hot cooked rice (optional)
Sliced kiwi fruit and star fruit (optional)

◆ Chicken Kabobs with Lime and Chutney Sauce

Rinse chicken; pat dry with paper towels. Cut chicken into 1-inch chunks. Set aside.

In a medium bowl stir together chutney, lime juice, oil, and curry powder. Stir in chicken pieces. Cover and refrigerate 2 to 4 hours.

On eight 6-inch wooden skewers, alternately thread chicken pieces with mango or papaya and sweet pepper. Arrange skewers in a 2-quart rectangular baking dish. Brush with any remaining marinade mixture. Cover with waxed paper. Micro-cook on 100% power (high) for 6 to 7 minutes or till chicken is no longer pink, turning dish and rearranging kabobs once. If desired, serve with hot cooked rice. Garnish with sliced fruit, if desired. Makes 4 servings.

Note: Recipe is not recommended for low-wattage ovens.

Nutrition facts per serving: 298 cal., 7 g total fat (1 g sat. fat), 45 mg chol., 54 mg sodium, 42 g carbo., 2 g fiber; 17 g pro. Daily Value: 33% vitVit. A, 86% vit. C, 9% iron.

$200 WINNER
Norma J. Keleher, Pacific Grove, Calif.

Tropical Fruit Soup

FOR A SPECIAL SPRING CELEBRATION, SERVE THIS FRUIT SOUP AS A REFRESHING FIRST-COURSE APPETIZER OR AS A LUSCIOUS LIGHT DESSERT—

2 cups cubed canteloupe, papaya, mango, and/or guava
1½ cups cubed pineapple
¾ cup guava, papaya, or pear nectar
2 teaspoons snipped fresh mint
¾ cup lime-flavored seltzer water, chilled
Sliced strawberries (optional)
Mint leaves (optional)

In blender container or food processor bowl combine *half* of the fruit, *half* the nectar, and *1 teaspoon* of the mint. Cover; blend or process till smooth. Transfer to a large bowl. Repeat with remaining fruit, nectar, and mint; add to pureed fruit in bowl. Cover; chill 4 to 24 hours. Just before serving, stir in seltzer water. Ladle into bowls. Garnish with sliced strawberries and mint, if desired. Makes 4 servings.

Nutrition facts per serving: 83 cal., 1 g total fat (0 g sat. fat), 0 mg chol., 20 mg sodium, 21 g carbo., 2 g fiber, 1 g protein. Daily Value: 33% vit. A, 74% vit. C, 5% iron.

$200 WINNER

Mary Anne Scarr, Oakland, Calif.

Chilled Spanish Soup

THE TANGY SOUR CREAM, ROASTED SWEET PEPPERS AND HEAT OF THE CHILI PEPPERS COMPLEMENT EACH OTHER DELICIOUSLY IN THIS SOUP. SERVE IT AS THE FIRST COURSE TO A SPICY SUPPER—

1 14-ounce can artichoke hearts, drained
1 cup roasted red sweet peppers, drained
1 cup salsa
1 Anaheim chili pepper, seeded and chopped (about ¼ cup) or one 4-ounce can diced green chili peppers, drained
1¼ cups dairy sour cream
⅛ teaspoon ground cumin
⅛ teaspoon black pepper
4 cups chicken broth
Dairy sour cream (optional)
Milk (optional)
Thinly sliced jalapeño pepper (optional)

Combine the artichokes, red peppers, salsa, and chili pepper. Place *half* of the

continued on page 96

◆ Tropical Fruit Soup

◆ Chilled Spanish Soup

May
95

continued from page 97

mixture in a blender container or food processor bowl. Cover and blend or process till smooth. Transfer mixture to a large bowl. Repeat with remaining artichoke hearts, red peppers, salsa, and chili pepper. Add sour cream, cumin, and black pepper to blender. Cover and blend or process till mixture is smooth. Add to pepper mixture in bowl. Stir in broth. Cover and chill 2 to 24 hours. To serve, divide soup among eight bowls.

If desired, thin additional sour cream with a little milk; dollop onto each serving. Garnish with jalapeño pepper, if desired. Makes 8 side-dish servings.

Nutrition facts per serving: 127 cal. 9 g total fat (5 g sat. fat) 16 mg chol. 560 mg sodium, 9 g carbo. 1 g fiber, 5 g pro. Daily Value: 34% vit. A, 124% vit. C, 8% calcium.

$100 WINNER

Laura Sabo, Portland, Oreg.

♦ Quick Chicken Mole

Quick Chicken Mole

MOLE (PRONOUNCED MO LAY), A CLASSIC MEXICAN SAUCE, USUALLY CONTAINS TOMATOES, CHILI PEPPERS, AND CHOCOLATE. JUST A LITTLE COCOA LENDS RICHNESS TO THIS SAUCE—

2 teaspoons unsweetened cocoa powder
1½ teaspoons chili powder
½ teaspoon ground cumin
½ teaspoon dried oregano, crushed
¼ teaspoon salt
1 8-ounce can tomato sauce
¼ cup finely chopped onion
3 cloves garlic, minced
1 pound skinless, boneless chicken breast halves, cut into bite-sized strips

1 4-ounce can diced green chili peppers, drained
Toasted sliced almonds (optional)
Flour tortillas or hot cooked rice
Chopped tomato, shredded lettuce, and sliced avocado (optional)

In a 1½-quart microwave-safe casserole combine cocoa powder, chili powder, cumin, oregano, and salt. Stir in tomato sauce, onion, and garlic. Microcook, covered, on 100% power (high) for 2 to 3 minutes or till mixture is bubbly around edges, stirring once. Stir in chicken and chili peppers. Cover; cook on high for 8 to 10 minutes (10 to 12 minutes for low-wattage ovens) or till chicken is tender and no longer pink inside, stirring every 3 minutes. Garnish with almonds, if desired. Serve with warm tortillas or hot cooked rice, tomato, lettuce, and avocado, if desired. Makes 4 servings.

Nutrition facts per serving: 253 cal., 5 g total fat (1 g sat. fat), 59 mg chol., 700 mg sodium, 2 g fiber, 25 g carbo., 26 g pro. Daily Value: 29% vit. A, 29% vit. C, 11% calcium, 19% iron.

$100 WINNER

Maureen Valentine, Seatac, Wash.

June

Celebrate Summer

Prize Tested Recipes

Celebrate
Summer

By Lisa Holderness

Western BBQ

Round up family and friends for a wild-West chuck-wagon dinner. With your backyard as your prairie and our Texas-style menu for the grub, create a finger-lickin cookout, complete with sizzling steak, zesty beans, and all the trimmings. Because more than half the recipes are grilled, even the cooks get to join in the outdoor fun. The other dishes can be made ahead, leaving plenty of time for horsin' around. To capture the spirit of the West, dress the part with cowboy boots, shirts, and hats. Decorate the table with cactus centerpieces and use bandannas for napkins.

Texas Barbecue Beef

THE BRUSH-ON SAUCE FLAVORS AND MOISTENS THE MEAT WHILE GRILLING. THE SOPPIN' SAUCE IS A SECOND DOSE OF ZESTY TASTE—

¼ cup Worcestershire sauce
3 tablespoons vinegar
1 teaspoon ground cumin
1 teaspoon dry mustard
½ teaspoon bottled hot pepper sauce
¼ teaspoon ground cinnamon
1½ pounds beef flank or round steak, cut about ¾ inch thick
1 recipe Hobo Vegetables (optional) (see recipe, page 100)
Red jalapeño peppers (optional)
Fresh cilantro sprigs (optional)
1 recipe Soppin' Sauce or purchased barbecue sauce

For brush-on sauce, in a small bowl combine Worcestershire sauce, vinegar, cumin, dry mustard, hot pepper sauce, and cinnamon.

For direct grilling, place the meat on an uncovered grill directly over *medium* coals. Brush *some* of the brush-on sauce over the meat. Grill meat for 12 to 14 minutes for medium doneness or longer for desired doneness, turning once and brushing frequently with brush-on sauce.

Or, for indirect grilling, in a covered grill arrange *medium-hot* coals around a drip pan. Place steak on the grill rack over the drip pan. Brush *some* of the brush-on sauce over the meat. Cover and grill over *medium* heat for 18 to 22 minutes or till desired doneness, turning

continued on page 100

◆ Cowboy Beans

◆ Texas Barbecue Beef
with Soppin' Sauce

continued from page 98

once and brushing frequently with brush-on sauce.

Remove meat from the grill and allow meat to stand, covered loosely with foil, about 10 minutes for easier carving. Thinly slice the meat across the grain. Arrange on platter with Hobo Vegetables, if desired. Garnish with red jalapeño peppers and fresh cilantro. Serve with Soppin' Sauce. Makes 6 main-dish servings.

Soppin' Sauce: In a small saucepan combine ½ cup *catsup;* ¼ cup *water;* 2 tablespoons finely chopped *onion;* 2 tablespoons *apple jelly;* 1 tablespoon *vinegar;* 1 tablespoon *Worcestershire sauce;* 1 *jalapeño pepper,* finely chopped; and ⅛ teaspoon *salt.* On the grill or stove top, bring the sauce to boiling. (If grilling, bring sauce to boiling over direct heat, then place over indirect heat to simmer.) Simmer, uncovered, about 15 minutes or to desired consistency. To make ahead, prepare sauce, then cover and chill for up to 2 days. Before serving, heat through. Makes about 1 cup.

Nutrition facts per serving with Soppin' Sauce: 220 cal., 8 g total fat (3 g sat. fat), 53 mg chol., 475 mg sodium, 14 g carbo., 0 g fiber, 23 g pro. Daily Value: 7% vit. A, 56% vit. C, 4% calcium, 24% iron.

Cowboy Beans

2 15-ounce cans pinto beans, rinsed and drained
¾ cup beer or water
½ cup finely chopped onion
½ cup coarsely chopped ham or crumbled, crisp-cooked bacon (4 to 5 slices)
1 4-ounce can diced green chili peppers
⅓ cup molasses
¼ cup catsup
1 tablespoon chili powder

In a 1½-quart casserole or bean pot combine beans, beer or water, onion, ham or bacon, *undrained* chili peppers, molasses, catsup, and chili powder. Stir to mix thoroughly*.

Bake, uncovered, in a 350° oven for 1 to 1½ hours or till desired consistency, stirring occasionally. Makes 6 to 8 side-dish servings.

***To make ahead:** Combine ingredients as directed. Cover and chill till cooking time, up to 24 hours.

Nutrition facts per serving: 216 cal., 1 g total fat (0 g sat. fat), 6 mg chol., 818 mg sodium, 41 g carbo. 8 g fiber, and 12 g pro. Daily Value: 14% vit. A, 17% vit. C, 6% calcium, 17% iron.

Hobo Vegetables

KIDS LIKE EATING VEGETABLES FROM THEIR OWN FOIL PACKETS. COOL THE PACKETS SLIGHTLY AND OPEN THEM CAREFULLY TO AVOID ANY HOT STEAM BURNS—

4 medium potatoes, thinly sliced
2 medium red onions, cut into thin wedges
2 medium carrots, cut into julienne strips
¼ cup margarine or butter, melted
1 clove garlic, minced

½ teaspoon salt
¼ teaspoon pepper
2 tablespoons snipped parsley (optional)

Cut six 18x12-inch pieces heavy foil. Divide potatoes, onions, and carrots evenly among pieces of foil, placing vegetables in center of each piece.

In a small bowl stir together margarine or butter, garlic, salt, and pepper. Brush mixture over vegetables in each packet, using all of the mixture. Bring up long sides of foil and, leaving space for steam, seal tightly with a double fold. Fold short ends to seal.

Grill foil packets, on an uncovered grill, directly over medium coals for 25 minutes or till vegetables are tender, turning packets over half way through. Serve in the foil packets or transfer the vegetables to a serving platter. Sprinkle with parsley, if desired. Makes 6 side-dish servings.

Nutrition facts per serving: 186 cal., 8 g total fat (1 g sat. fat), 0 mg chol., 289 mg sodium, 28 g carbo., 2 g fiber, 3 g pro. Daily Value: 78% vit. A, 27% vit. C, 3% calcium, 4% iron.

Corn on the Cob

COOK THE SWEET CORN INDOORS, LEAVING ROOM ON THE GRILL FOR THE BEEF, VEGETABLES, AND BREAD—

6 to 8 fresh ears of corn
2 to 3 tablespoons margarine or butter, softened

Remove the husks and silks from the corn; scrub with a stiff brush to remove all silks. Rinse.

In a Dutch oven cook corn, covered, in a small amount of lightly salted boiling water for 5 to 7 minutes or till tender. Transfer corn to a serving platter. Brush corn with margarine or butter. Serve hot. Makes 6 to 8 side-dish servings.

Nutrition facts per serving: 117 cal., 5 g total fat (1 g sat. fat), 0 mg chol., 58 mg sodium, 19 g carbo., 7 g fiber, 3 g pro. Daily Value: 6% vit. A, 5% vit. C.

Summer Slaw

FOR A LIGHTER SALAD, USE REDUCED-CALORIE OR FAT-FREE SALAD DRESSING—

½ of a 16-ounce preshredded coleslaw mix (about 4 cups)
1 medium orange, peeled, sliced, and quartered, or 1 small red sweet pepper, seeded and cut into bite-size pieces
½ of a jicama, peeled and cut into julienne strips (1½ cups)
⅔ cup creamy cucumber, creamy Italian, buttermilk ranch salad dressing, or coleslaw dressing
⅓ cup toasted pecan pieces

In a large bowl combine coleslaw mix, orange or pepper, and jicama.

Pour dressing over coleslaw mixture and toss to coat. Cover and chill for 1 to 24 hours. Stir in pecans before serving. Makes 6 side-dish servings.

Nutrition facts per serving: 200 cal., 18 g total fat (2 g sat. fat), 0 mg chol., 349 mg sodium, 11 g carbo, 2 g fiber, 2 g pro. Daily Value: 49% vit. A, 52% vit. C, 3% calcium. 5% iron.

Texas Toast

WHEN THE HOBO VEGETABLES COME OFF THE GRILL PLACE THICK SLICES OF SOURDOUGH BREAD OVER THE HOT COALS TO TOAST. SERVE THE BREAD WITH HONEY-CITRUS BUTTER—

¼ cup margarine or butter
2 tablespoons honey
1 teaspoon finely shredded lemon or orange peel
⅛ teaspoon ground cinnamon
Finely shredded lemon or orange peel (optional)
1 1-pound loaf sourdough bread, cut into 1-inch thick slices

For honey-citrus butter, beat margarine or butter till fluffy. Beat in honey, the 1 teaspoon finely shredded lemon or orange peel, and cinnamon till combined. Transfer honey-citrus butter to a small serving dish. Sprinkle with additional lemon or orange peel, if desired.

Grill bread slices, on an uncovered grill, directly over *medium* coals for 1 to 2 minutes or till golden. Turn and grill other side for 1 to 2 minutes or till golden. Serve warm with honey-citrus butter. Makes 16 slices.

Nutrition facts per slice: 114 cal., 3 g total fat (1 g sat. fat), 0 mg chol., 201 mg sodium, 19 g carbo., 0 g fiber, 3 g pro. Daily Value: 4% vit. A, 0% vit. C, 0% calcium, 5% iron.

Strawberry-Fudge Mud Pie

FOR A LIGHTER VERSION, USE CHOCO-
LATE AND STRAWBERRY LOW-FAT OR
FAT-FREE FROZEN DESSERTS AND SKIP
THE WHIPPED CREAM—

*1½ cups finely crushed chocolate wafers
(30 wafers)
6 tablespoons margarine or butter, melted
1 pint chocolate ice cream or coffee-
flavored ice cream*
½ cup toasted coarsely chopped almonds
1 pint strawberry ice cream
⅓ cup fudge ice-cream topping
Whipped cream (optional)
Whole strawberries (optional)*

In a medium bowl stir together the crushed wafers and melted margarine or butter. Turn the chocolate crumb mixture into a 9-inch pie plate. Spread crumb mixture evenly in pie plate. Press on bottom and sides to form a firm, even crust. Chill about 1 hour till firm.

In a medium mixing bowl soften chocolate or coffee-flavored ice cream, using a wooden spoon to stir and press against side of bowl. Spread softened chocolate or coffee-flavored ice cream evenly atop cookie crust; sprinkle with toasted almonds. Freeze till firm (about 1 hour).

In a clean bowl soften strawberry ice cream as described above. Remove pie from freezer and spread strawberry ice cream atop almond layer. Return to freezer.

In a small saucepan heat and stir the fudge topping just till heated through. Cool the topping slightly. Remove the pie from the freezer and drizzle the top of pie with fudge topping in a lacy design. Return to freezer immediately.

◆ Strawberry Fudge Mud Pie

Freeze for 4 hours or till firm. To freeze longer, cover the pie with freezer wrap or foil and freeze for up to 1 month.

To serve, let pie stand at room temperature about 10 minutes. Garnish pie with whipped cream and whole strawberries, if desired. For easier slicing, place pie plate atop a warm, wet towel. Slice the pie and serve immediately. Makes 8 servings.

*Note: For this versatile pie, you can vary the flavors of ice cream and ice-cream topping.

Nutrition facts per serving: 339 cal., 21 g total fat (4 g sat. fat), 17 mg chol., 258 mg sodium, 34 g carbo., 1 g fiber, 5 g pro. Daily Value: 20% vit. A, 5% vit. C, 12% calcium, 7% iron.

Celebrate Summer
Country Garden Party

When the family gathers for a dressier occasion, it's the little extras that make the day memorable. With our help, planning your celebration can be almost as much fun as the party itself. Choose from 10 appetizer and dessert recipes to create a menu that fits your party size and theme. Each recipe is designed for busy hosts (and can stand up to the midday sun). With your freshly trimmed yard as the setting, fill in with a few finishing touches from the Country Garden Party Tips.

Menu

Confetti Vegetable Terrine
Combine the richness of cheesecake with a sprinkling of vegetables in this savory, make-ahead spread.

Grilled Seafood Platter
The aroma of succulent shrimp, scallops, and salmon on the grill will draw guests in search of a sample.

Bite-Size Herb Biscuits
Stuff mini biscuits with a variety of fillings. Party-goers love 'em, because they're easy to eat and taste so delicious.

Easy Antipasto Sampler
Start with Italian Caponata and Herbed Goat Cheese, then fill in with favorite fruits, bread, and tomatoes.

Confetti Vegetable Terrine

2 8-ounce packages cream cheese, softened
½ cup crumbled feta cheese
¼ teaspoon garlic powder
⅛ teaspoon ground red pepper
½ cup dairy sour cream
2 eggs
1½ teaspoons finely shredded lemon peel
¼ cup thinly sliced green onion
½ cup chopped roasted sweet peppers or canned pimiento
⅓ cup chopped ripe olives
½ cup snipped parsley
Edible flowers, such as snapdragons or pansies (optional)*
Chives (optional)
Purple kale or leaf lettuce (optional)
Assorted crackers

Line bottom of an 8x4x2-inch loaf pan with foil. Grease sides; set aside.

In a medium mixing bowl beat cream cheese till smooth. Add feta cheese, garlic powder, and ground red pepper. Beat well. Add sour cream, eggs, and lemon peel. Beat just till blended. *Do not overbeat.* Stir in onion, sweet pepper or pimiento, and olives. Pour into prepared pan; spread evenly. Place loaf pan in a larger baking pan. Pour boiling water into the larger pan to a depth of 1 inch.

Bake in a 325° oven for 50 minutes or till center is soft set and stays firm when shaken. Transfer loaf pan to a wire cooling rack; cool completely (about 1 hour). Cover and chill for 4 to 24 hours.

To serve, slip a knife around the sides of the pan to loosen, then invert onto a serving platter. Remove foil. Gently press parsley onto sides of the terrine, leaving top plain. Garnish the top with edible flowers and chives for the stems, if desired. Sprinkle more edible flowers on

◆ Confetti Vegetable Terrine

the platter. Line the edge of the platter with purple kale or leaf lettuce, if desired. Serve with crackers. Makes about 20 appetizer servings.

*Note: When decorating food with flowers, make sure that the flowers you choose are safe to eat and were grown without pesticides. Your safest sources are from the supermarket and your own garden.

Nutrition facts per 1 tablespoon atop a cracker: 31 cal., 2 g total fat (1 g sat. fat), 6 mg chol., 40 mg sodium, 3 g carbo., 0 g fiber, 1 g pro. Daily Value: 2% vit. A, 2% vit. C, 0% calcium.

Grilled Seafood Platter

HAVE THE SAUCES, SEAFOOD, VEGETABLES, AND COALS ALL READY TO GO WHEN GUESTS ARRIVE. WHEN IT'S TIME TO GRILL, ENLIST THEIR HELP. GRILL ONLY ENOUGH SEAFOOD AND VEGETABLES TO FILL A PLATTER, THEN GRILL MORE DURING THE PARTY AS NEEDED—

1½ pounds fresh or frozen large shrimp in shells and/or sea scallops
1 1- to 1½-pound fresh or frozen salmon fillet
1 red sweet pepper, cut into 1-inch pieces
1 medium red onion, cut into bite-size pieces
1 small zucchini, halved lengthwise and cut into ½-inch slices
1 small yellow summer squash, halved lengthwise and cut into ½-inch-thick slices
⅓ cup olive oil or cooking oil
3 tablespoons lemon juice
2 cloves garlic, minced
1 tablespoon snipped fresh dill or
1 teaspoon dried dillweed, crushed
¼ teaspoon pepper
Curly endive or leaf lettuce (optional)
Fresh dill sprigs (optional)
Caper Mayonnaise, Honey-Lime Dipping Sauce, and/or Strawberry-Basil Sauce (optional)

Thaw shrimp and/or scallops and salmon, if using frozen. Cover and chill till needed.

Soak 12 to 15 four-inch wooden skewers in water for 20 to 30 minutes; drain. Set aside for vegetable kabobs.

Meanwhile, peel shrimp, if using, leaving tails intact. Devein. Thread shrimp and/or scallops on several 12- to 15-inch metal or wooden skewers (if using wood, soak as directed). If using both shrimp and scallops, thread on separate skewers

◆ Grilled Seafood Platter

because scallops cook faster. Cover and chill till needed, up to 4 hours.

For vegetable kabobs, on *each* of the presoaked 4-inch skewers thread *1 piece each* of sweet pepper, onion, zucchini, and summer squash. Cover and chill till needed, up to 4 hours.

In a small bowl stir together oil, lemon juice, garlic, dill, and pepper.

At serving time, brush salmon on both sides with *some* of the oil mixture. Place salmon on a piece of heavy foil or on a fish grilling rack.

Brush shrimp and/or scallop skewers and vegetable kabobs with remaining oil mixture.

Grill seafood and vegetable kabobs, uncovered, directly over *medium-hot* coals. For shrimp, grill for 10 to 12 minutes or till pink, turning once. For scallops, grill 5 to 8 minutes or till opaque, turning once. For salmon, grill 4 to 6 minutes per ½-inch thickness of fish. For vegetable kabobs, grill for 6 to 8 minutes or till squash is tender and onion is crisp-tender.

To serve, line 1 or 2 large platters with endive. Using a large fork, push cooked shrimp and scallops off skewers. Arrange kabobs on platters. Garnish with dill sprigs. Serve with Caper Mayonnaise, Honey-Lime Dipping Sauce, and Strawberry-Basil Sauce. Makes 12 to 15 appetizer servings.

Nutrition facts per serving without sauce: 115 cal., 6 g total fat (1 g sat. fat), 72 mg chol., 99 mg sodium, 2 g carbo., 0 g fiber, 13 g pro. Daily Value: 6% vit. A, 21% vit. C, 2% calcium, 9% iron.

◆ Bite-Size Herb Biscuits

Honey-Lime Dipping Sauce

½ teaspoon finely shredded lime peel
3 tablespoons lime juice
3 tablespoons honey
⅛ teaspoon ground cinnamon
⅓ cup salad oil
1½ teaspoons chopped fresh or canned jalapeño pepper

In a blender container combine lime peel, lime juice, honey, and cinnamon. With blender running, add salad oil in a steady stream through opening in lid. Add chopped jalapeño pepper; blend just till combined. Cover and chill for up to 24 hours.

Nutrition facts per teaspoon: 23 cal., 2 g total fat (0 g sat. fat), 0 mg chol., 0 mg sodium, 2 g carbo., 0 g fiber, 0 g pro.

Strawberry-Basil Sauce

¾ cup cut-up fresh or frozen unsweetened strawberries
4 teaspoons lemon juice
1 tablespoon chopped green onion
1 to 1½ teaspoons sugar
¼ teaspoon pepper
1 tablespoon finely snipped fresh basil or oregano

In a blender container combine strawberries, lemon juice, green onion, sugar, and pepper. Cover and blend till smooth. Stir in basil or oregano. Cover; chill for up to 24 hours.

Nutrition facts per teaspoon: 1 cal., 0 g total fat (0 g sat. fat), 0 mg chol., 0 mg sodium, 0 g carbo., 0 g fiber, 0 g pro.

Caper Mayonnaise
¾ cup mayonnaise or salad dressing
4 teaspoons capers, chopped
2 teaspoons white wine Worcestershire sauce

In a small bowl stir together mayonnaise or salad dressing, capers, and white wine Worcestershire sauce. Cover and chill till serving time, up to 24 hours.

Nutrition facts per teaspoon: 33 cal., 4 g total fat (1 g sat. fat), 3 mg chol., 34 mg sodium, 0 g carbo., 0 g fiber, 0 g pro.

Bite-Size Herb Biscuits

MAKE AND FREEZE THE BISCUITS AHEAD SO THAT ON PARTY DAY, ALL YOU HAVE TO DO IS THAW THE BISCUITS AND ADD THE FILLINGS—

2 cups all-purpose flour
1 tablespoon baking powder
2 teaspoons sugar
½ teaspoon cream of tartar
¼ teaspoon salt
½ cup shortening, margarine, or butter
⅔ cup milk
2 tablespoons finely chopped green onion
1 tablespoon finely snipped parsley
Garden Cheese Filling, Pesto-Chicken Salad, and Meat and Cheese Filling

Combine flour, baking powder, sugar, cream of tartar, and salt. Cut in shortening, margarine, or butter till mixture resembles coarse crumbs. Make a well in center; add milk, onion, and parsley all at once. Stir till dough clings together.

On a lightly floured surface, knead dough gently 10 to 12 strokes. Roll or pat dough to ½-inch thickness. Cut dough with a 1½-inch round cutter, dipping cutter into flour between cuts. Reroll dough as needed. Transfer biscuits to an ungreased baking sheet.

Bake in a 450° oven for 6 to 8 minutes or till golden. Transfer biscuits to a wire rack to cool slightly.*

To assemble, split biscuits in half horizontally. Fill a *third* of the biscuits with Garden Cheese Filling and a *third* with Pesto-Chicken Salad, using about 1 rounded *teaspoon* of filling per biscuit. Fill the remaining *third* of the biscuits with Meat and Cheese Filling.

Serve immediately or cover and chill for up to 2 hours. To serve, arrange on a platter with *basil sprigs*, if desired. Makes 24 to 28 appetizers.

*To make biscuits ahead: Cool biscuits completely. Place biscuits in a freezer container. Cover and freeze for up to 2 months. Thaw before filling.

Nutrition facts per biscuit filled with Garden Cheese Filling: 133 cal., 9 g total fat (4 g sat. fat), 15 mg chol., 120 mg sodium, 10 g carbo., 0 g fiber, 2 g pro. Daily Value. 22% vit. A, 4% vit. C.

Garden Cheese Filling: In a small bowl pour enough boiling water over 2 tablespoons finely snipped *dried tomatoes* to cover. Let stand 5 minutes; drain tomatoes thoroughly. Rinse and dry bowl. In same bowl combine drained tomatoes, ½ of an 8-ounce container *soft-style cream cheese with chives and onions*, and 2 tablespoons finely shredded *carrot*. Stir till thoroughly combined. Cover and chill till needed, up to 4 hours. (To make up to 24 hours ahead, reserve drained tomatoes and add up to 4 hours ahead because the red color tends to bleed.) Makes ⅔ cup.

Pesto-Chicken Salad: Measure 2 tablespoons purchased *pesto*. If necessary, drain off any excess oil. In a small bowl stir together the pesto and 2 tablespoons *mayonnaise or salad dressing*. Stir in ½ cup finely chopped cooked *chicken* or *half* of a 3-ounce can *chunk-style chicken*, drained. Cover and chill till needed, up to 24 hours. Makes about ½ cup.

Meat and Cheese Filling: Divide 2 ounces *thinly sliced cooked roast beef, turkey,* or *ham,* cut to fit, among about 8 of the biscuit bottoms. Top each with a very thin slice of desired *cheese,* a dab of purchased *horseradish sauce or honey mustard,* and the biscuit tops.

Easy Antipasto Sampler

1 tablespoon olive oil or cooking oil
1 clove garlic, minced
1 8-ounce package Italian bread shells
(2 shells) (Boboli brand)
Italian Caponata
Bibb lettuce or Boston lettuce (optional)
Herbed Goat Cheese
5 to 6 figs, cut into wedges, or ½ of a
medium cantaloupe, scooped into
melon balls
Assorted fruits and vegetables such as
pear-shaped yellow and/or red tomatoes,
tomato wedges, pickled baby corn, pickled
peppers, grapes, and/or strawberries

Combine olive oil and garlic. Place bread shells on a baking sheet and brush with oil mixture. Bake in a 400° oven 10 to 15 minutes or till golden. Cut bread shells into wedges; set aside.

Spoon Italian Caponata into a small bowl and place on a large serving platter. Line the rest of the platter with lettuce. Arrange Herbed Goat Cheese, figs or melon, and desired fruits and vegetables on the platter. Serve with bread wedges. Makes 12 to 15 appetizer servings.

Nutrition facts per serving: 146 cal. 7 g total fat (2 g sat. fat), 4 mg chol., 282 mg sodium, 18 g carbo., 2 g fiber, 5 g. pro. Daily Value: 4% vit. A, 27% vit. C, 4% calcium, 7% iron.

◆ Easy Antipasto Sampler

Italian Caponata

1 small eggplant, peeled and cut into ½-
inch cubes (4 cups)
½ cup chopped onion
2 tablespoons olive oil or cooking oil
2 medium tomatoes, chopped
½ cup chopped yellow and/or green sweet
pepper
3 tablespoons wine vinegar
2 tablespoons tomato paste
1 teaspoon sugar
½ teaspoon salt
Dash ground red pepper
½ cup sliced pitted ripe olives
1 tablespoon snipped fresh parsley or basil
1 tablespoon drained capers
Fresh parsley sprigs (optional)

In a large skillet cook eggplant and onion in hot oil over medium heat for 5 to 6 minutes or till just tender. Stir in tomatoes, sweet pepper, wine vinegar, tomato paste, sugar, salt, and ground red pepper. Cook, uncovered, over low heat for 3 minutes, stirring occasionally. Remove from heat.

Stir in olives, parsley or basil, and capers. Cover; chill 2 to 24 hours. Let stand at room temperature for 30 minutes before serving. Top with fresh parsley sprigs, if desired. Makes 12 to 15 appetizer servings (2⅔ cups).

Nutrition facts per serving: 49 cal., 3 g total fat (0 g sat. fat), 0 mg chol., 152 mg sodium, 6 g carbo., 1 g fiber, 1 g pro. Daily Value: 3% vit. A, 14% vit. C, 12% calcium, 0% iron.

Herbed Goat Cheese

A DELICIOUS ADDITION TO THE EASY ANTIPASTO SAMPLER, THIS SIMPLE CHEESE LOG CAN STAR INDEPENDENTLY AS WELL. SERVE WITH CELERY STICKS, CUCUMBER SLICES, CARROT SLICES, OR CRACKERS FOR SPREADING—

3 ounces semisoft goat cheese (chèvre)
2 teaspoons snipped fresh basil or
½ teaspoon dried basil, crushed
¼ teaspoon onion powder
Dash pepper

In a small bowl combine goat cheese, basil, onion powder, and pepper. Stir till thoroughly combined. If dry, stir in a little *milk* (2 to 3 teaspoons) till of desired consistency.

Shape into a 4-inch log. Cover with plastic wrap and chill till needed, up to 1 week. Makes 12 to 15 appetizer servings.

Nutrition facts per serving: 19 cal., 1 g total fat (1 g sat. fat), 3 mg chol., 26 mg sodium, 0 g carbo., 0 g fiber, 1 g pro.

DESSERTS
Menu

Devonshire Cream Trifle
Layer this gorgeous fruit, cake, and cream dessert the day before your party.

Fudge Brownie Tarts
You're in for a delicious dose of dense, rich chocolate with these little nuggets.

Miniature Almond Cakes
Use cookie cutters to shape these cakes, then decorate with frosting, berries, and nuts.

Strawberry Daiquiri Punch
Mix pitchers of both the rum and non-alcoholic versions of this refreshing punch.

Chocolate-Dipped Berries
Take advantage of one of summer's most delicious gifts—juicy, ruby-red berries.

Queen of Heart Pastries
Elegant, and easy too; these hearts start with purchased puff pastry.

◆Devonshire Cream Trifle

Vibrant fresh fruits and flowers take center stage at the dessert table. With platters full of sweet miniatures, guests can sample a bite of everything, from peach and blueberry filled pastries to brownie cups and dipped strawberries. And, don't forget a spoonful of sumptuous summer fruit trifle.

Devonshire Cream Trifle

DEVONSHIRE, ENGLAND, IS KNOWN FOR ITS THICK, RICH, CLOTTED CREAM. THIS FRUIT-FILLED TRIFLE USES A COMBINATION OF WHIPPING CREAM AND SOUR CREAM TO REPLICATE THIS BEST-LOVED TREAT—

1 teaspoon unflavored gelatin
1 cup whipping cream
¼ cup sugar
2 teaspoons vanilla
1 8-ounce carton dairy sour cream
4 cups assorted fresh fruit such as raspberries, sliced strawberries, chopped peeled nectarines or peaches*, and cut-up peeled kiwi fruit
2 tablespoons sugar

◆ Fudge Brownie

◆ Miniature Almond Cakes

◆ Queen of Hearts Pastries

◆ Chocolate-Dipped Berries

*Hot Milk Sponge Cake or one 10¾ ounce
frozen loaf pound cake, thawed
¼ cup peach brandy, amaretto, orange
liqueur, or orange juice
Grated chocolate (optional)*

For Devonshire cream, in a small saucepan combine gelatin in ½ cup *cold water*; let stand 5 minutes to soften. Heat and stir over medium heat till gelatin dissolves. Cool.

In a chilled medium mixing bowl beat whipping cream, the ¼ cup sugar, and vanilla with an electric mixer on medium-low speed till soft peaks form (tips curl). Do not overbeat.

Combine cooled gelatin mixture and sour cream; mix well. Fold the sour cream mixture into the whipped cream. Chill for 30 to 45 minutes or till mixture is thickened and will mound on a spoon.

Meanwhile, for fruit filling, in a large mixing bowl combine the fresh fruit and the 2 tablespoons sugar. Let stand for 10 minutes.

Cut the Hot Milk Sponge Cake or pound cake into 2x½-inch strips. In a 2 ½- or 3-quart clear glass serving bowl or a soufflé dish arrange *half* of the cake strips on the bottom. Arrange *half* of the fruit atop the cake strips. Sprinkle with 2 *tablespoons* of the brandy, liqueur, or juice.

Spoon *half* of the Devonshire cream on top. Repeat layers, piping or dolloping remaining Devonshire cream atop.

Cover and chill for 2 to 24 hours. Sprinkle with chocolate. Serves 12.

*****Note:** If using peaches or nectarines, dip slices in a mixture of 1 cup *water* and 1 tablespoon *lemon juice* to prevent them from discoloring.

***Nutrition facts per serving:** 231 cal., 13 g total fat (7 g sat. fat), 54 mg chol., 60 mg sodium, 24 g carbo., 2 g fiber, 3 g pro. Daily Value: 20% vit. A, 18% vit. C, 8% calcium, 4% iron.

June

Hot Milk Sponge Cake

½ cup all-purpose flour
½ teaspoon baking powder
Dash salt
1 egg
½ cup sugar
¼ cup milk
1 tablespoon margarine or butter

Grease and lightly flour a 9x1½-inch or 8x1½-inch round baking pan. In a small mixing bowl stir together flour, baking powder, and salt. Set pan and flour mixture aside.

In a medium mixing bowl beat egg with an electric mixer on high speed for 3 to 4 minutes or till thick and lemon-colored. Gradually add sugar, beating on medium speed 4 to 5 minutes or till sugar is almost dissolved. Add flour mixture. Beat on low to medium speed just till combined.

In a small saucepan heat the milk and margarine or butter just till margarine or butter melts. Stir warm milk mixture into egg mixture. Pour batter into prepared pan; spread evenly.

Bake in a 350° oven about 18 minutes or till cake top springs back when touched. Cool cake in pan on a wire rack for 10 minutes. Loosen cake from sides of pan. Invert cake onto a wire rack and cool completely.

To make ahead, wrap cooled cake in freezer wrap or foil and freeze for up to 1 month. Thaw at room temperature before using. Serves 8.

Nutrition facts per serving: 104 cal., 3 g total fat (1 g sat. fat), 27 mg chol., 66 mg sodium, 18 g carbo.. 0 g fiber, 2 g pro. Daily Value: 3% vit. A, 0% vit. C, 1% calcium, 3% iron.

Fudge Brownie Tarts

5 ounces unsweetened chocolate, chopped
⅓ cup margarine or butter
1 cup sugar
2 beaten eggs
1 teaspoon vanilla
½ cup all-purpose flour
Pecan halves (optional)
Vanilla Icing (optional)
Milk chocolate (optional)
Whole hazelnuts (optional)

In a heavy medium saucepan melt the unsweetened chocolate with the margarine or butter over low heat till smooth, stirring constantly. Remove from heat. Stir in sugar, eggs, and vanilla. Using a wooden spoon, lightly beat the mixture just till combined. Stir in the flour.

Line 1¾-inch muffin pans with 1¾-inch paper bake cups. Spoon batter into bake cups, spreading so that the tops are smooth. If desired, top with a pecan half.

Bake in a 350° oven for 10 to 12 minutes or till edges are set. (Centers should be soft.) Transfer tarts, in the paper bake cups, to a wire rack to cool. If making ahead, store in a covered container for up to 24 hours at room temperature. Or, transfer to a freezer container and freeze for up to 1 month. Thaw at room temperature before decorating.

To decorate, spoon Vanilla Icing into a pastry bag, fitted with a small round tip. Pipe icing atop cooled tarts. Or, drizzle icing atop cooled tarts with a spoon.

For chocolate-dipped hazelnuts, melt milk chocolate in a small heavy saucepan over low heat till smooth, stirring constantly. Remove from heat. Working quickly, use your thumb and forefinger to dip hazelnuts, one at a time, in the melted chocolate. Cover about *half* of each nut with chocolate. Transfer to a piece of waxed paper to dry. Attach dry, dipped nuts to tarts with a dab of icing or melted chocolate. Makes 30 tarts.

Nutrition facts per tart: 77 cal., 4 g total fat (0 g sat. fat), 14 mg chol., 28 mg sodium, 11 g carbo., 0 g fiber, 1 g pro. Daily Value: 4% vit. A., 2% iron.

Vanilla Icing: In a small bowl combine 1 cup sifted *powdered sugar*, ¼ teaspoon *vanilla*, and 1 tablespoon *milk*. Stir in enough additional *milk*, 1 teaspoon at a time, till of piping or drizzling consistency. Makes ½ cup.

Miniature Almond Cakes

1½ cups all-purpose flour
2½ teaspoons baking powder
¼ teaspoon salt
1 8-ounce package almond paste
1½ cups sugar
6 eggs
1 cup margarine or butter, softened
Whipped Cream Frosting, Chocolate
Whipped Cream Frosting, Raspberry
Whipped Cream Frosting, or Simple
Designer Frosting (see recipe, page 114)
Assorted toppings, such as raspberries,
chocolate curls, grated chocolate, sliced
almonds, mint leaves, and chocolate-
dipped hazelnuts (optional)

In a small mixing bowl combine flour, baking powder, and salt.

Crumble the almond paste into a large mixer bowl. Add the sugar and 2 of the eggs. Beat with an electric mixer* on low speed till thoroughly combined and no lumps of almond paste remain (about 3 minutes.) Add the margarine or butter; beat on medium-low speed for 3 minutes. Add remaining eggs, one at a time, beating for 1 minute after each addition.

Fold in the flour mixture. Pour ⅔ of the batter (about 4 cups) into a greased and floured 13x9x2-inch baking pan and the remaining batter into a greased and floured 8x8x2-inch baking pan. Spread batter evenly in pans.

Bake in a 350° oven for 18 to 20 minutes or till toothpick inserted near center of each pan comes out clean. Cool for 10 minutes in pans (cakes may sink slightly in center). Loosen sides and invert cakes onto wire racks; cool thoroughly. If desired, wrap with plastic wrap or foil and chill till needed, up to 24 hours.

To assemble, using 2-inch round, star, and/or diamond-shaped cookie cutters with fluted or straight sides, cut about 35 cake pieces from the 2 cakes. Pipe or dollop desired frostings atop cakes. (Leave the sides of the cakes unfrosted so they are easy to pick up.) Decorate with assorted toppings, if desired. Makes 35 cakes.

*Note: Because of the length of beating time, we recommend a full-size stand mixer instead of a hand mixer.

Note: If you're running short on time, use a cake mix instead of the recipe above. Prepare 1 package 2-layer-size *white or chocolate cake mix* according to package directions except pour ⅔ of the batter into a greased and floured 13x9x2-inch baking pan and ⅓ of the batter in an 8x8x2-inch baking pan. Bake in a 350° oven 20 to 22 minutes or till toothpick inserted near centers comes out clean. Continue as directed for Miniature Almond Cakes.

Nutrition facts per cake with Whipped Cream Frosting: 153 cal., 9 g total fat (2 g sat. fat), 41 mg chol., 113 mg sodium, 16 g carbo., 0 g fiber, 3 g pro. Daily Value: 10% vit. A, 0% vit. C, 2% calcium, 4% iron.

Whipped Cream Frosting

YOU CAN FREEZE THIS FROSTING IN A COVERED CONTAINER FOR UP TO 1 MONTH. BEFORE USING, THAW THE FROZEN FROSTING FOR SEVERAL HOURS IN THE REFRIGERATOR, THEN STIR VIGOROUSLY TILL SMOOTH—

2 teaspoons cold water
¼ teaspoon unflavored gelatin
½ cup whipping cream
1 tablespoon sugar

In a 1-cup glass measuring cup combine cold water and gelatin. Let stand 2 minutes. In a small saucepan bring about 2 inches water to boiling. Place measuring cup in saucepan of boiling water. Heat and stir about 1 minute or till the gelatin is completely dissolved. Remove.

In a bowl beat whipping cream and sugar with an electric mixer on medium speed while gradually drizzling the gelatin over the cream mixture. Continue beating till stiff peaks form. Makes 1 cup frosting.

Chocolate Whipped Cream Frosting: Prepare Whipped Cream Frosting as directed *except* increase sugar to 4 teaspoons. Mix the sugar with 1 tablespoon *unsweetened cocoa powder* before beating with the cream. Makes 1 cup frosting.

Raspberry Whipped Cream Frosting: Prepare Whipped Cream Frosting as directed except beat in 2 tablespoons *raspberry liqueur* or *seedless raspberry jam* with the cream and sugar. If desired, add a few drops of red food coloring. Makes about 1 cup frosting.

◆ Strawberry Daiquiri Punch

Simple Designer Frosting

1 16-ounce can milk chocolate frosting or vanilla frosting
2 tablespoons strong coffee or coffee liqueur, kirsch, amaretto, orange liqueur, or milk
Food coloring (optional)

For mocha frosting, combine the milk chocolate frosting and coffee or coffee liqueur. If needed, add more liquid to make of piping or spreading consistency.

For cherry, amaretto, orange, or vanilla frosting, combine vanilla frosting with kirsch, amaretto, orange liqueur, or milk. If needed, add more liquid to make of piping or spreading consistency. Makes 2 cups frosting.

Nutrition facts per 2 teaspoons mocha frosting: 38 cal., 2 g total fat (1 g sat. fat), 0 mg chol., 16 mg sodium, 6 g carbo., 0 g fiber, 0 g pro. Daily Value: 0% vit. A, 0% vit. C.

Strawberry Daiquiri Punch

6 cups fresh or frozen unsweetened strawberries
1 6-ounce container frozen limeade concentrate
¾ cup light rum or unsweetened pineapple juice
1 16-ounce bottle lemon-lime carbonated beverage, chilled
2 cups ice cubes
Fresh strawberries (optional)

If using fresh strawberries, remove stems and caps. For frozen strawberries, thaw the berries after measuring; do not drain.

Place strawberries, *half* at a time, in a blender container or food processor bowl. Cover; blend or process till smooth. Transfer blended berries to a large pitcher. Stir in limeade concentrate and light rum or pineapple juice. Cover; chill till serving time.

Just before serving, stir in the lemon-lime beverage and the ice. Garnish with whole berries, if desired. Makes 8 to 12 servings.

Nutrition facts per serving: 144 cal., 0 g total fat, 0 mg chol., 8 mg sodium, 24 g carbo., 3 g fiber, 1 g pro. Daily Value: 0% vit.L A, 110% vit. C, 2% calcium, 3% iron.

Chocolate-Dipped Berries

MAKE SURE THAT YOUR STRAWBERRIES ARE COMPLETELY DRY BEFORE DIPPING OR THE CHOCOLATE OR COATING MAY CLUMP. DIP BERRIES NO MORE THAN 2 HOURS BEFORE SERVING—

Vanilla-flavored candy coating (at least 2 ounces)
Fresh strawberries, rinsed and patted dry
Semisweet chocolate or chocolate-flavored candy coating (at least 2 ounces)

In a small saucepan melt the vanilla candy coating over low heat, stirring constantly. Remove from heat. Holding a berry by its green cap, dip a portion of the berry into the melted vanilla coating.

Let excess coating drip off berry; place on a baking sheet lined with waxed paper. Let dry. Working quickly, repeat with more berries.

In another small saucepan melt chocolate over low heat, stirring constantly. Dip additional strawberries in melted chocolate. Or, for double-dipped berries, dip the dry, vanilla-coated berries in the melted chocolate, leaving part of the vanilla coating showing. Let dry. Chill.

Nutrition facts per large berry: 108 cal., 6 g total fat (4 g sat. fat), 0 mg chol., 1 mg sodium, 16 g carbo., 1 g fiber, 0 g pro. Daily Value: 0% vit. A, 29% vit. C, 1% calcium, 1% iron.

Queen of Hearts Pastries

1 17¼-ounce package frozen puff pastry (2 sheets)
⅓ cup peach or apricot all-fruit spread or preserves
1 teaspoon finely shredded lemon peel
1 cup peeled and finely chopped peaches (about 2)
1 cup blueberries
1 8-ounce package cream cheese, softened
¼ cup packed brown sugar
1 teaspoon vanilla
Powdered sugar

Thaw and unfold puff pastry sheets onto a lightly floured surface. Using a floured, 2-inch heart-shaped cookie cutter or a sharp small knife and a heart pattern, cut pastry into about 45 heart shapes (do not reroll scraps). Place pastry hearts on an ungreased baking sheet.

Bake in a 375° oven for 10 to 12 minutes or till puffed and golden. Cool on a wire rack. If desired, store, tightly covered, at room temperature for up to 12 hours.

In a small saucepan combine fruit spread or preserves and lemon peel. Heat and stir till melted; cool.

In a large mixing bowl combine peaches and blueberries. Add spread or preserves mixture and gently toss to combine; set aside.

In a medium mixer bowl beat cream cheese, brown sugar, and vanilla with an electric mixer on medium-high speed till fluffy.

To assemble pastries, with a serrated knife, cut pastry hearts in half horizontally. Spread each of the bottom halves with about *1 teaspoon* cream cheese mixture. Top each with a spoonful of fruit mixture and a pastry top. Serve immediately or cover and chill for up to 4 hours. Just before serving, dust with powdered sugar. Makes about 45 pastries.

Nutrition facts per pastry heart: 82 cal., 5 g total fat (1 g sat. fat), 6 mg chol., 57 mg sodium, 8 g carbo., 0 g fiber, 1 g pro. Daily Value: 3% vit. A, 1% vit. C, 1% calcium.

Prize Tested Recipes®

Chicken Fajita Potato

A CHICKEN FAJITA MIXTURE BECOMES A TOPPER FOR POTATOES IN THIS MEXICAN-STYLE MAIN DISH—

4 large baking potatoes (2 pounds)
1 medium red or green sweet pepper, cut into bite-size strips
1 small onion, chopped (¼ cup)
2 tablespoons margarine or butter
1 tablespoon taco seasoning mix*
6 ounces cooked chicken breast, cut into bite-size strips
½ cup shredded cheddar cheese (2 ounces)
½ cup shredded Monterey Jack cheese (2 ounces)
1 2¼-ounce can sliced pitted ripe olives, drained
2 tablespoons canned diced green chili peppers
1 cup salsa
Dairy sour cream, guacamole, and salsa (optional)

Scrub potatoes with a brush. Pat dry. Prick skins with a fork. Place potatoes in a microwave-safe 9-inch pie plate. Cover with waxed paper. Micro-cook on 100% power (high) for 15 to 18 minutes or till tender, turning dish twice.

Meanwhile, in a medium saucepan cook sweet pepper and onion in hot margarine or butter over medium heat till tender. Add taco seasoning mix. Cook and stir for 1 minute. Remove from heat. Stir in chicken, cheeses,

◆ Chicken Fajita Potato

olives, and chili peppers. Cut a lengthwise slit in the top of each potato. Press potatoes open. Divide chicken mixture among potatoes. Spoon ¼ *cup* salsa over each. Cover; cook on high 5 to 7 minutes or till heated through. Serve with sour cream, guacamole, and salsa, if desired. Makes 4 servings.

*Note: Stir any leftover taco seasoning mix into ground beef for tacos.

Nutrition facts per serving: 461 cal., 16 g total fat (7 g sat. fat) 57 mg chol., 763 mg sodium, 61 g carbo., 5 g fiber, 25 g pro. Daily Value: 32% vit. A, 116% vit. C.

$200 WINNER
Marilee Baas, Hales Corners, Wis.

Peanutty Ice-Cream Pie

A CRUNCHY PEANUT CRUST IS ONE
SECRET TO HYACINTH'S PEANUT-BUTTER-
SWIRLED ICE-CREAM PIE—

1½ cups coarsely ground peanuts
3 tablespoons margarine or butter, melted
2 tablespoons sugar
¼ cup flaked coconut
¼ cup light corn syrup
¼ cup peanut butter
3 tablespoons chopped peanuts
1 quart vanilla ice cream
Chopped candy-coated milk chocolate
pieces or peanuts (optional)

Lightly grease a 9-inch pie plate. In a
medium mixing bowl combine ground
peanuts, margarine or butter, and sugar.
Press mixture firmly onto bottom and
up sides of the pie plate. Refrigerate for
15 minutes. For filling, in a small mixing
bowl combine coconut, corn syrup,
peanut butter, and the 3 tablespoons
chopped peanuts.

Place ice cream in a large chilled bowl;
stir ice cream just to soften. Stir in the
peanut mixture just till combined.
Spoon into chilled crust. If desired,
sprinkle chopped chocolate pieces or
peanuts atop pie. Cover; freeze till firm
(about 5 hours). Remove from freezer
and let stand 10 minutes before cutting
into wedges. Makes 8 servings.

Nutrition facts per serving: 420 cal.,
31 g total fat (9 g sat. fat), 30 mg chol.,
149 mg sodium, 28 g carbo., 3 g fiber,
12 g pro. Daily Value. 15% vit. A, 15%
calcium.

$200 WINNER
Hyacinth Rizzo, Snyder, N.Y.

◆ Peanutty Ice-Cream Pie

Mocha Fudge Swirl Ice Cream

THIS COFFEE-FLAVORED CHOCOLATE ICE
CREAM IS SWIRLED WITH FUDGE RIBBONS
OF HOMEMADE CHOCOLATE SAUCE—

Hot Fudge Sauce (see recipe, page 118) or
1 cup purchased chocolate fudge
ice-cream topping
3 beaten eggs
2 cups milk
1 cup sugar
3 tablespoons unsweetened cocoa powder
1 to 2 tablespoons instant coffee crystals
2 cups half-and-half or light cream

Prepare Hot Fudge Sauce, if desired.
Cool to room temperature. In a medium
saucepan combine eggs and milk. Stir in
sugar, cocoa powder, and coffee crystals.
Cook and stir over medium heat till
continued on page 118

◆ Mocha Fudge Swirl Ice Cream

continued from page 117

mixture coats a metal spoon (about 5 minutes). Stir in half-and-half or light cream. Cool. Freeze in 4- to 5-quart ice-cream freezer according to manufacturer's directions. Remove ice-cream paddle. Stir in 1 cup Hot Fudge Sauce or ice-cream topping just till swirled. Serve with additional Hot Fudge Sauce, if desired. Makes about 3 quarts (24 servings).

Hot Fudge Sauce: In a small saucepan melt 2 squares (2 ounces) *unsweetened chocolate* and ¼ cup *margarine* or *butter* over low heat, stirring constantly. Stir in 1 cup *sugar* and ⅓ cup *unsweetened cocoa powder* till nearly smooth. Stir in one 5-ounce can (⅔ cup) *evaporated milk*. Heat and stir till smooth. Stir in ½ teaspoon *vanilla*. Store, covered, in the refrigerator for up to 3 weeks. Makes 1½ cups.

Nutrition facts per ½-cup serving: 127 cal., 6 g total fat (3 g sat. fat) 40 mg chol., 44 mg sodium, 17 g carbo., 0 g fiber, 3 g pro. Daily Value: 8% vit. A, 10% calcium, 3% iron.

$100 WINNER
Pamela B. Fisher, Randallstown, Md.

Dilly Cabbage Potatoes

PATRICIA ADAPTED AN IRISH DISH MADE OF MASHED POTATOES ONION AND CABBAGE (CALLED COLCANNON) AND TURNED IT INTO A STUFFED POTATO. TRY IT WITH BARBECUE CHICKEN—

4 large baking potatoes (2 pounds)
3 cups shredded cabbage
½ cup chopped onion
1 tablespoon olive oil or cooking oil
¼ cup water

◆ Dilly Cabbage Potatoes

1 tablespoon soy sauce
½ teaspoon dillseed
2 tablespoons margarine or butter
1 teaspoon lemon juice
¼ teaspoon salt
¼ teaspoon pepper
2 to 4 tablespoons milk
Dairy sour cream (optional)
Snipped fresh dill or chives (optional)

Scrub potatoes with a brush. Pat dry. Prick skins with a fork. Bake in a 425° oven for 40 to 60 minutes or till tender. Meanwhile, cook cabbage and onion in hot oil for 5 minutes. Add water, soy sauce, and dillseed; bring to boiling. Simmer, covered, about 10 minutes. Cut a thin lengthwise slice from the top of each potato. Using a spoon, gently scoop out pulp leaving a ¼-inch-thick shell. Mash potato pulp; stir in margarine or butter, lemon juice, salt, and pepper. Stir in cabbage mixture. Add milk to desired consistency. Spoon mixture into shells. Place potatoes in a shallow baking pan. Bake, uncovered, in a 425° oven 15 minutes or till hot. To serve, top with sour cream and snipped dill or chives, if desired. Makes 4 side-dish servings.

Nutrition facts per serving: 332 cal., 10 g total fat (2 g sat. fat), 1 mg chol., 488 mg sodium, 57 g carbo., 6 g fiber, 6 g pro. Daily Value: 10% vit. A, 81% vit. C, 6% calcium.

$100 WINNER
Patricia J. Daley, Akron, Ohio

July

No-Cook Summer Meals

Prize Tested Recipes

No-Cook Summer Meals

By Julia Malloy

Tex-Mex Tortilla Stack

THE LAYERED LOOK IS "IN" FOR SUMMER
DINING, ESPECIALLY WHEN THE LAYERS
BOAST MEXICAN-STYLE INGREDIENTS—

1 9-ounce package (2 cups) frozen chopped
cooked chicken
1 cup finely chopped, peeled jicama
½ cup taco sauce
8 10-inch flour tortillas
1 6-ounce container frozen avocado
dip, thawed
2 cups chopped lettuce
16-ounce can refried beans with green
chili pepper or Mexican-style beans,
drained and mashed
1 8-ounce carton reduced-fat or regular
dairy sour cream
⅓ cup chopped red sweet pepper
⅓ cup sliced green onion
1 cup shredded lower-fat or regular
cheddar cheese, Cojack cheese, or Monterey
Jack cheese with jalapeño peppers
¼ cup sliced pitted ripe olives
Taco sauce (optional)

Thaw chicken. In a medium mixing
bowl combine chicken, jicama, and the
½ cup taco sauce; set aside.

Place *one* of the flour tortillas on a
platter. Spread with *half* of the chicken
mixture. Spread *half* of the avocado dip
onto a second tortilla; place, avocado
side up, atop chicken. Sprinkle with *half*

◆ Tex-Mex Tortilla Stack

of the lettuce. Top with a third tortilla; spread with half of the beans. Top with another tortilla; add *half each* of the sour cream, red pepper, green onion, and cheese.

Repeat layers, ending with remaining sour cream, red pepper, green onion, and cheese. Sprinkle with olives. Serve right away or cover and chill for up to 3 hours.

To serve, cut into wedges. Pass taco sauce. Makes 8 main-dish servings.

Nutrition facts per serving: 392 cal., 15 g total fat (3 g sat. fat), 42 mg chol., 566 mg sodium, 42 g carbo., 4 g fiber, 24 g pro. Daily Values: 13% vit. A, 26% vit. C, 29% calcium, 24% iron.

Seafood Cocktail Salad

THE PERFECT PARTNER FOR THIS FRUIT-FUL TWIST ON CLASSIC SHRIMP COCKTAIL? SHELL SHAPED CRACKERS, OF COURSE!

1 8 ounce package frozen shrimp and/or crab-flavored salad-style fish (surimi)*
1 8 ounce package fresh or frozen peeled, cooked shrimp
⅓ cup nonfat or regular French or Russian salad dressing
¼ cup cocktail sauce
1 medium avocado, halved, seeded, peeled, and chopped
Lettuce leaves
½ of a small honeydew melon, seeded, peeled, and sliced
½ of a small cantaloupe, seeded, peeled, and sliced
1 orange, peeled and sliced crosswise
12 strawberries, halved
½ teaspoon poppy seed

◆ Seafood Cocktail Salad

Thaw fish and shrimp, if frozen; set aside. For dressing, stir together salad dressing and cocktail sauce. If necessary, stir in a little *water* to make of pouring consistency. Cover and chill till serving time.

In a medium mixing bowl toss together shrimp and/or fish, avocado, and *3 tablespoons* of the dressing.

Arrange lettuce leaves on 4 dinner plates. Spoon seafood mixture onto let-tuce. Arrange melon, orange slices, and berries around seafood. Sprinkle with poppy seed. Serve with remaining dressing. Makes 4 main-dish servings.

*Note: You can cut 300 milligrams of sodium by using an additional 8 ounces fresh or frozen shrimp instead of the surimi.

Nutrition facts per serving: 308 cal., 10 g total fat (1 g sat. fat), 108 mg chol., 851 mg sodium, 39 g carbo., 5 g fiber, 19 g pro. Daily Value: 53% vit. A, 171% vit. C, 10% calcium, 18% iron.

◆ Smoked Turkey Salad Sandwich

Smoked Turkey Salad Sandwich

AFTER YOU TASTE THIS SALAD SEASONED WITH CORN RELISH, PLAIN CHICKEN SALAD MAY SEEM A LITTLE HO-HUM.

¼ cup nonfat or regular mayonnaise
or salad dressing
¼ cup plain nonfat yogurt
½ cup corn relish

2 cups chopped fully cooked smoked turkey
1 stalk celery, thinly sliced (½ cup)
4 kaiser rolls, split; or lettuce leaves
1 medium tomato, sliced

For dressing, in a small mixing bowl stir together mayonnaise or salad dressing and yogurt. Stir in corn relish.

In a large mixing bowl combine turkey and celery. Add dressing; toss gently to coat. Serve on rolls or on lettuce leaves with tomato slices. Makes 4 main-dish servings.

Nutrition facts per serving: 292 cal., 10 g total fat (1 g sat. fat), 0 mg chol., 527 mg sodium, 3 g carbo., 2 g fiber, 18 g pro. Daily Value: 3% vit. A, 12% vit. C, 25% calcium, 16% iron.

Black Bean Gazpacho

CANNED CONVENIENCE GETS FRESH WITH GARDEN VEGETABLES IN THIS SPUNKY CHILLED SOUP—

3 cups chopped, peeled, and seeded tomatoes
1 12-ounce can (1½ cups) hot-style vegetable juice cocktail*
1 cup cubed fully cooked ham
1 15-ounce can black beans or garbanzo beans, rinsed and drained
½ cup chopped seeded cucumber, yellow summer squash, and/or zucchini
¼ cup chopped green or yellow sweet pepper
¼ cup thinly sliced green onion
2 tablespoons Italian salad dressing
Bottled hot pepper sauce (optional)

In a large bowl combine tomatoes, juice, ham, beans, cucumber or squash, chopped pepper, green onion, and dressing. Cover and chill for 2 to 24 hours. If desired, serve with bottled hot pepper sauce. Makes 4 main-dish servings.

*Note: If you're not so hot about hot and spicy food, you can use regular vegetable juice cocktail, or even the reduced-sodium version.

Nutrition facts per serving: 201 cal., 6 g total fat (1 g sat. fat) 11 mg chol., 1,247 mg sodium, 25 g carbo., 8 g fiber, 17 g pro. Daily Value: 17% vit. A, 82% vit. C, 8% calcium 19% iron.

◆ Black Bean Gazpacho

Chicken and Cheddar Pasta Toss

YES YOU CAN ENJOY A PASTA DINNER EVEN WHEN YOU'RE NOT IN THE MOOD TO COOK: JUST POUR BOILING WATER OVER NO-BOIL NOODLES—

6 ounces no-boil pasta ribbons or no-boil lasagna noodles, broken
1 8¼-ounce package frozen mesquite grilled chicken tenders or one 9-ounce package frozen chopped cooked chicken, slightly thawed
3 ounces reduced-fat cheddar or American cheese, cut into ¾-inch cubes
1 medium green, yellow, or red sweet pepper, cut into strips
1 ounce pepperoni, chopped
1 8-ounce bottle nonfat Italian salad dressing
⅛ teaspoon cracked black pepper
5 cups torn curly endive
1 cup red or yellow cherry tomatoes, halved

In a large mixing bowl cover noodles with boiling water. Let stand for 10 minutes, separating the noodles occasionally with a fork. Drain. Rinse with cold water and drain again. If using chicken tenders, halve them crosswise.

Return noodles to boil; stir in chicken, cheese, pepper strips, and pepperoni. Add dressing and black pepper; toss gently to coat. Cover and chill for 2 hours or overnight. Before serving, add endive and tomatoes; toss gently to mix. Makes 6 main-dish servings.

Nutrition facts per serving: 252 cal., 7 g total fat (2 g sat. fat), 36 mg chol., 792 mg sodium, 28 g carbo., 1 g fiber; 19 g pro. Daily Value: 17% vit. A, 31% vit. C, 16% calcium, 8% iron.

◆ Chicken and Cheddar Pasta Toss

◆ Greek Pita Platter

Greek Pita Platter

A QUICK STOP AT YOUR FAVORITE DELI IS ALL IT TAKES TO STAGE THIS MAKE-YOUR-OWN SANDWICH PLATTER—

1 8-ounce carton plain nonfat yogurt
⅓ cup crumbled feta cheese
2 teaspoons snipped fresh oregano or mint or ½ teaspoon dried oregano or mint, crushed
1 pint deli-style marinated vegetables
6-ounce package very thinly sliced fully cooked beef
8 whole Greek olives or ⅓ cup pitted ripe olives
4 whole wheat or plain pita bread rounds, halved crosswise, or eight 6-inch flour tortillas

For sauce, in a blender container or food processor bowl combine yogurt, feta cheese, and oregano or mint. Cover and blend or process till smooth. If desired, cover and chill till serving time. To serve, place sauce in a small serving bowl. If desired, garnish with additional oregano or mint.

Drain vegetables; discard marinade. On a large platter arrange serving bowl of sauce, vegetables, meat, olives, and pita halves or tortillas.

To assemble, fill pita pockets or tortillas with desired fillings and sauce. Makes 4 main-dish servings.

Nutrition facts per serving: 392 cal., 21 g total fat, (8 g sat. fat), 49 mg chol., 502 mg sodium, 31 g carbo., 3 g fiber; 20 g pro. Daily Value: 137% vit. A, 54% vit. C, 29% calcium, 18% iron.

Deli Chicken with Pea Pesto

A PRETTY PLATTER THAT'S PERFECT FOR A LUNCH OR LIGHT SUPPER. POOL THE PESTO ON YOUR PLATE FOR A DIP 'N' EAT SAUCE—

6 ounces fresh pea pods or sugar snap peas
(1½ cups)
1 cup frozen peas, thawed
¼ cup purchased or homemade pesto
¼ cup milk
12 ounces thinly sliced fully cooked chicken
breast (12 slices), rolled up
2 ounces semisoft goat cheese (chévre) or
mozzarella cheese, sliced
8 radishes, each cut into eighths
Cracked pepper
Fresh basil (optional)

Place pea pods in a medium mixing bowl. Add enough boiling water to cover; let stand for 2 minutes. Drain. Rinse with cold water; drain again. Set aside.

For sauce, in a blender container or food processor bowl combine thawed peas, the pesto, and milk; cover and blend or process till smooth.

To serve, pour one-fourth of the sauce onto each of 4 dinner plates. Arrange pea pods, chicken, cheese, and radishes on plate. Sprinkle with black pepper. If desired, garnish with basil. Makes 4 main-dish servings.

Nutrition facts per serving: 380 cal., 26 g total fat (2 g sat. fat), 10 mg chol., 209 mg sodium, 15 g carbo., 3 g fiber, 23 g pro. Daily Value: 5% vit. A, 52% vit. C, 3% calcium, 19% iron.

◆Deli Chicken with Pea Pesto

◆ Almond-Dill Spinach Soup

Almond-Dill Spinach Soup

ALMONDS, YOGURT, AND EVAPORATED MILK MAKE THIS A HEARTY, RICH-TASTING MEAL—

*10 ounces fresh spinach leaves
(about 7 cups) or one 10-ounce package
frozen chopped spinach, thawed
2¼ cups (18 ounces) evaporated skim
milk, chilled
1 small onion, cut up
2 teaspoons snipped fresh dill or
½ teaspoon dried dillweed
1 teaspoon lemon-pepper seasoning
1 8-ounce carton plain nonfat yogurt
¼ cup toasted slivered almonds
Fresh dill (optional)
Rose petals (optional)**

In a blender container or food processor bowl combine about *one-third* of the fresh spinach or *half* the undrained thawed spinach, *1½ cups* of the evaporated milk, the onion, dill, and lemon-pepper seasoning. Cover and blend or process till nearly smooth. Add another third of the fresh spinach (if you're using fresh); cover and blend or process till smooth. Pour the mixture into a large storage container.

In the blender container or food processor bowl combine remaining fresh or thawed spinach, remaining evaporated milk, and the yogurt; cover and blend or process till nearly smooth. Stir into the mixture in the storage container. Cover and chill till serving time.

To serve, ladle soup into bowls; top with almonds. If desired, garnish with fresh dill and rose petals. Makes 4 main-dish servings.

*Note: To use rose petals as a garnish, make sure they are not poisonous and that they are free from pesticides. Gently wash them and pat dry with paper towels.

Nutrition facts per serving: 207 cal., 4 g total fat (1 g sat. fat), 6 mg chol., 534 mg sodium, 26 g carbo., 2 g fiber, 17 g pro. Daily Value: 89% vit. A, 19% vit. C, 80% calcium, 14% iron.

Nutty Coleslaw Spring Rolls

AS STIFF AS LASAGNA NOODLES WHEN DRY, EDIBLE RICE PAPERS SOFTEN IN WATER. YOU'LL FIND THEM IN ORIENTAL FOOD MARKETS—

¼ cup soy sauce
2 tablespoons rice vinegar or vinegar
½ teaspoon sesame oil
¼ teaspoon sesame seed
2 cups coleslaw mix (shredded cabbage and carrot)
1 10½-ounce package firm tofu (fresh bean curd), drained and diced
⅓ cup toasted chopped nuts
⅓ cup sweet-and-sour sauce
8 9-inch round dried rice papers
Fresh cilantro leaves (optional)
8 10-inch-long chives or four 10-inch-long green onion tops
Chinese cabbage leaves (optional)

For dipping sauce, in a small bowl stir together soy sauce, vinegar, sesame oil, and sesame seed; set aside.

For filling, in a bowl combine coleslaw mix, tofu, and nuts. Add sweet-and-sour sauce; toss to coat. Set aside.

Pour *warm water* into a large shallow dish. Dip rice papers into water; let excess drain off. Place papers between damp cotton dish towels; let stand for 10 minutes. In the center of each rice paper, place a cilantro leaf, if desired. Top with about ⅛ *cup* of the filling. Fold one edge over the filling; fold in the sides. Roll up.

Cut green onions in half lengthwise, if using. Pour boiling water over chives or green onion strips to cover; let stand for 1 minute. Drain. Wrap or tie a chive or

◆ Nutty Coleslaw Spring Rolls

onion strip around each bundle. If desired, cover and chill till serving time, up to 4 hours.

To serve, arrange bundles on a cabbage-lined platter and garnish with cilantro, if desired. Serve with sauce. Makes 4 main-dish servings.

Nutrition facts per serving: 262 cal., 13 g total fat (2 g sat. fat), 0 mg chol., 643 mg sodium, 23 g carbo., 3 g fiber, 16 g pro. Daily Values: 30% vit. A, 39% vit. C, 23% calcium, 57% iron.

◆ Super Submarine with Summer Fruit Relish

Super Submarine with Summer Fruit Relish

CHOOSE FAVORITE CHEESES AND FRUIT FOR YOUR MEATLESS MEAL-IN-A-BUN—

¼ cup lower-fat or regular creamy
cucumber salad dressing
¾ cup Boursin or soft-style cream cheese
with garlic and herbs
¾ cup finely chopped fresh fruit
(peach, plum, or tomato)
¾ cup finely chopped seeded cucumber
2 tablespoons toasted chopped pecans
2 tablespoons snipped parsley
1 loaf unsliced Italian bread
Lettuce leaves
6 ounces sliced lower-fat or regular cheese
(Swiss, Monterey Jack, mozzarella,
Havarti, fontina, provolone, or Jarlsberg)

For relish, in a medium mixing bowl stir together salad dressing and ¼ cup of the Boursin or cream cheese. Stir in chopped fruit, cucumber, pecans, and parsley. Set aside.

Slice bread in half horizontally. Hollow out halves, leaving l-inch thick shells; spread cut sides with remaining cheese mixture. Line bread bottom with lettuce leaves; add relish and cheese slices. Place bread top on cheese. To serve, cut into individual slices. Makes 6 main-dish servings.

Nutrition facts per serving: 393 cal., 14 g total fat (1 g sat. fat), 40 mg chol., 660 mg sodium, 49 g carbo., 3 g fiber, 19 g pro. Daily Values: 15% vit. A, 9% vit. C, 39% calcium, 14% iron.

Prize Tested Recipes.

Garbanzo Bean and Sweet Pepper Salad

A LIGHT MINT AND LEMON DRESSING COMPLEMENTS THIS SUMMER-FRESH VEGETABLE COMBO. TOTE IT TO YOUR NEXT POTLUCK PICNIC, AND WATCH IT GO FAST—

*2 medium red sweet peppers or one
7-ounce jar roasted red sweet peppers,
drained and chopped
4 cups cooked garbanzo beans
(about 1½ cups dry) or two 15-ounce cans
garbanzo beans, rinsed and drained
½ cup sliced green onion
½ cup finely chopped celery
2 tablespoons capers, drained
1 clove garlic, minced
3 tablespoons snipped fresh mint or
1½ teaspoon dried mint, crushed
3 tablespoons olive oil or salad oil
3 tablespoons lemon juice or vinegar
⅛ teaspoon salt
⅛ teaspoon pepper
Lettuce leaves (optional)*

To roast fresh sweet peppers, halve, then remove stems, membranes, and seeds. Place pepper halves, cut side down, on a foil-lined baking sheet. Bake in a 425° oven for 20 to 25 minutes or till skin is bubbly and dark. Place peppers in a clean paper bag; close bag and let stand for 20 minutes or till cool enough to handle. With a knife, pull off skin gently and slowly. Chop roasted peppers.

◆ Garbanzo Bean and Sweet Pepper Salad

In a large bowl combine sweet peppers, cooked or canned beans, green onion, celery, and capers. In a screw-top jar combine garlic, mint, oil, lemon juice or vinegar, salt, and pepper; cover and shake well. Pour over bean mixture. Toss to coat. Cover and chill 4 to 24 hours. To serve, line a platter with lettuce leaves, if desired. Spoon bean mixture atop lettuce. Makes 6 side-dish servings.

Nutrition facts per serving: 234 cal., 9 g total fat (1 g sat. fat), 0 mg chol., 351 mg sodium, 30 g carbo., 6 g fiber, 9 g pro. Daily Value: 19% vit. A, 73% vit. C, 78% calcium.

$200 WINNER
Karen Kaleta Johnson, Franklin, N.C.

◆ Raspberry Summer Delight

◆ Raspberry Cheesecake

Raspberry Summer Delight

WHAT MAKES THIS RECIPE SUCH A
DELIGHT? IT'S A SIMPLE, WONDERFUL,
AND LIGHT WAY TO ENJOY FRESH RASP-
BERRIES—

2 beaten egg yolks
¼ cup water
3 tablespoons sugar
2 teaspoons lemon juice
1 8-ounce carton vanilla yogurt
1 teaspoon finely shredded lemon peel
2 cups fresh raspberries
Fresh raspberries (optional)
Fresh mint leaves (optional)

In a small heavy saucepan combine
egg yolks, water, sugar, and lemon juice.
Cook and stir over medium heat till
mixture just comes to boiling. Cool mixture to room temperature quickly by
placing pan in a sink or bowl of ice
water, stirring constantly.

In a small bowl combine yogurt and
lemon peel; stir in cooled yolk mixture.
Cover; chill 4 to 24 hours. To serve,
divide berries among 4 dessert dishes or
wine glasses. Spoon yogurt mixture atop.
Garnish with additional raspberries and
fresh mint, if desired. Makes 4 servings.

Nutrition facts per serving: 154 cal.,
4 g total fat (1 g sat. fat), 110 mg chol.,
44 mg sodium, 26 g carbo., 3 g fiber, 5 g
pro. Daily Value: 7% vit. A, 29% vit. C,
14% calcium.
$200 WINNER
Audrey Thibodeau, Fountain
Hills, Ariz.

Raspberry Cheesecake

THIS RECIPE IS EVERYTHING A CHEESE-
CAKE SHOULD BE: CREAMY, CREAMY, AND
MORE CREAMY. RASPBERRY YOGURT AND
BERRY LIQUEUR INSIDE MAKE THE WIN-
NING DIFFERENCE—

1 cup finely crushed graham crackers
(about 14 crackers)
¼ cup finely chopped almonds
¾ cup sugar
4 tablespoons all-purpose flour
2 tablespoons margarine or butter, melted
3 8-ounce packages cream cheese, softened
¼ cup raspberry liqueur
1 tablespoon vanilla
2 eggs
1 8-ounce container plain yogurt
or raspberry yogurt
1 8-ounce container raspberry yogurt
Fresh raspberries and/or blackberries
Sifted powdered sugar (optional)

continued on page 132

continued from page 131

For crust, combine cracker crumbs, almonds, ¼ *cup* of the sugar, *2 tablespoons* of the flour, and margarine or butter. Press onto the bottom of a 9-inch springform pan. In a medium mixer bowl combine the remaining ½ cup sugar, remaining flour, the cream cheese, liqueur, and vanilla. Beat with an electric mixer till fluffy. Add eggs and yogurt, beating on low speed just till combined. (Do not overbeat.) Pour into pan. Place pan on a shallow baking pan in oven. Bake in a 375° oven for 50 to 55 minutes or till center appears nearly set when gently shaken. Cool 15 minutes. Loosen cake from sides of pan. Cool 30 minutes; remove sides of pan. Cool. Chill at least 4 hours. To serve, arrange berries atop cake. Dust with powdered sugar, if desired. Makes 12 servings.

Nutrition facts per serving: 395 cal., 25 g total fat (14 g sat. fat), 100 mg chol., 266 mg sodium, 32 g carbo., 1 g fiber, 9 g pro. Daily Value: 36% vit. A, 16% calcium, 10% iron.

$100 WINNER
Gene Sparks, LaPine, Oreg.

◆ Kidney Bean and Rice Salad

Kidney Bean and Rice Salad
BACKYARD BARBECUES ON HOT SUMMER DAYS CALL FOR COOL SALADS SUCH AS THIS ONE—

2 cups cooked long grain rice, chilled (about ¾ cup uncooked)
1 15½-ounce can red kidney beans, rinsed and drained
1 medium green apple (such as Granny Smith or Golden Delicious), cored and cut into julienne strips
1 medium avocado, seeded, peeled, and chopped (about 1 cup)
½ cup chopped red sweet pepper
⅓ cup chopped white or red onion
¼ cup snipped fresh parsley
¼ cup bottled Thousand Island salad dressing
2 tablespoons olive oil or salad oil
4 teaspoons lemon juice
1 tablespoon vinegar
1 teaspoon prepared mustard
Salt and pepper

Combine the rice, beans, apple, avocado, sweet pepper, onion, and parsley. Stir together bottled dressing, oil, lemon juice, vinegar, mustard, and salt and pepper to taste. Pour over salad; toss gently to coat. Cover and chill for 1 to 2 hours. Makes 8 side-dish servings.

Nutrition facts per serving: 221 cal., 10 g total fat (2 g sat. fat), 2 mg chol., 171 mg sodium, 30 g carbo., 5 g fiber, 6 g pro. Daily Value: 13% vit. A, 30% vit. C, 4% calcium, 12% iron.

$100 WINNER
Joanna Manoogia, San Francisco, Calif.

August

Best-of-Summer

Salads and Tarts

Prize Tested Recipes

Best-of-Summer
Salads and Tarts

By Lisa Holderness

Color-splashed garden salads go hand in hand with the relaxing days of summer. Tarts, with their flaky, golden pastries, showcase summer fruits in the most irresistible way.

When light sounds right for dinner or lunch, fresh and fruity Honey-Lime Turkey Breast Salad really hits the spot.

Honey-Lime Turkey Breast Salad

TOSS THIS CHUNKY TURKEY AND FRUIT SALAD WITH A REFRESHING YOGURT AND SOUR CREAM DRESSING. FOR AN EXTRA LOW-FAT VERSION USE THE NONFAT YOGURT AND LOW-FAT SOUR CREAM OPTIONS—

⅓ cup plain low-fat or nonfat yogurt
⅓ cup regular or lower-fat dairy sour cream
2 tablespoons honey
1½ teaspoons finely shredded lime peel
2 teaspoons lime juice
¼ teaspoon salt
¼ teaspoon pepper

2 cups cooked turkey or chicken breast cut into bite-size pieces
2 medium peaches, sliced, or 1 cup cubed mango or papaya
1 cup halved seedless red grapes
⅓ cup thinly sliced celery
2 tablespoons snipped fresh chives
Assorted greens such as Bibb and red leaf lettuce
Fresh fruit such as cherries, sliced kiwi fruit, and/or champagne grapes (optional)
Edible flowers such as chive blossoms (optional)

For dressing, in a small mixing bowl stir together yogurt, sour cream, honey, lime peel, lime juice, salt, and pepper.

In a large mixing bowl combine turkey or chicken; peaches, mango, or papaya; grapes; celery; and chives. Add dressing and stir gently to combine. Cover and chill for at least 1 hour or up to 24 hours.

Line 4 salad plates with assorted greens. Divide turkey mixture among the plates. Garnish with fresh fruit and edible flowers, if desired. Makes 4 main-dish servings.

Nutrition facts per serving: 245 cal., 5 g total fat (3 g sat. fat), 74 mg chol., 206 mg sodium, 25 g carbo., 2 g fiber, 26 g pro. Daily Value: 14% vit. A, 17% vit. C, 8% calcium, 11% iron.

◆ Honey-Lime Turkey Breast Salad

Potluck Pasta Salad

THIS MAKE-AHEAD SALAD TOTES EASILY TO SUMMER GATHERINGS. FOR LARGER GROUPS, SIMPLY DOUBLE THE INGREDIENTS—

4 ounces wagon wheel macaroni or desired pasta (1⅓ cups)
4 ounces tri-colored corkscrew macaroni or desired pasta
1 teaspoon crushed dried red pepper
1 medium red sweet pepper, cut into thin strips
1 medium yellow squash and/or zucchini, halved lengthwise and sliced
1 10-ounce package frozen peas, thawed, or 1½ cups cooked and cooled fresh peas (pods removed)
1 6-ounce can pitted ripe olives, drained
4 ounces smoked cheddar cheese, cubed
1 cup unblanched whole almonds, toasted
½ cup sliced green onion
2 tablespoons snipped fresh tarragon, oregano, basil, or dill
1 8-ounce bottle regular or nonfat Italian salad dressing

Cook pasta according to package directions *except* add crushed red pepper to the cooking water. Rinse with cool water and drain thoroughly. Cool pasta to room temperature.

In a large mixing bowl combine pasta, sweet pepper, yellow squash or zucchini, peas, olives, cheese, almonds, green onion, and herb.

Add dressing to pasta mixture. Toss gently to mix. Cover and chill for 2 hours or up to 24 hours. Makes 12 side-dish servings.

Nutrition facts per serving: 302 cal., 20 g total fat (4 g sat. fat), 10 mg chol., 293 mg sodium, 24 g carbo., 3 g fiber, 9 g pro. Daily Value: 19% vit. A, 27% vit. C, 15% calcium, 12% iron.

◆ Potluck Pasta Salad

Raspberry-Lemon Tartlets

TO SAVE TIME, MAKE THE LEMON CURD UP TO TWO DAYS AHEAD AND CHILL. YOU CAN ALSO PREPARE AND CHILL THE LEMON AND POPPY SEED PASTRY UP TO TWO DAYS AHEAD—

½ cup sugar
1 tablespoon cornstarch
1½ teaspoons finely shredded lemon peel
3 tablespoons lemon juice
3 tablespoons water
3 beaten egg yolks
¼ cup unsalted butter or lightly salted butter, cut into 4 pieces
Nonstick spray coating
Lemon and Poppy Seed Pastry

¼ cup apple jelly
2 teaspoons water
2 to 2½ cups fresh red, yellow, and/or black raspberries and/or blackberries

For lemon curd filling, in a small saucepan stir together sugar and cornstarch. Stir in the lemon peel, lemon juice, and the 3 tablespoons water. Cook and stir over medium heat till thickened and bubbly.

Slowly stir *half* of the lemon mixture into the 3 beaten egg yolks. Then return all of the egg yolk mixture to the saucepan. Cook and stir till mixture comes to a gentle boil. Cook and stir for

Use your fingers to press the lemon and Poppy Seed Pastry onto the bottom and up the sides of each tart pan.

Lemon and Poppy Seed Pastry

PREPARE THIS HOMEMADE SWEET PASTRY FOR THE RASPBERRY-LEMON TARTLETS. IT MAKES ENOUGH FOR FOUR SMALL TARTLETS OR ONE LARGE TART—

1 cup all-purpose flour
¼ cup sugar
⅓ cup cold unsalted or lightly salted butter
1 beaten egg yolk
1 tablespoon lemon juice
2 teaspoons poppy seed

In a medium mixing bowl stir together flour and sugar. Using a pastry blender, cut in the butter till pieces are the size of small peas.

In a small mixing bowl combine the egg yolk, lemon juice, and poppy seed. Gradually stir egg yolk mixture into the flour mixture. Dough will not be completely moistened. Using your fingers, gently knead dough just till a ball forms.

Use the dough immediately, or wrap it in plastic wrap and chill for up to 48 hours. (If chilling, bring the dough to room temperature before using.) Makes enough dough for four 4-to 4½-inch tarts or one 9-inch tart (8 servings).

Nutrition facts per serving: 90 cal., 2 g total fat (1 g sat. fat), 28 mg chol., 1 mg sodium, 17 g carbo., 0 g fiber, 2 g pro. Daily Value: 4% vit. A, 1% vit. C, 1% calcium, 5% iron.

◆ Raspberry Lemon Tartlets

2 minutes more. Remove from heat. Add butter all at once, stirring till completely melted. Cover surface with plastic wrap. Chill at least 1 hour or for up to 48 hours.

Spray nonstick coating onto four 4- to 4½-inch tart pans* with removable bottoms. Divide the Lemon and Poppy Seed Pastry into 4 equal portions. Using your fingers, press 1 portion onto the bottom and up the sides of each tart pan. Using the tines of a fork, generously prick bottom and sides of pastry in each tart pan. Line pastry shells with a double thickness of foil.

Bake in a 375° oven for 7 minutes. Remove foil. Bake for 9 to 10 minutes more or till golden. Completely cool pastry shells in pans on a wire rack.

In a small saucepan heat and stir apple jelly and the 2 teaspoons water till melted. Cool slightly.

Gently wash berries; drain atop several layers of paper towels till dry. This keeps berries from watering out when placed atop the tart filling.

Spread a fourth of the lemon curd filling into *each* pastry shell. Top each with berries. With a pastry brush, brush berries gently with the slightly cooled jelly. Loosen and remove sides of pans and bottoms, if desired. Serve immediately or cover and chill tarts for up to 4 hours. Cut each tartlet in half to serve. Makes 8 servings.

For one 9-inch tart: Spray non-stick coating onto a 9-inch round tart pan with removable bottom. Roll all of the Lemon and Poppy Seed Pastry between 2 sheets of waxed paper to an 11-inch circle. Remove top paper. Carefully invert pastry into the 9-inch tart pan. Remove remaining waxed paper while easing pastry into pan. If needed, trim pastry even with rim of pan. Continue as above. Serves 8.

Nutrition facts per serving: 318 cal., 17 g total fat (9 g sat. fat), 143 mg chol., 8 mg sodium, 41 g carbo., 2 g fiber, 3 g pro. Daily Value: 22% vit. A, 20% vit. C, 5% calcium, 9% iron.

Fresh Fruit Medley with Frosty Melon Dressing

SALAD DRESSING IN FROZEN, SORBETLIKE SCOOPS? SURE! IT'S FUN TO SERVE, AND AS THE DRESSING MELTS, IT COATS THE FRUIT—

¼ cup orange juice
1 teaspoon unflavored gelatin
1½ cups very ripe cantaloupe chunks
1 tablespoon honey
2 teaspoons white wine vinegar
⅛ teaspoon ground cinnamon
Kale and/or romaine (optional)
5 to 6 cups assorted fresh fruit such as sliced nectarines, peeled and sliced kiwi fruit, strawberries, seedless grapes, cherries, sliced pears, sliced plums, papaya chunks, yellow and red watermelon, honeydew melon, and/or cantaloupe

In a small saucepan combine orange juice and gelatin; let stand for 5 minutes to soften. Stir over low heat till gelatin is dissolved; set aside.

In a blender container or food processor bowl blend or process the 1½ cups cantaloupe, honey, vinegar, and cinnamon till smooth. Add orange juice mixture; process till combined.

Transfer melon mixture to an 8x4x2-inch or 9x5x3-inch loaf pan. Cover; freeze for 4 hours or till firm. Break frozen mixture into small chunks. Transfer melon mixture to a chilled mixing bowl. Beat with an electric mixer on medium-low speed till smooth but not melted. Rinse and dry the pan; line with plastic wrap. Return mixture to loaf pan. Cover and freeze till firm or for up to 2 weeks.

To serve, arrange kale or romaine on a serving platter or 6 salad plates. Place the desired fruit atop the greens.

◆ Fresh Fruit Medley with Frosty Melon Dressing

For dressing, use a melon baller or scrape a spoon across the top of the frozen melon mixture to make small scoops. (If too frozen to scoop or scrape, let frozen dressing sit at room temperature for 5 to 10 minutes to soften). Place frozen scoops of dressing atop fruit and serve immediately. Makes 6 side-dish servings.

Nutrition facts per serving: 85 cal., 1 g total fat (0 g sat. fat), 0 mg chol., 7 mg sodium, 21 g carbo., 2 g fiber, 2 g pro. Daily Value: 31% vit. A, 85% vit. C.

Remember this gorgeous platter for your next brunch or outdoor gathering. The frozen scoops of cantaloupe dressing slowly melt, coating favorite summer fruits with tangy sweetness.

Sesame Chicken Kabob Salad

4 medium skinless, boneless chicken breast
halves (1 pound)
16 fresh pineapple chunks (1 cup)
3 tablespoons salad oil
3 tablespoons rice vinegar or white
wine vinegar
1 tablespoon toasted sesame oil
1 tablespoon soy sauce
½ teaspoon dry mustard
1 tablespoon plum sauce or chili sauce
2 cups chopped red cabbage
2 cups chopped bok choy or iceberg lettuce
16 to 24 fresh pea pods, trimmed
½ cup enoki mushrooms or sliced white
mushrooms
½ cup sliced radishes*
Toasted sesame seed (optional)

◆ Sesame Chicken Kabob Salad

Rinse chicken and pat dry with paper towels. Cut *each* chicken breast half into 4 lengthwise strips. On *each* of *eight* 6-inch wooden skewers, thread 2 of the chicken strips and 2 pieces of pineapple. Place kabobs in a single layer in a 2-quart rectangular microwave-safe baking dish.

For dressing, in a screw-top jar combine salad oil, vinegar, sesame oil, soy sauce, and dry mustard. Cover and shake till combined. Reserve *2 tablespoons* dressing. Cover remaining dressing; chill till needed.

Stir together the 2 tablespoons reserved dressing and plum sauce or chili sauce. Brush kabobs with some of the mixture.

Micro-cook kabobs, covered with vented heavy plastic wrap, on 100% power (high) for 2 minutes. Turn kabobs over, rearrange in dish, and brush again with remaining sauce mixture. Micro-cook, covered, on high for 2 to 4 minutes more or till chicken is no longer pink.

Combine cabbage and bok choy or lettuce and divide among 4 dinner plates. Top with kabobs, pea pods, mushrooms, and radishes. Shake chilled dressing to combine; drizzle atop each salad. Sprinkle with sesame seed. Makes 4 main-dish servings.

*Note: For spinning-top radishes, thinly slice about 5 radishes. With a knife, make a notch in each slice, cutting from center to edge. Holding 2 radish slices, line up notches; press together, making a spinning top. Repeat with remaining radishes.

Nutrition facts per serving: 314 cal., 18 g total fat (3 g sat. fat), 59 mg chol., 344 mg sodium, 16 g carbo., 3 g fiber, 25 g pro. Daily Value: 130% vit. C.

Italian Mozzarella Salad

ONE BITE OF FRESH MOZZARELLA AND YOU'LL UNDERSTAND THE DIFFERENCE BETWEEN THIS AND THE FIRMER, MORE STRINGY, PACKAGED MOZZARELLA AVAILABLE IN MOST STORES. THE FRESH VERSION HAS A SOFT, MOIST TEXTURE AND A CREAMY-RICH TASTE. IT IS USUALLY MADE BY HAND SO IT TENDS TO BE EXPENSIVE. FOR THE FRESHEST FLAVOR, ENJOY THIS CHEESE WITHIN A WEEK OF PURCHASING, OR COVER AND FREEZE.

¼ cup red wine vinegar
¼ cup olive oil or salad oil
*1½ teaspoons snipped fresh basil or ½
teaspoon dried basil, crushed*
1 teaspoon Dijon-style mustard
¼ teaspoon crushed red pepper
1 small clove garlic, minced
*8 ounces round- or log-shaped mozzarella
(preferably fresh mozzarella) or
part-skim scamorza*
*1 15-ounce can black beans or
garbanzo beans*
*1 15-ounce can butter beans or great
northern beans*
*1 small cucumber, quartered lengthwise
and sliced (1 cup)*
2 red and/or yellow tomatoes, thinly sliced
½ cup thinly sliced green onion
Fresh basil sprigs (optional)

In a jar with a screw-top lid combine vinegar, oil, basil, mustard, crushed red pepper, and garlic. Cover and shake well to mix. Chill till needed, up to 48 hours.

Cut mozzarella or scamorza cheese into thin slices; set aside. Drain and rinse beans; drain thoroughly.

In a large mixing bowl combine beans and cucumber. Add dressing to bean mixture; toss. Divide among 4 dinner plates. Arrange cheese and tomato slices

◆ Italian Mozzarella Salad

alternately atop bean mixture. Sprinkle with sliced green onion. Garnish with basil sprigs, if desired. Makes 4 main-dish servings.

Note: Look for fresh mozzarella or scamorza (also spelled scamorze or scamorzo), in the specialty cheese department of your grocery store, gourmet stores, or Italian markets. Or, to order through the mail, call the Mozzarella Company in Dallas, Texas, at 800/798-2954. They sell their handmade fresh mozzarella for $7.50 per pound plus overnight shipping.

Nutrition facts per serving: 433 cal., 23 g total fat (8 g sat. fat), 32 mg chol., 834 mg sodium, 36 g carbo., 11 g fiber, 26 g pro. Daily Value. 24% vit. A, 41% vit. C, 56% calcium, 24% iron.

Garden Greens with Swordfish

*1 pound fresh or frozen swordfish or tuna
steaks, cut ½ to 1 inch thick*
1 tablespoon lemon juice
1 teaspoon dried Italian seasoning, crushed
¼ teaspoon garlic salt
Goat Cheese Croutons (optional)
*5 cups torn assorted salad greens such as
leaf lettuce, Belgian endive, radicchio,
and/or curly endive*
*1 cup torn arugula or torn assorted
salad greens*
*12 pear-shaped baby red and/or
yellow tomatoes, halved, or cherry
tomatoes, halved*
Roasted Pepper Dressing

Thaw fish, if frozen. Brush swordfish or tuna steaks with lemon juice. Combine Italian seasoning, garlic salt, and ⅛ teaspoon *pepper*; rub mixture all over fish. Measure thickness of fish. Place fish on the greased, unheated rack of a broiler pan.

Broil 4 inches from the heat for 4 to 6 minutes per ½-inch thickness. (If fish is 1 inch thick, turn over halfway through broiling.) Remove fish from rack and cut into strips. (Keep the broiler on and toast the croutons.)

Divide assorted greens and arugula among 4 dinner plates. Top with fish slices and tomatoes. Stir Roasted Pepper Dressing; drizzle atop salads. Serve with Goat Cheese Croutons, if desired. Makes 4 main-dish servings.

Nutrition facts per serving: 293 cal., 19 g total fat (3 g sat. fat), 45 mg chol., 396 mg sodium, 8 g carbo., 2 g fiber, 25 g pro. Daily Value: 62% vit. A, 102% vit. C, 10% calcium, 19% iron.

Goat Cheese Croutons: In a small bowl stir together 2 ounces *soft goat cheese (chèvre) or cream cheese* and ½ teaspoon snipped fresh *chives, basil, or parsley.* Place 8 very thin slices *baguette-style French bread* on the rack of a broiler pan. Broil 4 inches from heat for 30 to 60 seconds or till bread is lightly toasted, turning twice. Spread cheese mixture on one side of each bread slice. Makes 8 croutons.

Nutrition facts per crouton: 23 cal., 2 g total fat (1 g sat. fat), 6 mg chol., 41 mg sodium, 0 g carbo., 0 g fiber, 1 g pro.

◆ Garden Greens with Swordfish

Roasted Pepper Dressing

1 large red sweet pepper, roasted, or
½ of a 7-ounce jar roasted
sweet peppers, drained
¼ cup salad oil
3 tablespoons white wine vinegar
Dash ground red pepper*

In a blender container or food processor bowl combine roasted sweet pepper, salad oil, vinegar, ground red pepper, and ¼ teaspoon *salt*; cover and blend or process till nearly smooth. Transfer dressing to a covered pitcher or storage container; chill till serving time, up to 24 hours. Makes about 1 cup.

*To roast red sweet pepper: Cut pepper in half lengthwise. Remove seeds. Place pepper, cut side down, on a foil-lined baking sheet. Bake, uncovered, in a

Choose a shady spot outdoors for a refreshing salad supper. Dress up assorted crisp greens with slices of succulent swordfish and a colorful drizzle of red pepper dressing.

425° oven for 20 to 25 minutes or till skin is bubbly and brown. Place pepper in a clean paper bag; seal and let stand for 20 to 30 minutes or till cool enough to handle. Pull skin off gently and slowly using a paring knife.

Nutrition facts per tablespoon: 32 cal., 3 g total fat (0 g sat. fat), 0 mg chol., 36 mg sodium, 0 g carbo., 0 g fiber, 0 g pro. Daily Value: 1% vit. A, 18% vit. C, 0% calcium, 0% iron.

Warm Peach and Nutmeg Tart

1 recipe Homemade Pastry
(see recipe, right)
1 beaten egg
⅔ cup sugar
3 tablespoons all-purpose flour
1½ teaspoons finely shredded orange peel
¼ teaspoon ground nutmeg
4 cups peeled and sliced ripe
peaches (7 to 8 medium)
½ cup whipping cream
1 tablespoon sugar
½ teaspoon finely shredded orange peel
Coarsely shredded orange peel (optional)

For the crust, reserve *one-fourth* of the Homemade Pastry; cover and set aside. On a lightly floured surface, roll remaining pastry into a 13x10-inch rectangle. Ease pastry into an 11x8x1-inch rectangular tart pan with a removable bottom. (Or, roll pastry into a 12-inch circle. Ease the round pastry into a 10-inch round tart pan with a removable bottom.) Use your fingers to trim pastry from pan edge, reserving trimmings. Or, roll a rolling pin across the pan edge to remove excess pastry. Line pastry with a double thickness of foil; set aside.

On a lightly floured surface, roll reserved pastry and any pastry trimmings to ⅛-inch thickness. Using a small knife, cookie cutters, or your hands, shape or cut pastry into desired shapes, such as a bunch of grapes, peaches, cherries, branches, and leaves. Transfer shapes to an ungreased baking sheet. Use the dull edge of a butter knife to make decorative marks in pastry shapes, such as veins in leaves and indents in peaches. Brush with beaten egg; sprinkle with additional *sugar.*

Bake crust and pastry shapes in a 400° oven for 10 to 12 minutes or till pastry shapes are golden brown (if sizes of pastry shapes vary, smaller shapes may brown more quickly). Transfer pastry shapes to a wire rack. Carefully remove foil from crust; set crust, in the pan, on a wire rack.

For filling, in a large mixing bowl stir together the ⅔ cup sugar, flour, the 1½ teaspoons peel, and the nutmeg. Add peaches; toss gently to coat. Spoon mixture into pastry crust.

Bake in a 400° oven for 30 to 40 minutes or till pastry is golden. Cool slightly on a wire rack.

Top tart with pastry shapes; serve warm or cover and store at room temperature for up to 1 day. To store leftover tart longer, cover and chill for up to 3 days.

To serve, prepare orange whipped cream: In a chilled small mixing bowl beat whipping cream, the 1 tablespoon sugar, and the ½ teaspoon finely shredded orange peel with the chilled beaters of an electric mixer on medium-high speed just to soft peaks. Transfer to a serving bowl and top with coarsely shredded orange peel. Cut tart in squares; serve with orange whipped cream. Makes 8 servings.

Nutrition facts per serving: 348 cal., 19 g total fat (7 g sat. fat), 47 mg chol., 81 mg sodium, 42 g carbo., 2 g fiber, 4 g pro. Daily Value: 15% vit. A.

Homemade Pastry

THIS FLAKY PASTRY IS THE PERFECT SIZE FOR THE WARM PEACH AND NUTMEG TART AND THE COUNTRY CHERRY AND APRICOT TART—

1½ cups all-purpose flour
¼ teaspoon salt
½ cup shortening
4 to 5 tablespoons cold water

In a medium mixing bowl combine flour and salt. Using a pastry blender or two forks, cut in the shortening till pieces are the size of small peas. Sprinkle *1 tablespoon* of the water over part of the mixture, then gently toss with a fork. Push the moistened mixture to the side of the bowl. Repeat, using *1 tablespoon* of the water at a time, till all the dough is moistened.

Form the dough into a ball. Use as directed in the Warm Peach and Nutmeg Tart or Country Cherry and Apricot Tart. Makes enough dough for 1 of these 2 recipes.

Use the dull edge of a butter knife to make decorative marks in the pastry shapes, such as veins in leaves and indents in peaches.

◆ Warm Peach and Nutmeg Tart

Mixed Fruit Tart with Amaretto Crème

THIS LUSCIOUS ALMOND AND FRUIT TART
IS MADE IN A 9-INCH SPRINGFORM PAN,
INSTEAD OF A TART PAN—

*½ of a 15-ounce package folded
refrigerated unbaked piecrust (1 crust)
Milk
1 tablespoon granulated sugar
1 8-ounce package cream cheese, softened
1 3-ounce package cream cheese, softened
½ cup amaretto*
3 tablespoons brown sugar
½ cup toasted finely chopped almonds
3 to 4 cups chilled assorted fresh fruits such
as melon balls, seedless grapes, clumps of
champagne grapes, halved strawberries,
raspberries, and/or sliced peaches
1 tablespoon granulated sugar*

Let the piecrust sit for 20 minutes at
room temperature before using, following the package directions. On a lightly
floured surface, roll pastry to an 11-inch
circle and transfer to a 9-inch springform
pan. Press pastry evenly onto the bottom
and 1 inch up the sides of the pan. Flute
edge of pastry, if desired. With the tines
of a fork, generously prick sides and bottom. Line pastry shell in springform pan
with a double thickness of foil.

Bake in a 450° oven for 5 minutes.
Remove the foil and brush the edge of
the pastry with milk. Sprinkle pastry
with the first 1 tablespoon granulated
sugar. Bake for 7 to 9 minutes more or
till pastry is golden brown. Completely
cool pastry shell in pan on a wire rack.

In a small mixer bowl beat the cream
cheese, amaretto, and brown sugar with
an electric mixer on medium speed till
smooth. Stir in the almonds. Spread the

◆ Mixed Fruit Tart with Amaretto Crème

almond cream mixture evenly atop the
cooled pastry. At this point, you can
cover and chill for up to 4 hours.

Before serving, top almond cream
mixture with the desired fruits. Remove
sides of pan and bottom, if desired.
Sprinkle the fruit with the remaining
1 tablespoon sugar. Makes 8 servings.

*Note: You can substitute ¼ cup *milk*
and ¼ teaspoon *almond extract* for the
amaretto, if desired.

Nutrition facts per serving: 398 cal.,
26 g total fat (9 g sat. fat), 51 mg chol.,
226 mg sodium, 35 g carbo., 2 g fiber, 6
g pro. Daily Value: 35% vit. A, 14% vit.
C, 8% calcium, 7% iron.

*Line the pastry shell in the spring form
pan with a double thickness of heavy foil.
This prevents the pastry from puffing while
baking.*

Pour the filling into the pastry-lined dish. Fold the pastry border up and over the filling, pleating the pastry to fit. Lightly brush the pastry with milk.

Bake in a 375° oven for 45 to 50 minutes or till pastry is golden. Cool tart on a wire rack. Before serving, sift powdered sugar atop pastry edges. Serves 8.

Nutrition facts per serving: 350 cal., 16 g total fat (4 g sat. fat), 0 mg chol., 102 mg sodium, 47 g carbo., 2 g fiber, 3 g pro. Daily Value: 18% vit. A, 9% vit. C, 2% calcium, 8% iron.

◆ Country Cherry and Apricot Tart

To transfer the rolled pastry from the floured surface to the pie plate, loosely wrap the pastry around a rolling pin and gently unroll it onto the pie plate.

Country Cherry and Apricot Tart

¾ cup sugar
3 tablespoons cornstarch
¾ cup apricot nectar
3 tablespoons cherry or apricot brandy or orange juice
2 tablespoons margarine or butter
3 cups sliced fresh apricots (6 to 8)
2 cups pitted fresh sweet cherries (1 pound)
1 recipe Homemade Pastry
Milk
Powdered sugar

For filling, in a medium saucepan combine the sugar and cornstarch. Stir in the apricot nectar. Cook and stir over medium heat till thickened and bubbly. Cook and stir for 2 minutes more. Remove from heat. Stir in the brandy or orange juice and margarine or butter. Stir in apricots and cherries; set aside.

For pastry, on a lightly floured surface, use your hands to slightly flatten dough. Roll dough from center to the edge, forming a circle about 14 inches in diameter. Loosely wrap pastry around rolling pin. Unroll the pastry onto a 10-inch pie plate or quiche dish. Ease pastry into the plate or dish, being careful not to stretch it. Trim pastry to 1½ inches beyond the edge of the plate.

Using your fingers, fold the pastry border up and over the filling, pleating the pastry to fit.

Prize Tested Recipes.

Chili Pepper Cheeseburgers

HICKORY CHIPS IMPART A WONDERFUL SMOKY TASTE TO THESE SPICY BURGERS. THE REFRESHING LIME MAYONNAISE OFF-SETS THE "HEAT"—

2 cups hickory chips
⅓ cup finely chopped green onion
3 tablespoons nonfat plain yogurt
1 to 4 tablespoons finely chopped jalapeño peppers
½ teaspoon black pepper
2 pounds lean ground beef or turkey
6 ounces Monterey Jack cheese with jalapeño peppers, cut into 6 slices
8 Kaiser rolls, split and toasted
Leaf lettuce
Sliced tomato
1 recipe Lime Mayonnaise

At least 1 hour before needed, soak hickory chips in enough water to cover. In a medium bowl combine green onion, yogurt, jalapeño peppers, black pepper, and ½ teaspoon salt. Add beef or turkey; mix well. Shape mixture into 8 patties about ¾ inch thick. In a covered grill arrange preheated coals around a drip pan. Test for *medium* heat above pan. Drain chips and place on top of coals. Place burgers on grill rack above drip pan. Lower grill hood. Grill 20 to 24 minutes or till no pink remains, turning once. Top each patty with cheese the last 2 minutes of grilling time. Serve the beef or turkey patties on buns with lettuce,

◆ Chili Pepper Cheeseburgers

tomato, and Lime Mayonnaise. Makes 8 main-dish servings.

Lime Mayonnaise: In a small bowl combine ⅓ cup *reduced-fat mayonnaise* or *salad dressing*, ½ teaspoon finely shredded *lime peel*, 1 teaspoon *lime juice* and 1 teaspoon *Dijon-style mustard*. Cover; chill till serving time. Makes about ⅓ cup.

Nutrition facts per serving: 389 cal., 22 g total fat (9 g sat. fat) 94 mg chol. 511 mg sodium 19 g carbo. 1 g fiber; 29 g pro. Daily Value. 10% vit. A, 15% vit. C, 19% calcium, 22% iron.
$200 WINNER
Diane Halferty, Seattle, Wash.

◆ Stuffed Zucchini

◆ Zucchini and Feta Cheese Soufflés

Zucchini and Feta Cheese Soufflés

SERVE THESE MINI SOUFFLÉS WITH A FRESH FRUIT SALAD FOR BRUNCH OR AS A SIDE DISH TO FISH—

2 cups shredded zucchini
3 tablespoons margarine or butter
¼ cup all-purpose flour
¼ teaspoon dry mustard
1 cup milk
½ cup crumbled feta cheese
1 tablespoon grated Parmesan cheese
4 eggs, separated

Place shredded zucchini in a colander: sprinkle with 1 teaspoon *salt* and toss lightly. Let stand 30 minutes. Rinse and drain. Squeeze out excess liquid; set aside.

In a saucepan melt margarine or butter. Stir in flour and mustard. Add milk. Cook and stir till bubbly. Remove from heat. Stir in zucchini and cheeses. In a large bowl beat yolks with a fork. Gradually stir in zucchini mixture. In a mixing bowl beat whites with an electric mixer till stiff peaks form. Fold half of whites into zucchini mixture. Gently fold remaining whites into zucchini mixture. Spoon into six 6-ounce greased soufflé dishes or custard cups. Bake in a 375° oven 20 to 25 minutes or till a knife inserted near center comes out clean. Serve immediately. Makes 6 side-dish servings.

Nutrition facts per serving: 174 cal., 12 g total fat (4 g sat. fat) 154 mg chol., 276 mg sodium, 8 g carbo., 1 g fiber, 8 g pro. Daily Value. 18% vit. A, 4% vit. C, 11% calcium.

$200 WINNER
Karen E. Bosley, Lake Oswego, Oreg.

Stuffed Zucchini

WHILE DINING IN ITALY, TERRYE ENJOYED A SIDE DISH OF STUFFED ZUCCHINI CONTAINING CHEESE, BASIL, AND EGGS. AFTER RETURNING HOME, SHE CREATED THIS WINNING RECIPE—

2 medium zucchini (about 12 ounces)
⅓ cup finely chopped onion
1 tablespoon olive oil or cooking oil
2 teaspoons all-purpose flour
½ teaspoon dried basil, crushed
⅛ teaspoon pepper
½ cup milk
¼ cup frozen egg product,
*   thawed or 1 beaten egg*
⅓ cup grated Parmesan cheese

Cut zucchini in half lengthwise. Place, cut side down, in a microwave-safe 2-quart square baking dish. Micro-cook, covered, on 100% power (high) for 2 to *continued on page 148*

continued from page 147

3 minutes or till nearly tender. (Or, cook in boiling water for 3 to 4 minutes.) Scoop out pulp, leaving a ¼-inch-thick shell. Set shells aside. Finely chop the zucchini pulp; set aside.

In a medium saucepan cook onion in hot oil till tender but not brown. Add chopped zucchini; cook 1 minute more. Stir in flour, basil, and pepper. Add milk all at once. Cook and stir till thickened and bubbly. Cook and stir 1 minute more. Gradually add zucchini mixture to the egg product or egg. Stir in Parmesan. Spoon mixture into zucchini shells; place in a 2-quart square baking dish. Bake, uncovered, in a 350° oven for 25 to 30 minutes or till filling is lightly browned. Makes 4 side-dish servings.

Nutrition facts per serving: 131 cal., 8 g total fat (3 g sat. fat), 9 mg chol., 200 mg sodium, 8 g carbo., 0 g fiber, 7 g pro. Daily Value: 8% vit. A, 8% vit. C, 15% calcium, 5% iron.

◆ Chicken Burgers with Fresh Fruit Salsa

Chicken Burgers with Fresh Fruit Salsa

TOP THESE KNIFE-AND-FORK BURGERS WITH A PEACH-AND-PEAR CONDIMENT. PAIR THEM WITH GRILLED VEGETABLES FOR A FRESH SUMMERTIME MEAL—

⅓ cup purchased sweet-and-sour sauce
1 clove garlic, minced
2 teaspoons snipped fresh cilantro or parsley
1 teaspoon lemon juice
⅛ to ¼ teaspoon crushed red pepper
2 medium peaches, peeled, pitted, and chopped (about 1½ cups)
1 pear, cored and chopped (about 1 cup)

1 tablespoon finely chopped onion
1 pound ground raw chicken
½ cup finely chopped onion
2 teaspoons dried basil, crushed
½ teaspoon seasoned salt
¼ teaspoon black pepper
¼ teaspoon bottled hot pepper sauce

For salsa, in a medium bowl combine sweet-and-sour sauce, garlic, cilantro or parsley, lemon juice, and crushed red pepper. Stir in peaches, pear, and the 1 tablespoon chopped onion. Cover and chill till serving time.

In another bowl combine the chicken, remaining ½ cup onion, basil, seasoned

salt, black pepper, and hot pepper sauce; mix well. Shape into four ¾-inch-thick patties. Grill meat on the grill rack of an uncovered grill directly over *medium-hot* coals for 14 to 18 minutes or till no pink remains, turning once. (Or, grill, covered, indirectly over *medium* heat for 20 to 25 minutes.) Serve burgers with salsa. Makes 4 main-dish servings.

Nutrition facts per serving: 209 cal., 6 g total fat (2 g sat. fat), 54 mg chol., 282 mg sodium, 21 g carbo., 2 g fiber, 17 g pro. Daily Value: 5% vit. A, 14% vit. C, 9% iron.

$100 WINNER

Mrs. Marilyn Locche, New Hartford, Conn.

September

Eating Right
Here's How You Can
Do It

Prize Tested Recipes

Eating Right
Here's How You Can Do It

By Kristi Fuller, R.D.

What happened to the Hollingsworth family could happen to anyone. Caught in a whirlwind schedule of work, school, and activities, they seldom found time to eat right and keep fit. Mel, 42, and Joani Hollingsworth, 40, realized that their eating habits could lead to health problems for themselves and their children. "We wanted to change," said Joani, "but we weren't sure how." With a little help from their friends at *Better Homes and Gardens*, here's how they discovered a better way of eating and a new way of life.

Meet the Hollingsworth family: Mel, Joani, Megan, Libby, and Zach. Sixteen months ago they began to learn how to change their high-fat, high-calorie eating habits. Today, they look and feel better than ever! Mom Joani has even lost 25 pounds!

◆ Potato Bacon Soup

Potato Bacon Soup

<small>THIS HOLLINGSWORTH FAVORITE NOW HAS 20 FEWER GRAMS FAT AND 195 FEWER CALORIES PER SERVING—</small>

Nonstick spray coating
2 medium onions, chopped
½ of a 6-ounce package Canadian-style bacon, chopped (about ½ cup)
2 cups water
4 medium potatoes, cubed (about 1¼ pounds)
1 12-ounce can evaporated skim milk
1 ½-ounce package butter-flavored seasoning mix
¼ teaspoon salt
⅛ teaspoon pepper
Low-fat or nonfat dairy sour cream (optional)
Snipped fresh chives (optional)

Spray a 3-quart saucepan with nonstick coating. Add the chopped onions and bacon. Cook and stir over medium heat till onion is tender but not brown.

Stir in the water and potatoes. Bring to boiling; reduce heat. Cover and simmer for 10 to 15 minutes or till the potatoes are just tender.

Using a potato masher or a large fork, slightly mash some of the potatoes. Stir in the evaporated milk, butter-flavored seasoning mix, salt, and pepper. Cook and stir over medium heat till heated through. *Do not boil.*

To serve, ladle soup into bowls. Top with sour cream and chives, if desired. Makes 6 main-dish servings.

Nutrition information per serving: 181 cal., 2 g total fat (1 g sat. fat), 11 mg chol., 391 mg sodium, 32 g carbo, 11 g pro.

With the advice from BH&G Food Editor Kristi Fuller, a registered dietitian, the Hollingsworths adopted a whole new eating plan.

Identify Weak Areas

The first step the Hollingsworths took was identifying what needed changing. To do this, everyone in the family, even 6-year-old Zach, kept a "diet diary" of every single thing they ate for one week. The diaries revealed their problem areas. Because the whole family skipped meals and ate too many high-fat snacks, they concentrated on attacking these weaknesses first. "Going out for ice cream two or three times a week was normal," says Libby. "Now we have it maybe once a week, and we look for low-fat frozen yogurts. We didn't before!"

Set Manageable Goals

Early on, the Hollingsworths held a family powwow. They all agreed to eat on a more regular schedule and set a goal to have dinner at home together at least three times a week. Next came what Joani called "the fun part." New, more healthful recipes were put to the test. Mel, admitting to being a picky eater, said, "I was amazed at how good the lower-fat recipes tasted."

Joani also wanted to lose weight (permanently) and get more exercise. She set a modest, but obtainable, weight-loss goal. Because a person's weight fluctuates so much from day to day, Joani weighed herself monthly. "Weighing monthly, rather than weekly, took the pressure off," she says.

Cheesy Chicken Casserole

THE HOLLINGSWORTHS THOUGHT THIS MAKEOVER OF THEIR FAVORITE RECIPE TASTED BETTER THAN THE ORIGINAL!

Nonstick spray coating
1 8-ounce package light cream cheese (Neufchâtel), softened
1½ cups skim milk
1 10¾-ounce can reduced-sodium condensed cream of chicken soup
1 16-ounce package frozen mixed vegetables, such as broccoli, cauliflower, and carrots (about 4 cups), thawed
2 cups cubed cooked chicken
1 cup quick-cooking brown rice
⅓ cup grated Parmesan cheese
¼ teaspoon pepper
⅛ teaspoon garlic powder (optional)
1 tablespoon toasted wheat germ

Spray a 2-quart round casserole with nonstick coating. Place cream cheese in the casserole; stir in the milk. Stir in the soup till well-blended, then add the thawed vegetables, cooked chicken, uncooked rice, half of the Parmesan cheese, the pepper, and, if desired, the garlic powder.

Bake, covered, in a 350° oven for 30 minutes. Stir. Sprinkle with the remaining Parmesan cheese and the wheat germ. Bake, uncovered, about 20 minutes more or till heated through. Makes 6 main-dish servings.

Nutrition information per serving: 333 cal., 16 g total fat (8 g sat. fat), 84 mg chol., 566 mg sodium, 22 g carbo., 26 g pro.

◆ Cheesy Chicken Casserole

◆ Wild Rice and ChickenBake

Wild Rice and Chicken Bake

*1 6¼-ounce quick-cooking long grain
and wild rice
1½ cups water
1 10¾-ounce can reduced-sodium
condensed cream of mushroom soup
1 8-ounce can sliced water chestnuts,
drained
¾ cup frozen peas
1 medium carrot, shredded
3 whole medium chicken breasts (about 2
pounds total), skinned, boned, and halved
lengthwise
⅛ teaspoon paprika
⅛ teaspoon pepper*

Place uncooked rice and half of the flavor packet (about 1½ tablespoons*) in a 3-quart rectangular baking dish. Stir in water, soup, water chestnuts, frozen peas, and carrot. Arrange chicken over rice. Sprinkle chicken with paprika and pepper.

Bake, covered, in a 350° oven about 50 minutes or till chicken and rice are tender. Let stand, covered, 10 minutes. Makes 6 main-dish servings.

***Note:** Use remaining seasoning for another meal by stirring it into rice.

Nutrition information per serving: 151 cal., 4 g total fat (1 g sat. fat), 46 mg chol., 504 mg sodium, 34 g carbo., 1 g fiber, 21 g pro. Daily Value: 35% vit. A.

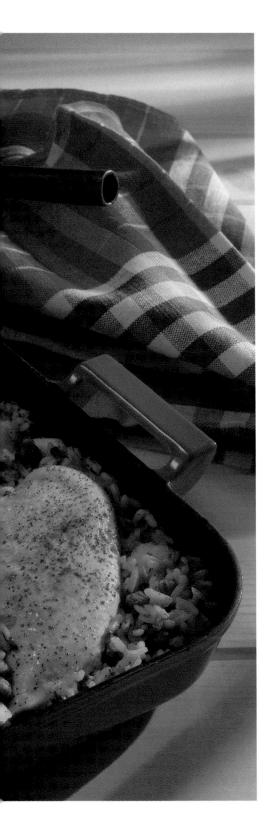

Lightened up recipes featured in this story had to first earn the status of "a keeper" from the Hollingsworths.

Make Wiser Choices

Food labels became a vital tool in helping the family shop smarter. After learning how to read labels to recognize lower-fat options, Joani began adapting favorite family recipes to make them more healthful. "You really can cut back on oil or fat used in recipes without much change in flavor. Many times I substitute lower-fat products, such as light sour cream, and no one even notices," she says.

The oldest children, Megan and Libby, got into the label-reading act too. "I now look for snacks that say 'low-fat' on the label," Libby says.

Take Your Time

"It has taken time, but our eating styles have really changed…forever," Joani says. "I realize now that you can't change your habits overnight." She began first by revising their favorite recipes to be more healthful. And, she slowly incorporated new foods into meals, such as a fish entrée or a vegetable they'd never tried before. Because both Joani and Mel set a goal to exercise more, they gradually increased the time spent exercising.

Spinach Salad

WE SUBSTITUTED PASTEURIZED REDUCED-CHOLESTEROL EGG PRODUCT FOR RAW EGGS IN THE ORIGINAL DRESSING. LOOK FOR THIS EGG PRODUCT NEXT TO REGULAR EGGS IN THE DAIRY CASE OF YOUR SUPERMARKET—

7 cups torn fresh spinach
1½ cups sliced fresh mushrooms
(about 4 ounces)
¼ cup sliced green onion (about 2 onions)
1 11-ounce can mandarin orange sections, drained
3 slices turkey bacon, diced
¼ cup refrigerated reduced-cholesterol egg product or frozen egg product, thawed
2 tablespoons lemon juice or herbed wine vinegar
2 tablespoons salad oil
2 teaspoons Dijon-style mustard
¼ teaspoon sugar
¼ teaspoon pepper
1 clove garlic, minced, or ⅛ teaspoon garlic powder

In a large salad bowl combine spinach, mushrooms, green onion, and orange sections; set aside. In a small skillet cook turkey bacon over medium heat till crisp. Remove from pan and drain on paper towels; set aside.

In a blender container combine egg product, lemon juice or vinegar, oil, mustard, sugar, pepper, and garlic. Cover and process till combined, about 1 minute.

To serve, pour dressing over the spinach mixture; toss gently to coat. Divide mixture among 6 salad plates. Top each serving with bacon pieces. Serve immediately. Makes 6 side-dish servings.

Nutrition information per serving: 106 cal., 7 g total fat (2 g sat. fat), 12 mg chol., 227 mg sodium, 11 g carbo., 2 g fiber, 5 g pro. Daily Value: 46% vit. A.

Mel's Spaghetti

WE REVAMPED MEL'S SPAGHETTI SPECIALTY AND MADE IT MORE HEALTHFUL. IF YOU'RE BUSY, MAKE A DOUBLE BATCH USING A 4-QUART DUTCH OVEN. SERVE HALF NOW AND FREEZE THE REST IN A FREEZER-SAFE CONTAINER FOR UP TO 6 MONTHS—

Nonstick spray coating
1 pound lean ground turkey or chicken
1 large onion, chopped (1 cup)
1 medium green pepper, chopped (¾ cup)
2 15-ounce cans low-sodium tomato sauce
2 4½-ounce jars sliced mushrooms, drained
1 6-ounce can Italian-style tomato paste
2 teaspoons dried Italian seasoning, crushed
2 teaspoons fennel seed, crushed
1 teaspoon sugar
½ teaspoon garlic salt
¼ teaspoon black pepper
¼ teaspoon ground red pepper (optional)
12 ounces spaghetti

Spray a 3-quart saucepan with nonstick coating. Add the ground turkey or chicken, onion, and green pepper. Cook and stir over medium heat till meat is no longer pink and vegetables are tender. Drain.

Stir tomato sauce, mushrooms, tomato paste, Italian seasoning, fennel seed, sugar, garlic salt, black pepper, and, if desired, ground red pepper into the meat mixture. Bring mixture to boiling; reduce heat. Cover and simmer for 30 minutes.

Meanwhile, cook spaghetti according to package directions, *except* omit any cooking oil and salt; drain. Serve hot pasta with sauce. Makes 6 main-dish servings.

Nutrition information per serving: 434 cal., 8 g total fat (2 g sat. fat), 28 mg chol., 690 mg sodium, 68 g carbo., 22 g pro.

Vegetable Pizza

THE MULTIGRAIN BISCUIT CRUST ADDS A DELICIOUS WHOLE WHEAT FLAVOR TO THIS GOOD-FOR-YOU SNACK—

Nonstick spray coating
1 package (8) refrigerated multigrain biscuits or buttermilk biscuits
½ of an 8-ounce package light cream cheese (Neufchâtel), softened
¼ cup reduced-calorie or nonfat mayonnaise or salad dressing
½ teaspoon dried dillweed
⅛ teaspoon onion powder
⅛ teaspoon garlic powder
¾ cup chopped fresh spinach
½ of a 7-ounce jar roasted red sweet peppers, drained and chopped (about ⅓ cup), or ⅓ cup diced pimiento
2 cups desired fresh vegetables, such as broccoli flowerets, sliced carrot, jicama strips, sliced green onions, green pepper strips, chopped yellow summer squash or zucchini, and/or cauliflower flowerets

Spray a 12-inch pizza pan with nonstick spray coating. For crust, place 7 biscuits in the pan near the edge forming

◆ Vegetable Pizza

◆ Spinach Salad

◆ Mel's Spaghetti

a circle; place 1 biscuit in the center. Using fingers, press biscuits in pan to form one single crust. Bake in a 375° oven for 12 to 15 minutes or till light brown. Cool in pan.

Meanwhile, in a medium mixing bowl stir together cream cheese, mayonnaise or salad dressing, dillweed, onion pow-der, and garlic powder. Add spinach and red sweet pepper or pimiento, stirring just till combined.

Spread the cream cheese mixture onto the cooled crust. Arrange vegetables atop cream cheese mixture. To serve, cut into wedges. Serve immediately. Or, cool then cover and chill up to 24 hours. Makes 12 snack servings.

Nutrition information per serving: 99 cal., 5 g total fat (1 g sat. fat), 9 mg chol., 197 mg sodium, 12 g carbo., 1 g fiber, 3 g pro. Daily Value: 12% Vit. A, 21% vit. C, 17% calcium, 37% iron.

Beef Ragout

TO ENJOY LOWER-FAT MEALS, YOU NEEDN'T CUT RED MEAT OUT OF YOUR DIET. JUST USE LEAN CUTS OF MEAT AND TRIM ANY FAT—

1½ pounds boneless beef top round steak, cut 1 inch thick
Nonstick spray coating
1 11-ounce can condensed cheddar cheese soup
½ cup water
¼ cup dried minced onion
3 tablespoons tomato paste
½ teaspoon lemon-pepper seasoning
½ cup buttermilk
1 tablespoon cornstarch
1 9-ounce package frozen Italian-style green beans
2 cups fresh small whole mushrooms, halved
10 ounces fettuccine, cooked

Trim fat from beef. Cut meat into 1-inch pieces. Spray a *cold* 4-quart Dutch oven with nonstick coating. Preheat over medium heat. Brown meat, *half* a time.

Return all meat to pan. Stir in soup, water, onion, tomato paste, and lemon-pepper. Bring to boiling; reduce heat. Simmer, covered, for 1½ hours.

Stir together buttermilk and cornstarch; stir into meat mixture. Add frozen green beans and mushrooms. Cover; simmer 10 to 15 minutes or till beans are crisp-tender. Serve over fettuccine. Makes 6 main-dish servings.

Crockery cooker directions: Brown meat as directed. Omit water and cornstarch. Place meat in a 3½- or 4-quart crockery cooker. In a bowl combine soup, onion, tomato paste, and lemon-pepper seasoning. Pour mixture over the meat. Add mushrooms. (*Do not* add green beans or buttermilk at this point.) Cover; cook on low-heat setting for 8 to 10 hours or on high-heat setting for 4 to 5 hours. To serve, if cooking on low, turn crockery cooker heat to high. Run frozen beans under cold running water to separate; add to crockery cooker. Stir in buttermilk. Cook, covered, on high-heat setting for 30 minutes more. Serve as directed.

Nutrition information per serving: 470 cal., 12 g total fat (5 g sat. fat), 86 mg chol., 614 mg sodium, 52 g carbo., 1 g fiber, 38 g pro. Daily Value: 37% iron.

◆ Beef Ragout

The Hollingsworth children, Zach, age 6, Megan, 10 and Libby, 12, often pitch in at mealtime. This makes them more enthusiastic about trying new foods.

Pizza Fish Fillets

HEALTH EXPERTS SAY WE ALL NEED TO EAT MORE FISH. THAT'S EASY WHEN IT'S AS TASTY AS THESE FILLETS—

1½ pounds fresh or frozen fish fillets (such as haddock, cod, or orange roughy), ½ to ¾ inch thick
Nonstick spray coating
½ teaspoon lemon-pepper seasoning
2 cups sliced fresh mushrooms
1 medium green pepper, chopped (1 cup)
1 medium onion, chopped
¼ cup water
1 8-ounce can pizza sauce
½ cup shredded part-skim mozzarella cheese (2 ounces)
Hot cooked spinach fettuccine

Thaw fish, if frozen. Cut the fish into 6 serving-size pieces. Spray a 2-quart rectangular baking dish with nonstick coating. Measure the thickness of the fish. Place fish in the prepared baking dish, tucking under any thin edges. Sprinkle with the lemon-pepper seasoning.

Bake fish, uncovered, in a 450° oven till fish just flakes easily with a fork (allow 6 to 9 minutes per ½-inch thickness). Drain off any liquid.

Meanwhile, in medium saucepan cook mushrooms, green pepper, and onion in the ¼ cup water, covered, about 5 minutes or just till tender. Drain; add pizza sauce. Heat through.

Spoon sauce over fish. Sprinkle with cheese. Bake 1 minute more or till cheese is melted. Serve with fettuccine. Makes 6 main-dish servings.

Nutrition information per serving: 159 cal., 4 g total fat (1 g sat. fat), 50 mg chol., 585 mg sodium, 9 g carbo., 23 g pro.

◆ Pizza Fish Fillets

Were the Changes Worth It?

For Joani, the changes they've made have resulted in a loss of 25 pounds—without feeling deprived or having to eat foods that differ from the rest of the family. She now realizes that changing her eating habits and adopting a healthful eating plan—not going on a diet—is the secret to long-term changes. Having tried numerous weight-loss diets, she has lost and gained more weight than she cares to remember. "I have been up and down in weight since I was 15," she says.

"Now that I'm 40, I think I've finally learned the secret. I'm a slow learner, but a thankful one!"

In thinking about the past year, Mel remembers a saying that expresses his feelings: "'As the twig is bent, so grows the tree.' Joani and I are role models for our children. We don't want them to fight weight or health problems. Teaching our children good eating habits will affect them for the rest of their lives."

◆Orange-Chocolate Cake

Orange-Chocolate Cake

Unsweetened cocoa powder
1 package 2-layer-size devil's food
cake mix
1 8-ounce carton low-fat or nonfat
plain yogurt
2 tablespoons finely shredded orange peel
½ cup orange juice
1 egg
2 egg whites
2 tablespoons cooking oil
1 teaspoon ground cinnamon
Chocolate Icing
Orange Icing

Spray a 10-inch fluted tube pan or a 13x9x2-inch baking pan with non-stick coating; dust with unsweetened cocoa powder. Set aside.

In a large mixer bowl combine cake mix, yogurt, orange peel, orange juice, egg, egg whites, cooking oil, cinnamon, and ½ cup *water*. Beat with an electric mixer on low speed for 4 minutes. Pour into prepared pan.

Bake in a 350° oven 40 to 50 minutes for fluted pan or 35 to 40 minutes for 13x9x2-inch pan or till a toothpick inserted near center comes out clean. Cool in pan 10 minutes. Remove cake from tube pan, if using; cool completely. Drizzle icings over cake. Serves 12.

Chocolate Icing: In a small mixing bowl combine ½ cup sifted *powdered sugar*, 1 tablespoon *unsweetened cocoa powder*, 2 teaspoons *orange juice*, and ¼ teaspoon *vanilla*. Stir in additional *orange juice* till of drizzling consistency. Makes about 2 tablespoons.

Orange Icing: In another small mixing bowl combine ½ cup sifted *powdered sugar*, 1 teaspoon *orange juice*, and ¼ teaspoon *vanilla*. Stir in additional *orange juice* till of drizzling consistency. Makes about 2 tablespoons.

Nutrition information per serving: 267 cal., 8 g total fat (3 g sat. fat), 36 mg chol., 428 mg sodium, 46 g carbo., 4 g pro.

◆Refrigerator Apple Muffins

Refrigerator Apple Muffins

STIR UP THE MUFFIN BATTER AND KEEP IT
ON HAND IN THE REFRIGERATOR. MAKE
AS MANY MUFFINS AS YOU WANT ON JUST
A MOMENT'S NOTICE—

*1½ cups multigrain oatmeal
(with rolled rye oats, barley, and wheat)
1 cup whole wheat flour
1 cup packed brown sugar
¾ cup all-purpose flour
⅓ cup toasted wheat germ
1 tablespoon baking powder
1 tablespoon apple pie spice
½ teaspoon baking soda
½ teaspoon salt
1½ cups chopped baking apple
(such as Jonathan, Granny Smith, or
Golden Delicious)
1¼ cups skim milk
⅓ cup cooking oil
3 slightly beaten egg whites or 2 slightly
beaten eggs
Coarse sugar or granulated sugar*

In a large mixing bowl combine the
multigrain oatmeal, whole wheat flour,
brown sugar, all-purpose flour, wheat
germ, baking powder, apple pie spice,
baking soda, and salt; stir to combine.
Add the chopped apple; stir to coat with
flour mixture.

In a small mixing bowl combine the
milk, cooking oil, and egg whites or
whole eggs. Add to the flour mixture;
stir just till moistened. Place the muffin
batter in an airtight container; cover and
seal. Store batter, refrigerated, for up to
3 days.

To bake, spray a 6- or 12-cup muffin
pan with nonstick coating or line with
paper bake cups. Gently stir batter.
Spoon the batter into the cups, filling
cups full. Sprinkle muffin tops with
some of the sugar.

Bake in a 400° oven for 18 to 20 minutes or till done. Cool slightly on a rack.
Serve warm. Makes 18 muffins.

Microwave directions: Line desired
number of 6-ounce custard cups or a
microwave-safe muffin pan with paper
bake cups. For each muffin, spoon 2
slightly rounded *tablespoons* of batter into
the cups. For custard cups, arrange the
cups in a ring on a large plate. Cook,
uncovered, on 100% power (high) for
specified time (see timings *below*) or till
done, giving the plate a half-turn every
minute. (To test muffins for doneness,
scratch the surfaces with a wooden pick.
The muffins should be cooked under-
neath.) If using custard cups, remove
each muffin from the oven as it becomes
done. Remove muffins from the cups or
pan. Let stand on wire rack for 5 minutes. Serve warm.

Microwave muffin cooking times:
For 1 Muffin: Cook on high for 30 to 60
seconds.
For 2 Muffins: Cook on high for 1 to 2
minutes.
For 4 Muffins: Cook on high for 1½ to
2½ minutes.
For 6 Muffins: Cook on high for 2 to 3½
minutes.

Nutrition information per muffin:
175 cal., 5 g total fat (1 g sat. fat), 24 mg
chol., 120 mg sodium, 29 g carbo., 1 g
fiber, 4 g pro. Daily Value: 2% vit. A,
0% vit. C, 4% calcium, 10% iron.

Mexican Stromboli

FOR THESE STUFFED PIZZA DOUGH BUN-
DLES, JOANI MAKES THE MOST OF
FAT-FREE BEANS AND SALSA AND OPTS
FOR LOW-FAT CHEESES AND LEAN
GROUND TURKEY—

1 pound lean ground turkey or ground beef
1 5-ounce can dark red kidney beans or
pinto beans, rinsed and drained
1½ cups salsa
Nonstick spray coating
2 10-ounce packages refrigerated pizza
dough
¾ cup shredded low-fat Monterey Jack
cheese (3 ounces)
Milk
1 tablespoon yellow cornmeal

For filling, in a large skillet cook the
turkey or beef till no longer pink; drain
off fat. Stir in *half* of the beans and all of
the salsa. Mash the remaining beans with
a fork or potato masher; add beans to the
meat mixture. Bring to boiling; reduce
heat. Simmer, uncovered, about 5 minutes or till most of the liquid has
evaporated. Cool about 5 minutes.

Spray a 15x10x1-inch baking pan with
nonstick coating; set aside. On a lightly
floured surface, roll one sheet of pizza
dough into a 12x10-inch rectangle. Trim
dough to a 10-inch square, reserving
trimmings.

Spoon *half* of the shredded cheese
down the center of the dough square.
Spoon *half* of the meat mixture over the
cheese. Moisten the dough edges with
milk. Bring the side edges of dough
together over the filling; stretch and
pinch to seal well. Fold the ends up and

◆ Mexican Stromboli

over the seam; seal well. Repeat with remaining dough, cheese, and meat to make another stromboli roll.

Arrange stromboli rolls, seam side down, on the prepared baking pan. Prick the tops with a fork. Brush the tops with milk. If desired, cut trimmings with a knife or small cookie cutter into shapes (such as stars, half-moons, or flowers). Place the shapes atop rolls; brush shapes with milk. Sprinkle the tops of the rolls with cornmeal. Bake, uncovered, in a 375° oven for 25 to 30 minutes or till light brown. Makes 8 main-dish servings.

Note: For any leftovers, wrap cooled stromboli in foil and refrigerate up to three days. To reheat, place unwrapped stromboli on a baking pan. Bake in a 375° oven about 25 minutes or till heated through.

Nutrition information per serving: 424 cal., 13 g total fat (3 g sat. fat), 29 mg chol., 749 mg sodium, 59 g carbo., 5 fiber, 22 g pro.

12 Steps to a Lifetime of Healthful Eating

THESE TIPS HELPED THE HOLLINGSWORTHS TURN THEIR DECISION TO CHANGE THEIR EATING HABITS INTO REALITY. THEY CAN HELP YOU AND YOUR FAMILY TOO.

1. Take stock. Inventory your eating habits and the items in your pantry. Write down all of the foods you eat for one week and how much you eat of them. All family members must participate. Review your diaries to see what high-fat foods you eat, then seek out alternatives. Do you eat too many chips for snacks? Eat pretzels instead. Do you love ice cream? Try frozen nonfat yogurt or ice milk. You don't have to eliminate your favorite foods. Just learn to have them less often or choose a lower-fat version.

2. Keep a journal. Joani found a journal helpful in tracking their progress. When someone raved about her new, slim self, for example, she wrote it down. When the family tried a new healthful recipe and the comments were, "Great! It's a keeper!" she jotted down their reactions. If she was feeling discouraged, she'd read her journal to remind herself how far she and her family had come.

3. Learn the basics. Find a good book on how to eat healthfully. Books such as *The New American Diet System* or *The American Heart Association Cookbook* are two examples. They can help you learn how to reduce fat in your meals.

continued on page 162

continued from page 161

4. Read labels. Zero in on the fat content of foods. For a 2,000 calorie a day diet, strive to eat less than 65 grams of fat. When reading labels, keep that total daily gram number in mind for comparison. If a food has 25 grams of fat, realize that this amount is nearing half your daily fat allowance. If this is how you want to spend your fat budget, be sure to choose low-fat foods the rest of the day.

5. Plan healthful snacks for kids. For children older than age two, the American Academy of Pediatrics recommends providing a diet similar to the diet recommended for adults (no more than 30% of calories coming from fat). Children over age two can eat the same lower-fat foods as the rest of the family. Just make sure to watch their weight. Children should not lose weight. They may need healthful snacks (for example, low-fat cheese and wheat crackers, skim milk and fruit muffins, or fresh fruit) several times a day to make up for their high-energy needs.

6. Plan ahead. Take it from Joani: "Things go to pot when I haven't taken the time to plan meals." Sit down and plan a menu for the week and make a gro-cery list. It will take the stress out of weekday cooking and leave less chance for running out for fast food or making less healthful meals.

7. Be realistic. It takes time to break old habits. Make your changes a little at a time. Begin eating on a regular schedule. No meal skipping allowed! Limit snacks to certain times of the day. Make a promise to exercise at least three times a week. Try cutting back the amount of margarine or butter in favorite recipes or using the lower-fat alternatives in place of foods your family likes, such as high-fat dressings or cheeses. If you're trying to lose weight, set a reasonable goal, such as no more than 5 pounds per month. Setting your goals too high can lead to letdown and the feeling of failure.

8. Stick with the familiar. Don't change your whole menu by throwing out all the recipes your family loves. Improve on those favorites. Cut the amount of cheese used, bake meats rather than fry them, and look for other ways to cut fat from recipes. Then, add some new healthful recipes to the menu for fun.

9. Involve the family in planning. Armed with new, health-focused cookbooks, Joani asked each child to choose new recipes they wanted to try. It became fun for the whole family to try the new recipes they had chosen. If your child is old enough, allow them to make some of the recipes.

10. Expect setbacks. Nobody is perfect. Everyone has times when they don't want to think about eating at all—never mind how healthful. That's OK. Just keep a positive attitude. It's not the end of the world if you have had a less than healthful meal. Forget it and move forward.

11. Reward yourself and your family. Do something for the whole family. Go see a movie or save for a vacation.

12. Seek support. If, like Joani, you're trying to lose weight as well as change your eating habits, you may need someone who can help you get started. A registered dietitian can lend you support, advice on choosing foods wisely, and guidance. If you'd like to find a registered dietitian in your area, call The American Dietetic Association, 800/366-1655.

Ham and Black-Eyed Pea Soup

*¾ pound dry black-eyed peas or
navy beans (2 cups)
2 14½-ounce cans reduced-sodium
chicken broth
1½ cups water
6 ounces reduced-sodium ham, cut into
½-inch pieces (about 1 cup)
4 medium carrots, sliced ½ inch thick
(2 cups)
2 stalks celery, sliced (1 cup)
¼ cup dried minced onion
1 teaspoon dried sage, crushed
1 teaspoon dried thyme, crushed
¼ teaspoon ground red pepper
1 tablespoon lemon juice*

In a 3-quart saucepan bring 4 cups *water* and black-eyed peas or navy beans to boiling. Boil, uncovered, for 10 minutes. Drain and rinse.

◆ Ham and Black Eyed Pea Soup

In a 4-quart electric slow crockery cooker combine broth, the 1½ cups water, ham, carrots, celery, onion, sage, thyme, and red pepper. Stir in drained peas or beans.

Cover and cook on low-heat setting for 11 to 12 hours or on high-heat setting for 4½ to 5½ hours. To serve, stir in the lemon juice. Makes 6 main-dish servings.

Range-top directions: In a 4-quart Dutch oven bring 4 cups water and black-eyed peas or beans to boiling. Boil,

uncovered, for 10 minutes. Drain and rinse; return peas or beans to Dutch oven. Stir in remaining ingredients except lemon juice; bring to boiling. Reduce heat to medium-low and simmer, covered, for 45 to 50 minutes or till peas or beans are tender, stirring occasionally. Stir in lemon juice.

Nutrition information per serving: 251 cal., 3 g total fat (0 g sat. fat), 12 mg chol., 753 mg sodium, 41 g carbo., 9 g fiber, 19 g pro.

Crockery Cooker Note:

Our crockery cooker recipes are tested only in cookers with heating elements that wrap around the sides of the pot. These pots have very low wattages and the elements remain on continuously during cooking. They can be identified by the heat control with one or two fixed settings, a *Low* and a *High*.

Prize Tested Recipes.

Banana Streusel Pie

A BANANA LOVER'S DELIGHT! THE MACADAMIA NUT STREUSEL MAKES THIS PIE OUTSTANDING—

Pastry for single-crust pie
4 cups sliced ripe bananas (about 5)
½ cup unsweetened pineapple juice
2 tablespoons lemon juice
1½ teaspoons finely shredded lemon peel
¼ cup granulated sugar
½ teaspoon ground cinnamon
1 teaspoon cornstarch
½ cup all-purpose flour
½ cup packed brown sugar
⅓ cup chopped macadamia nuts or almonds
1 teaspoon ground cinnamon
¼ cup margarine or butter

Prepare and roll out pie crust. Place pastry in a 9-inch pie plate. Line the unpricked pastry shell with a double thickness of foil. Bake in a 450° oven for 8 minutes. Remove foil. Bake 4 to 6 minutes more or till pastry is golden. Remove from oven. Reduce oven temperature to 375°.

Meanwhile, in a bowl gently toss together bananas, pineapple juice, and lemon juice. Drain, reserving juices. Gently toss bananas with lemon peel, granulated sugar, and the ½ teaspoon cinnamon. Spoon mixture into pastry shell. In a saucepan combine the reserved juices and cornstarch. Cook and stir over medium heat till thickened and bubbly.

◆Banana Streusel Pie

Pour over banana mixture in shell.

For streusel, combine the flour, brown sugar, nuts, and the 1 teaspoon cinnamon. With a pastry blender or 2 forks, cut in the margarine or butter till mixture resembles coarse crumbs. Sprinkle over banana mixture. Cover the edge of pie with foil. Bake in a 375° oven for 40 minutes or till topping is golden and edges are bubbly. Cool on wire rack. Makes 8 servings.

Nutrition information per serving: 406 cal., 18 g total fat (4 g sat. fat), 0 mg chol., 141 mg sodium, 60 g carbo., 2 g fiber, 4 g pro. Daily Value: 8% vit. A, 16% vit. C, 3% calcium.

$200 WINNER
Terry Thompson, Aiea, Hawaii

◆ Pork and Green Chili Casserole

◆Ham and Potato Au Gratin

Pork and Green Chili Casserole

THIS ZESTY RICE, BEAN, AND PORK DISH WILL RATE TOPS WITH THOSE WHO LOVE MEXICAN FOOD—

1½ to 1¾ pounds boneless pork shoulder
roast, trimmed of fat
1 tablespoon cooking oil
1 15-ounce can black beans or pinto
beans, rinsed and drained
1 10¾-ounce can condensed cream of
chicken soup
1 14½-ounce can diced tomatoes
2 4-ounce cans diced green chili
peppers, drained
1 cup quick-cooking brown rice
¼ cup water
1 to 2 tablespoons salsa
1 teaspoon ground cumin
½ cup shredded cheddar cheese

Cut pork into bite-size strips. In a large skillet stir-fry pork, *half* at a time, in hot oil till no longer pink. Drain. Return all meat to skillet. Stir in remaining ingredients *except* cheese. Heat and stir just till bubbly; pour into a 2-quart casserole. Bake, uncovered, in a 375° oven for 25 minutes or till rice is tender. Sprinkle with cheese. Bake 3 to 4 minutes more or till cheese is melted. Makes 6 main-dish servings.

Nutrition information per serving: 327 cal., 16 g total fat (6 g sat. fat), 64 mg chol., 1,022 mg sodium, 27 g carbo., 5 g fiber, 23 g pro. Daily Value: 28% vit. A, 37% vit. C.

$200 WINNER
Betty Cornelison, Portland, Oreg.

Ham and Potato Au Gratin

FROZEN HASH BROWN POTATOES SIMPLIFY THIS FAMILY FAVORITE DISH—

3 tablespoons margarine or butter
3 tablespoons all-purpose flour
1¾ cups milk
2 beaten eggs
1½ cups shredded cheddar cheese
(6 ounces)
¼ cup dry sherry or milk or 2 tablespoons
of each
1 tablespoon Dijon-style mustard
¼ teaspoon ground nutmeg
¼ teaspoon pepper
2 small onions, thinly sliced
2 tablespoons olive oil or cooking oil
1 10-ounce package frozen chopped
spinach, thawed and drained
12 ounces fully cooked ham, cut into
julienne strips
1 24-ounce package frozen shredded
hash brown potatoes (8 patties), thawed
¼ cup grated Parmesan cheese
continued on page 166

continued from page 165

In a large saucepan melt margarine or butter; stir in flour. Add milk all at once. Cook and stir till bubbly; cook 1 minute more. Remove from heat. Stir *1 cup* of the hot mixture into beaten eggs; return mixture to saucepan. Stir in cheddar cheese, sherry and/or milk, mustard, nutmeg, and pepper. Set aside. In a large skillet cook onion in hot oil till tender, about 5 minutes. Stir in spinach; set aside. Place *half* of the ham in an ungreased 2-quart rectangular baking dish or casserole. Break up hash brown patties and place *half* atop ham. Spoon *half* of the cheese sauce atop potatoes. Spoon the spinach mixture atop cheese in dish. Repeat layers with remaining ham, potatoes, and sauce. Sprinkle with Parmesan cheese. Bake, uncovered, in a 350° oven about 30 minutes. Let stand 10 minutes before serving. Makes 8 main-dish servings.

Nutrition information per serving: 369 cal., 21 g total fat (8 g sat. fat), 95 mg chol., 862 mg sodium, 24 g carbo., 3 g fiber, 22 g pro. Daily Value: 46% vit. A, 40% vit. C.

$100 WINNER
Diana Elliott, Rolling Hills, Calif.

Mango Cream Pie

YOU CAN USE FRESH MANGOES OR REFRIGERATED MANGO SLICES (FOUND IN YOUR SUPERMARKET PRODUCE SECTION) FOR THIS CREAMY CUSTARD-LIKE PIE—

*Pastry for single-crust pie or 1 baked
9-inch pie shell
1 cup sugar
¼ cup cornstarch
2½ sliced ripe mango (about 1½ mangoes)*

♦ Mango Cream Pie

*3 egg yolks
1½ cups plain yogurt or dairy sour cream
1 tablespoon lime juice
Fresh raspberries, kiwi fruit, and/or
blueberries (optional)*

Prepare pastry for a single-crust pie, if using. Roll dough into a 13-inch circle. Ease pastry into an ungreased 11-inch tart pan with a removable bottom. Press pastry into pan; trim edges. Prick pastry; line with a double thickness of foil. Bake in a 450° oven for 8 minutes. Remove foil; bake 5 to 6 minutes more or till lightly browned. Cool.

For filling, in a heavy medium saucepan stir together sugar, cornstarch, and ¼ teaspoon *salt*. In a blender container or food processor bowl place sliced mango. Cover; blend or process mango till smooth (should have 1½ cups). Stir mango and yogurt or sour cream into sugar mixture. Cook and stir mixture over medium heat till thickened and bubbly; then cook and stir 2 minutes more. Remove from heat. Stir about *1 cup* of the hot mixture into the egg yolks. Return mixture to the saucepan. Bring mixture to a gentle boil, stirring constantly. Cook and stir for 2 minutes more. Remove from heat. Stir in lime juice. Pour into baked pastry shell. Cool on wire rack 1 hour. Cover and chill at least 4 hours. To serve, garnish with berries or kiwi fruit, if desired. Serves 8.

Nutrition information per serving: 32 cal., 11 g total fat (3 g sat. fat) 83 mg chol. 173 mg sodium 51 g carbo., 1 g fiber, 5 g pro. Daily Value: 28% vit. A, 19% vit. C.

$100 WINNER
Robbie Melton, Washington, D.C.

October

How to Cook Like Grandma When You're Short on Time

Prize Tested Recipes

How To Cook Like Grandma
When You're Short On Time

BY JULIA MALLOY

With flour up to her elbows, Grandma cooked all day to fill her generous table. Wouldn't it be nice to serve the same comforting foods to your family without spending your life in the kitchen? We'll show you how.

To flute edge of crust, press dough with thumb (from outside the pie plate) between the thumb and forefinger of the other hand (from inside the pie plate). Continue around the edge.

No-Peel Apple Pie

THE SECRET TO NO-PEEL APPLE PIE LIES IN USING TENDER-SKINNED BAKING APPLES. OPT FOR VARIETIES SUCH AS GOLDEN DELICIOUS, JONAGOLD, OR JONATHAN—

1 15-ounce package folded refrigerated unbaked piecrust (2 crusts)
6 large apples, such as Golden Delicious, Jonagold, or Jonathan
½ cup water
2 tablespoons lemon juice
½ cup sugar
2 tablespoons all-purpose flour
1½ teaspoons apple pie spice
Whipping cream or milk
Coarse and/or granulated sugar
Whipped cream (optional)

Let piecrusts stand at room temperature according to package directions. Meanwhile, core and slice unpeeled apples (you should have 8 cups). In a large mixing bowl combine apples with water and lemon juice; toss to coat.

For filling, in a large mixing bowl stir together the ½ cup sugar, flour, and spice. Drain apples well; add to sugar mixture and toss gently to coat. Set aside.

Unfold 1 piecrust; sprinkle with flour according to package directions. Center crust, floured side down, in a 9-inch pie plate. Ease pastry evenly into the pie plate, being careful not to stretch or tear it. Cut out desired shapes from center of remaining crust; set aside.

Spoon the apple filling into the pastry-lined pie plate. Trim pastry even with rim of pie plate. Moisten edges with water. Center top crust atop filling. Fold top crust under bottom crust. With fingers, seal and flute edges. Brush the top crust with whipping cream or milk. If desired, top with reserved pastry cutouts; brush cutouts with cream or milk. Sprinkle the pie with coarse and/or granulated sugar. Cover the edge of the pie with foil to prevent overbrowning.

Bake the pie in a 375° oven for 30 minutes. Remove foil. Bake about 30 minutes more or till the top crust is golden. Cool slightly on a wire rack before serving. Serve pie warm with whipped cream, if desired. Serves 8.

Nutrition facts per serving: 373 cal., 16 g total fat (1 g sat. fat), 18 mg chol., 212 mg sodium, 57 g carbo., 3 g fiber, 3 g pro. Daily Value: 1% vit. A, 1% vit. C, 1% calcium, 4% iron.

◆ No-Peel Apple Pie

The Sunday-Best Dinner

With a houseful of relatives, Grandma cooked oodles for Sunday dinner. You can pick from these streamlined favorites to feed your family fast.

Menu 1: Southern-Style Chicken Dinner

OVEN-FRIED CHICKEN
WITH BUTTERMILK GRAVY
CREAMY MASHED POTATOES
HOMESTYLE VEGETABLES
HONEY AND POPPY SEED BISCUITS

Menu 2: Heartland Sampler

SWIFT SWISS STEAK
CROUTON-TOPPED NOODLES
STEAMED GREEN BEANS
CANDIED SQUASH

Oven-Fried Chicken with Buttermilk Gravy

WANT OLD-FASHIONED TASTE IN LESS THAN 10 MINUTES? FOLLOW THE QUICK BROILING METHOD FOR THIN BONELESS BREASTS—

½ cup fine dry seasoned bread crumbs
2 tablespoons grated Parmesan cheese
½ teaspoon paprika
3 pounds meaty chicken pieces (with bone)
3 tablespoons margarine or butter, melted
1 1-ounce envelope chicken gravy mix
1⅓ cups buttermilk

In a shallow dish combine bread crumbs, Parmesan cheese, and paprika; set aside. Rinse chicken; pat dry with paper towels. Brush chicken with some of the melted margarine or butter. If desired, sprinkle with salt and pepper. Dip chicken into crumb mixture, turning to coat.

Arrange chicken in a shallow baking pan. Bake, uncovered, in a 425° oven for 30 to 35 minutes or till tender and no longer pink.

For gravy, in a small saucepan prepare chicken gravy mix according to package directions, except use the 1⅓ cups buttermilk in place of the water called for in the package directions. Serve with chicken. Makes 6 main-dish servings.

Quick broiling directions: Use 6 skinless, boneless *large chicken breast halves* (1½ pounds total), instead of the meaty chicken pieces. Coat as above; arrange on the unheated rack of a broiler pan. Drizzle with any remaining margarine or butter. Broil 4 to 5 inches from the heat for 7 to 9 minutes or till tender and no longer pink, turning once during broiling.

Nutrition facts per serving: 325 cal., 15 g total fat (4 g sat. fat), 93 mg chol., 732 mg sodium, 12 g carbo., 0 g fiber, 34 g pro. Daily Value: 12% vit. A, 2% vit. C, 9% calcium, 9% iron.

Honey and Poppyseed Biscuits

Candied Squash

Homestyle Vegetables

Crouton-Topped Noodles

Creamy Mashed Potatoes

Swift Swiss Steak

Oven-Fried Chicken with
Buttermilk Gravy

Sunday Dinner Suggestions

Lucky you. Fixing Sunday Dinner in the '90s is much easier with our streamlined recipes. And, if your family is small, you can scale back the number of dishes you serve. In fact, you can create two totally different meals from our Sunday-Best Dinner.

Swift Swiss Steak

CUBED STEAK, ALREADY POUNDED AND TENDERIZED, GIVES YOU A BREAK FROM POUNDING THE STEAKS YOURSELF—

2 tablespoons all-purpose flour
½ teaspoon onion salt
¼ to ½ teaspoon pepper
6 beef cubed steaks (about 1½ pounds total)
4 teaspoons cooking oil
1 14½-ounce can Italian-style stewed tomatoes
1 8-ounce can tomato sauce
½ teaspoon dried savory or marjoram, crushed
1 medium green sweet pepper, cut into strips
Fresh marjoram (optional)
1 recipe Crouton-Topped Noodles (see recipe, right) or 4½ cups hot cooked noodles

In a shallow dish stir together flour, onion salt, and pepper. Dip steaks into flour mixture, coating both sides. In a large skillet brown meat, *half* at a time, in hot oil. Drain off fat.

Add *undrained* tomatoes, tomato sauce, and savory or marjoram to skillet. Bring to boiling; reduce heat. Cover and simmer for 25 minutes, stirring occasionally. Add green pepper; cover and simmer for 5 to 7 minutes more or till meat and green pepper are tender.

Transfer meat to a serving platter, reserving juices. Keep warm. Skim fat from juices; pour juices over meat. If desired, garnish with fresh marjoram. Serve meat with noodles. Makes 6 main-dish servings.

Nutrition facts per serving with ¾ cup Crouton-Topped Noodles: 487 cal., 17 g total fat (4 g sat. fat), 77 mg chol., 832 mg sodium, 47 g carbo., 1 g fiber, 34 g pro. Daily Value: 16% vit. A, 31% vit. C, 2% calcium, 37% iron.

Crouton-Topped Noodles

JUST POUR BOILING WATER OVER NO-COOK NOODLES. THEY'RE READY IN 6 MINUTES—

4½ cups no-boil noodles*
3 tablespoons margarine or butter
½ cup seasoned miniature croutons or ¼ cup fine dry seasoned bread crumbs

Prepare noodles according to package directions; drain. Stir in *1 tablespoon* of the margarine or butter.

In a small microwave-safe bowl micro-cook the remaining margarine or butter, uncovered, on 100% power (high) for 20 to 30 seconds or till melted. Add croutons or bread crumbs; toss gently to coat.

To serve, spoon the noodles into a serving dish. Sprinkle crouton or bread crumb mixture atop. Makes 6 side-dish servings.

Note: To use regular noodles instead of no-boil noodles, cook them according to package directions first.

Nutrition facts per serving: 238 cal., 6 g total fat (1 g sat. fat), 0 mg chol., 193 mg sodium, 37 g carbo., 0 g fiber, 7 g pro. Daily Value: 7% vit. A, 0% vit. C, 0% calcium, 13% iron.

Creamy Mashed Potatoes

CREAM CHEESE TURNS INSTANT POTA-TOES INTO AN INCREDIBLY DELICIOUS SIDE DISH. YOUR MICROWAVE OVEN MAKES THEM EVEN MORE "INSTANT"—

2 cups water
¾ to 1 cup milk
2 tablespoons margarine or butter
¼ teaspoon salt
2 cups instant mashed potato flakes
½ of an 8-ounce container soft-style cream cheese with chives and onion
Margarine or butter (optional)
Snipped chives (optional)

In a 1½-quart microwave-safe casse-role combine water, ¾ cup milk, margarine or butter, and salt. Stir in potato flakes. Cook, covered, on 100% power (high) for 5 to 7 minutes or till heated through.

Stir to rehydrate potatoes. Stir in cream cheese. Add milk, if necessary, till of desired consistency. Cook, covered, on high about 1 minute or till heated through. If desired, top with margarine or butter and chives. Makes 6 side-dish servings.

Nutrition facts per serving: 186 cal., 10 g total fat (4 g sat. fat), 22 mg chol., 258 mg sodium, 18 g carbo., 1 g fiber, 3 g pro. Daily Value: 11% vit. A, 0% vit. C, 4% calcium, 0% iron.

Homestyle Vegetables

READY-TO-COOK FROZEN VEGETABLES GET SPUNKY WITH BOTTLED SALAD DRESSING—

1 16-ounce package loose-pack frozen brussels sprouts, cauliflower, and carrots
2 tablespoons water
3 tablespoons Italian salad dressing

In a 1½-quart microwave-safe casse-role cook vegetables, covered, in the water on 100% power (high) for 7 to 9 minutes or till crisp-tender, stirring once. Drain.

Add salad dressing; toss gently to coat. Cook, covered, on high about 1 minute more or till heated through. Makes 4 side-dish servings.

Nutrition facts per serving: 74 cal., 4 g total fat (1 g sat. fat), 0 mg chol., 88 mg sodium, 9 g carbo., 4 g fiber, 3 g pro. Daily Value: 88% vit. A, 90% vit. C, 1% calcium, 4% iron.

Candied Squash

SQUASH COOKS FIVE TIMES FASTER IN YOUR MICROWAVE THAN IN YOUR OVEN—

1 1-pound acorn and/or butternut squash
1 tablespoon brown sugar
1 tablespoon maple syrup or maple-flavored syrup
1 teaspoon butter-flavored mix or 1 tablespoon margarine or butter, melted
Dash ground nutmeg

Halve squash lengthwise. Scoop out seeds and discard. Arrange squash halves in a 2-quart square microwave-safe bak-ing dish. Cover with microwave-safe plastic wrap; turn back one corner to vent. Cook on 100% power (high) for 7 to 9 minutes or till tender, giving dish a half-turn once. Drain.

Meanwhile, combine brown sugar, syrup, butter-flavored mix or margarine, and nutmeg. Slice squash halves cross-wise. Arrange in dish. Pour or spoon syrup mixture over squash. Cook, uncovered, on high for 60 seconds more. Makes 4 side-dish servings.

Nutrition facts per serving: 89 cal., 0 g total fat (0 g sat. fat), 0 mg chol., 14 mg sodium, 23 g carbo., 0 g fiber, 1 g pro. Daily Value: 83% vit. A, 24% vit. C, 6% calcium, 6% iron.

Honey and Poppy Seed Biscuits

LITTLE EXTRAS MAKE BISCUIT MIX TASTE LIKE BISCUITS FROM SCRATCH—

½ cup cream-style cottage cheese
¼ cup milk
2 tablespoons honey
2¼ cups packaged biscuit mix
1 tablespoon poppy seed

In a food processor bowl or blender container combine cottage cheese, milk, and honey. Cover and process or blend till nearly smooth.

Prepare biscuit mix for rolled or dropped biscuits according to package directions, *except* substitute the pureed mixture and poppy seed for the liquid. Bake as directed on the package direc-tions. Makes 12 to 14 biscuits.

Nutrition facts per biscuit: 124 cal., 4 g total fat (0 g sat. fat), 2 mg chol., 323 mg sodium, 19 g carbo., 1 g fiber, 3 g pro. Daily Value: 1% vit. A, 0% vit. C, 2% calcium, 1% iron.

So-Quick Seafood Chowder

GRANDMA'S CHOWDER ALWAYS INCLUD-
ED BACON. OPEN A CAN OF COOKED
REAL BACON PIECES AND FORGET THE
FRYING—

12 ounces fresh or frozen fish fillets (such as
salmon, orange roughy, or cod)
½ of a 24-ounce package frozen hash
brown potatoes with onions and
peppers (3 cups)
1 cup water
1 12-ounce can evaporated milk*
1 10¾-ounce can condensed cream of
shrimp or potato soup
⅓ of a 3-ounce can cooked bacon pieces
(¼ cup)
2 teaspoons snipped fresh dill or
¾ teaspoon dried dillweed
¼ teaspoon pepper
1 2-ounce jar diced pimiento, drained
Fresh dill (optional)

Thaw fish, if frozen.** Rinse and
drain. Cut fish into 1-inch pieces. Set
aside.

Meanwhile, in a large saucepan combine potatoes and water. Bring to
boiling; reduce heat. Cover and simmer
about 5 minutes or till tender.

Stir in evaporated milk, condensed
soup, bacon, dill or dillweed, and pepper. Return to boiling. Add fish and
pimiento; reduce heat. Cover and simmer for 3 to 5 minutes more or till fish
flakes easily when tested with a fork.

To serve, ladle into bowls. If desired,
garnish each serving with additional
fresh dill. Makes 6 main-dish servings.

*Note: Cut about 5 grams of fat per
serving by using evaporated skim milk.

**Note: To thaw fish, place
unwrapped fish in a 2-quart square

♦ So-Quick Seafood Chowder

microwave-safe baking dish. Cover and
cook on 30% power (medium-low) for 5
to 6 minutes, turning and separating fillets after 3 minutes. When thawed, the
fish should be pliable and cold on the
outside, but still slightly icy in the center
of the thick areas.

Nutrition facts per serving: 253 cal.,
10 g total fat (5 g sat. fat), 39 mg chol.,
671 mg sodium, 24 g carbo., 0 g fiber,
17 g pro. Daily Value: 11% vit. A, 25%
vit. C, 23% calcium, 8% iron.

*Cover the meat filling crosswise with
three lasagna noodles. Make sure the noodles do not touch the edge of the dish, so
they can rehydrate properly.*

Shortcut Lasagna

IF YOU LIKE, YOU CAN ASSEMBLE AND CHILL THIS FEED-A-CROWD FAVORITE A DAY AHEAD. TO SERVE, SIMPLY INCREASE THE FIRST BAKING TIME TO 40 MINUTES (20 TO 25 MINUTES FOR THE MICROWAVE OVEN), THEN CONTINUE AS THE RECIPE DIRECTS—

½ pound ground beef
½ pound bulk Italian sausage
1 15-ounce can regular or low-sodium tomato sauce
1 14½-ounce can Italian-style stewed tomatoes
1 6-ounce can tomato paste
1½ teaspoons dried Italian seasoning, crushed
½ teaspoon pepper
1 egg
2 cups ricotta cheese or cream-style cottage cheese
9 no-boil lasagna noodles
1 8-ounce package sliced mozzarella cheese
¼ cup grated Parmesan cheese
Fresh basil (optional)

In a large saucepan cook beef and sausage till brown. Drain off fat. Stir in tomato sauce, undrained tomatoes, tomato paste, Italian seasoning, and pepper; bring the mixture to boiling.

Meanwhile, in a mixing bowl beat egg slightly with a fork. Stir in ricotta or cottage cheese.

To assemble, spread about *1 cup* of the hot meat mixture in the bottom of a 3-quart rectangular baking dish (for microwave cooking, the dish should be microwave safe). Cover with 3 lasagna noodles, making sure that noodles *do not touch the edge of the dish* (see photograph, page 174). Cover with another *1 cup* of meat mixture, *one-third* of the ricotta

◆ Shortcut Lasagna

mixture, and *one-third* of the mozzarella cheese. Repeat with 2 more layers of noodles, meat mixture, ricotta cheese, and mozzarella. Sprinkle with Parmesan cheese. Bake or micro-cook as directed.

Baking directions: Cover with foil. Bake in a 350° oven for 30 minutes. Uncover and bake for 10 to 15 minutes more or till cheese is brown and noodles are tender. Let stand for 5 minutes before serving. If desired, garnish with basil. Makes 8 main-dish servings.

Microwave directions: Cover with microwave-safe plastic wrap; turn back one corner to vent. Cook on 100% power (high) for 17 to 20 minutes or till hot in center, turning the dish twice. Let stand for 5 minutes before serving. If desired, garnish with basil. Makes 8 main-dish servings.

Nutrition facts per serving: 482 cal., 26 g total fat (13 g sat. fat), 117 mg chol., 918 mg sodium, 25 g carbo., 1 g fiber, 37 g pro. Daily Value: 31% vit. A, 29% vit. C, 53% calcium, 20% iron.

Cranberry-Pear Cobbler

SPEED-COOK THE FRUITY FILLING IN THE MICROWAVE, THEN BAKE THE BISCUIT TOPPER TILL CRISP AND GOLDEN—

3 cups sliced, peeled, and cored pears
1 16-ounce can whole cranberry sauce
¼ cup sugar
1 package (6) refrigerated biscuits
1 tablespoon margarine or butter, melted
1 tablespoon sugar
¼ teaspoon ground nutmeg
Half-and-half or light cream (optional)
Fresh mint (optional)

In a 1½-quart microwave-safe casserole combine pears, cranberry sauce, and ¼ cup sugar. Micro-cook, covered, on 100% power (high) for 8 to 10 minutes or till mixture is bubbly and pears are slightly tender, stirring once.

Meanwhile, with scissors, snip edges of biscuits to within ½ inch of center to form flower petals. Place biscuits atop hot filling (see photograph, right). Brush with melted margarine or butter. In a small mixing bowl combine the 1 tablespoon sugar and nutmeg; sprinkle over biscuits.

Bake, uncovered, in a 400° oven for 10 to 12 minutes or till biscuits are golden. Serve warm.

To serve, spoon fruit and biscuits into serving bowls. If desired, serve with half-and-half or light cream. Garnish with fresh mint. Makes 6 servings.

Nutrition facts per serving: 278 cal., 3 g total fat (0 g sat. fat), 0 mg chol., 225 mg sodium, 65 g carbo., 3 g fiber, 2 g pro. Daily Value: 3% vit. A, 12% vit. C, 1% calcium, 5% iron.

◆ Cranberry-Pear Cobbler

Arrange the flower-shaped biscuits on top of the hot cooked filling.

Always Room for Dessert

Just when you thought you couldn't eat one more bite, Grandma would walk in with one of her irresistible home-baked desserts. Well, loosen your belt once again. It's time for these luscious, but now time-efficient, favorites from long ago.

Plump Apple Dumplings with Caramel Sauce

REMEMBER TO THAW ONE SHEET OF PUFF PASTRY 20 MINUTES AHEAD. KEEP THE REMAINING SHEET IN THE FREEZER—

1 sheet frozen puff pastry
4 medium cooking apples (such as Golden Delicious or Jonathan)
1 tablespoon sugar
1 teaspoon ground cinnamon
1 slightly beaten egg
1 teaspoon water
½ cup caramel ice-cream topping
⅓ cup toasted chopped pecan halves

Thaw and unfold puff pastry according to package directions. On a lightly floured surface, roll pastry into a 16-inch square. Trim to four 7-inch squares, using a fluted pastry cutter or table knife. Reserve pastry trimmings. Set aside.

Core apples. If necessary, trim bottoms of apples so they stand upright. Place one apple in the center of each pastry square. Combine sugar and cinnamon; spoon into centers of apples.

Combine beaten egg and water. Moisten the edges of the pastry with egg mixture; fold corners to center atop fruit. Pinch to seal, pleating and folding pastry along seams as necessary. Place dumplings in an ungreased 13x9x2-inch baking pan.

Using a knife or small cookie cutter, cut leaf shapes from pastry trimmings; score veins in leaves. For curved leaves, drape leaves over crumpled foil on another baking sheet (see photograph, right).

Brush wrapped apples and leaf cutouts with egg mixture. Sprinkle leaves with sugar.

◆ Plump Apple Dumplings with Caramel Sauce

Bake dumplings in a 400° oven about 35 minutes or till fruit is tender and pastry is brown. Add pastry leaves the last 5 minutes of baking.

Meanwhile, for sauce, in a 2-cup glass measure combine caramel topping and pecans. Micro-cook, uncovered, on 100% power (high) for 30 to 60 seconds or till heated through.

To serve, moisten the bottoms of baked pastry leaves with caramel sauce; place on top of the baked dumplings, gently pressing in place. Serve dumplings warm with caramel-pecan sauce. Makes 4 servings.

Nutrition facts per serving: 534 cal., 27 g total fat (1 g sat. fat), 53 mg chol., 389 mg sodium, 72 g carbo., 3 g fiber, 6 g pro. Daily Value: 3% vit. A, 1% vit. C, 3% calcium, 5% iron.

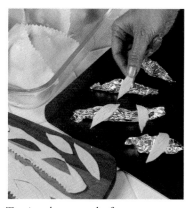

To give the pastry leaf cutouts a natural curl, drape them over crumpled foil on a baking sheet.

Coffeetime Favorites

Put on a pot of coffee, bake one of these quick-and-easy breads or cakes, and invite a friend for a cozy kitchen chat.

Short 'N' Sweet Caramel Bubble Ring

SERVE THIS STICKY PULL-APART BREAD FOR BRUNCH OR BREAKFAST. BOTH ADULTS AND KIDS WILL LOVE IT—

⅓ cup chopped pecans
¾ cup sugar
4 teaspoons ground cinnamon
2 11-ounce packages (16) refrigerated breadsticks
⅓ cup margarine or butter, melted
½ cup caramel ice-cream topping
2 tablespoons maple-flavored syrup

Generously grease a 10-inch fluted tube pan. Sprinkle about half of the pecans in the bottom of the pan. Set aside. Stir together sugar and cinnamon; set aside.

Separate each package of dough into 8 pieces, making 16 total. *Do not unroll.* Cut the pieces in half crosswise. Dip each piece of dough into melted margarine or butter, then roll in sugar mixture. Arrange dough pieces, spiral side down, in the prepared pan (see photograph, right).

Sprinkle with remaining pecans. In a measuring cup stir together caramel topping and maple-flavored syrup; drizzle over dough in pan.

◆ Short 'N' Sweet Caramel Bubble Ring

Bake in a 350° oven about 35 minutes or till dough is light brown, covering with foil the last 10 minutes to prevent overbrowning.

Let stand for 1 minute only. (If it stands for more than 1 minute, the ring will be difficult to remove from pan.) Invert onto a serving platter. Spoon any topping and nuts remaining in the pan onto rolls. Serve warm. Makes 10 to 12 servings.

Nutrition facts per serving: 347 cal., 12 g total fat (3 g sat. fat), 0 mg chol., 503 mg sodium, 57 g carbo., 0 g fiber, 5 g pro. Daily Value: 8% vit. A, 1% vit. C, 2% calcium, 14% iron.

Place the cinnamony dough spirals, flat side down, atop the nuts in the bottom of the tube pan.

◆ One Bowl Chocolate Cake

One-Bowl Chocolate Cake

STIR UP THIS SCRATCH CAKE IN NEARLY
THE SAME TIME AS A MIX—

2 cups all-purpose flour
2 cups sugar
1/2 cup unsweetened cocoa powder
1 teaspoon baking powder
3/4 teaspoon baking soda
1/4 teaspoon salt
1 1/2 cups milk
1/2 cup margarine or butter, softened
1 teaspoon vanilla
2 eggs
1 recipe No-Cook Chocolate Frosting

Grease and flour two 9x1½-inch round baking pans; set aside. In a large mixing bowl stir together flour, sugar, cocoa powder, baking powder, baking soda, and salt. Add milk, margarine or butter, and vanilla. Beat with an electric mixer on low speed till combined. Beat on high speed for 2 minutes more. Add eggs; beat for 2 minutes more.

Pour batter into prepared pans. Bake in a 350° oven about 35 minutes or till a toothpick inserted near the center comes out clean.

Cool in pans on a wire rack for 10 minutes. Remove from the pans. Cool completely on the wire rack.

To frost, place one layer of cake top side down, on a serving platter. Spread about ½ cup of the No-Cook Chocolate Frosting on top of the cake layer. Place the second cake layer, top side up, on top of the frosted layer. Spread sides with a thin layer of frosting to seal in crumbs. Add another layer to the sides; spread remaining frosting on top of the cake. Makes 12 servings.

No-Cook Chocolate Frosting: In a large mixing bowl stir together 3 cups unsifted *powdered sugar* and ½ cup *unsweetened cocoa powder*. Add ½ cup cut-up *margarine or butter*, ⅓ cup boiling *water*, and 1 teaspoon *vanilla*. Beat with an electric mixer on low speed till combined. Beat for 1 minute on medium speed. Cool for 20 to 30 minutes or till frosting is of spreading consistency. Frosts top and sides of two 8- or 9-inch cake layers.

Nutrition facts per serving: 482 cal., 18 g total fat (4 g sat. fat), 38 mg chol., 329 mg sodium, 77 g carbo., 1 g fiber, 6 g pro. Daily Value: 28% vit. A, 1% vit. C, 17% calcium, 13% iron.

Spirited Chocolate Cake: Prepare as directed, *except* decrease milk to 1¼ cups and add ¼ cup *liqueur* (such as hazelnut, crème de cacao, coffee, amaretto, cherry, or raspberry). For the frosting, decrease the boiling water to ¼ cup and substitute 1 tablespoon *liqueur* for the vanilla.

Nutrition facts per serving: 504 cal., 18 g total fat (3 g sat. fat), 37 mg chol., 6 g pro., 80 g carbo., 1 g fiber, 327 mg sodium. Daily Value: 27% vit. A, 0% vit. C, 16% calcium, 13% iron.

Amazing Banana Nut Roll

SHAPING A JELLY ROLL USED TO BE A MULTI-STEP PROCESS—ROLLING, COOLING, FILLING, AND REROLLING. NOW YOU BAKE THE CAKE AND FILLING TOGETHER AND ROLL JUST ONCE—

1 8-ounce package cream cheese, softened
1 3-ounce package cream cheese, softened
½ cup sugar
1 egg
3 tablespoons milk

• • •

½ cup all-purpose flour
½ teaspoon baking powder
¼ teaspoon baking soda
4 egg yolks
½ teaspoon vanilla
⅓ cup sugar
1 large banana, mashed (about ½ cup)
½ cup finely chopped walnuts or pecans
4 egg whites
½ cup sugar
1 recipe Cream Cheese Frosting
Chocolate-flavored syrup (optional)

Lightly grease a 15x10x1-inch baking pan. Line bottom with waxed paper; grease paper. Set aside.

For filling, in a small mixing bowl combine cream cheese and ½ cup sugar; beat with an electric mixer on medium speed till smooth. Add whole egg and milk; beat till combined. Spread in the prepared pan; set aside.

For cake, in a medium mixing bowl stir together flour, baking powder, and baking soda; set aside.

In a small mixer bowl beat egg yolks and vanilla on medium speed about 5 minutes or till thick and lemon colored. Gradually add the ⅓ cup sugar, beating till sugar is dissolved. Stir in banana and nuts.

Thoroughly wash the beaters. In a large mixing bowl beat the egg whites on medium speed till soft peaks form (tips curl). Gradually add the ½ cup sugar, beating on high speed till stiff peaks form (tips stand straight).

Fold yolk mixture into egg whites. Sprinkle the flour mixture evenly over egg mixture; fold in just till blended.

Carefully spread the cake batter evenly over the cream cheese filling in the baking pan.

Carefully spread the batter evenly over the filling in the pan (see photograph, above). Bake in a 375° oven for 15 to 20 minutes or till the cake springs back when lightly touched.

Immediately loosen the cake from sides of pan and turn out onto a towel sprinkled with powdered sugar. Carefully peel off paper. Starting with narrow end, roll up cake using towel as a guide (see photograph, right). (Do not roll towel into cake.) Cool completely on a wire rack.

Spread top with Cream Cheese Frosting. If desired, drizzle with chocolate syrup. Makes 10 servings.

Cream Cheese Frosting: In a small mixing bowl combine *half* of a 3-ounce package *cream cheese*, softened, and ½ teaspoon *vanilla*; beat with an electric mixer on medium speed till light and fluffy. Gradually beat in 1 cup unsifted

◆ Amazing Banana Nut Roll

powdered sugar. Beat in enough *milk* (1 to 2 tablespoons) to make a frosting of spreading consistency. Makes about ½ cup frosting.

Nutrition facts per serving: 400 cal., 19 g total fat (9 g sat. fat), 146 mg chol., 162 mg sodium, 51 g carbo., 1 g fiber, 8 g pro. Daily Value: 29% vit. A, 2% vit. C, 4% calcium, 9% iron.

Starting with a narrow end, roll up the cake and filling, using a towel as a guide.

Three-in-One Oatmeal Cookies

REMEMBER TO THAW THE FROZEN DOUGH IN THE REFRIGERATOR THE NIGHT BEFORE YOU WANT TO BAKE YOUR CHOICE OF COOKIE FLAVORS—

1½ cups margarine or butter
3 cups all-purpose flour
2 cups packed brown sugar
1 cup sugar
2 eggs
¼ cup milk
2 teaspoons baking powder
2 teaspoons vanilla
½ teaspoon baking soda
2 cups rolled oats

In a very large mixing bowl beat margarine or butter with an electric mixer on medium to high speed for 30 seconds. Add about *half* of the flour, the brown sugar, sugar, eggs, milk, baking powder, vanilla, and baking soda. Beat till combined. Beat or stir in remaining flour. Use a wooden spoon to stir in oats.

Divide dough into 3 portions; form into balls. Wrap each in freezer wrap; seal, label, and freeze for up to 6 months.

Before baking, thaw dough overnight in the refrigerator. Choose one of the following cookie variations. Stir ingredients for desired cookie into one portion of thawed dough.

Drop dough onto an ungreased cookie sheet. (For large cookies, drop into scant ¼-cup mounds 4 inches apart; for small cookies, drop from a tablespoon 2 inches apart.) Bake in a 375° oven till edges are golden but centers are soft, allowing 13 to 15 minutes for large cookies and 9 to 11 minutes for small cookies. Cool on the cookie sheet for 1 minute. Cool on

◆ Three-in-One Oatmeal Cookies

wire rack(s). Makes about 11 large cookies or 32 small cookies.

Spicy Raisin Rounds: Stir in 1 cup *raisins or currants*, 1 teaspoon *ground cinnamon*, and ¼ teaspoon *ground cloves*. Continue as directed.

Nutrition facts per large cookie: 249 cal., 9 g total fat (2 g sat. fat), 13 mg chol., 145 mg sodium, 41 g carbo., 1 g fiber, 3 g pro. Daily Value: 14% vit. A, 1% vit. C, 5% calcium, 10% iron.

Nutty Brickle Chippers: Stir in 1 cup chopped *chocolate-covered English toffee or semisweet chocolate pieces* and ½ cup chopped *walnuts or hazelnuts*. Continue as directed.

Nutrition facts per large cookie: 325 cal., 17 g total fat (2 g sat. fat), 18 mg chol., 207 mg sodium, 41 g carbo., 1 g fiber, 4 g pro. Daily Value: 15% vit. A, 0% vit. C, 5% calcium, 9% iron.

Gumdrop Cookies: Stir in 1 cup snipped or chopped *gumdrops or candy-coated milk chocolate pieces*. Continue as directed.

Nutrition facts per large cookie: 268 cal., 9 g total fat (2 g sat. fat), 13 mg chol., 149 mg sodium, 45 g carbo., 1 g fiber, 2 g pro. Daily Value: 14% vit. A, 0% vit. C, 3% calcium, 8% iron.

Fix-and-Forget Pork Chops and Rice

NO BROWNING NEEDED. THESE CHOPS BAKE TENDER AND JUICY ON A CREAMY BED OF VEGETABLES AND RICE—

1½ cups quick-cooking rice
1⅓ cups water
1 11-ounce can whole kernel corn
with sweet peppers
1 medium carrot, shredded
1 tablespoon dried minced onion
¼ to ½ teaspoon dried thyme, crushed
1 10¾-ounce can low-fat, low-sodium
condensed cream of mushroom soup
4 pork chops, cut ½ inch thick
Dash salt
Dash pepper
¼ cup fine dry seasoned bread crumbs
½ teaspoon paprika
1 tablespoon margarine or butter, melted

In a medium saucepan combine *uncooked* rice, water, *undrained* corn, carrot, onion, and thyme; bring to boiling. Stir in soup. Transfer mixture to a 2-quart rectangular baking dish.

Trim excess fat from chops; sprinkle with salt and pepper. Arrange on rice mixture. Cover with foil. Bake in a 375° oven for 15 minutes.

Stir together bread crumbs and paprika. Add margarine or butter; toss gently to mix.

Remove foil from chops; sprinkle paprika mixture atop. Bake, uncovered, about 15 minutes more or till rice is tender and pork is slightly pink just near the bone. Makes 4 servings.

Nutrition facts per serving: 495 cal., 17 g total fat (5 g sat. fat), 76 mg chol., 898 mg sodium, 58 g carbo., 2 g fiber, 28 g pro. Daily Value: 57% vit. A, 16% vit. C, 4% calcium, 22% iron.

◆ Fix and Forget Pork Chops and Rice

Step-Saving Sweet Potato Bread

INSTEAD OF CARROT OR PUMPKIN, ADD SWEET POTATOES TO A QUICK BREAD MIX—

1 15- to 16-ounce package nut quick bread mix
2 teaspoons ground cinnamon
¼ teaspoon ground nutmeg
¼ teaspoon ground ginger or ⅛ teaspoon ground cloves
1 cup water
½ cup drained and mashed canned sweet potatoes or canned pumpkin
1 beaten egg
2 tablespoons cooking oil
1 recipe Orange Icing

Grease and lightly flour five 4½ x 2½ x 1½-inch loaf pans or one 8x4x2-inch loaf pan; set aside.

In a large mixing bowl stir together mix, cinnamon, nutmeg, and ginger or cloves. Add water, potato or pumpkin, egg, and oil. Stir just till moist.

Pour batter into pan(s). Bake in a 350° oven till a toothpick inserted near center(s) comes out clean, allowing 30 to 35 minutes for small pans or 60 to 65 minutes for large pan.

Cool in the pan(s) on a wire rack for 10 minutes. Remove from pans; cool completely on rack. If desired, wrap and store loaves overnight in a cool, dry place for easier slicing.

Before serving, drizzle loaves with Orange Icing. Makes 5 mini loaves (20 slices total) or 1 large loaf (16 slices).

Orange Icing: In a small mixing bowl stir together 1 cup unsifted *powdered sugar* and enough *orange juice* to make of drizzling consistency (about 1 table-spoon).

Nutrition facts per mini-loaf slice: 133 cal., 3 g total fat (1 g sat. fat), 11 mg chol., 110 mg sodium, 23 g carbo., 0 g fiber, 2 g pro. Daily Value: 14% vit. A, 4% vit. C, 1% calcium, and 4% iron.

◆ Step-Saving Sweet Potato Bread

Microwave Note

Our microwave recipes are thoroughly tested in a variety of microwave ovens, including high-wattage (600 to 700 watts) and low-wattage (400 to 500 watts) ovens. If the low-wattage cooking times differ from the high-wattage times, they appear in parentheses.

Prize Tested Recipes.

Chili Cornbread Pie

REFRIGERATED CORNBREAD TWISTS MAKE A QUICK CRUST FOR THIS TOP-NOTCH TEX-MEX PIE—

1 pound lean ground beef
½ cup chopped onion
½ cup coarsely chopped green
sweet pepper
1 15½-ounce can chili beans
1 8-ounce can tomato sauce
1 6-ounce can tomato paste
2 to 4 tablespoons chili powder
½ teaspoon ground cumin
½ teaspoon bottled hot pepper sauce
1 11½-ounce package (10) refrigerated
cornbread twists
1 8-ounce carton dairy sour cream
2 tablespoons all-purpose flour
1 cup shredded cheddar cheese
2 cups corn chips, coarsely crushed
(about 1 cup)
Chopped green pepper (optional)

◆ Chili Cornbread Pie

In a large skillet cook ground beef, onion, and the ½ cup green pepper till meat is no longer pink; drain off fat. Stir in *undrained* beans, tomato sauce, tomato paste, chili powder, cumin, and hot pepper sauce. Bring to boiling; reduce heat. Simmer, uncovered, for 5 minutes, stirring frequently.

Meanwhile, for crust, lightly grease a 9- or 10-inch pie plate. Unwrap and separate cornbread twists, but do not uncoil. Arrange biscuits in pie plate, pressing onto the bottom and up the sides of plate, extending biscuits about ½-inch above pie plate. Spoon ground beef mixture into crust. Combine sour cream and flour; spread atop beef mixture. Sprinkle with cheese and corn chips. Place on a baking sheet. Bake, uncovered, in a 375° oven for 30 minutes. Let stand 10 minutes before serving. Garnish with green pepper, if desired. Makes 8 main-dish servings.

Nutrition information per serving: 501 cal., 29 g total fat (11 g sat. fat) 63 mg chol., 739 mg sodium, 44 g carbo., 4 g fiber, 22 g pro. Daily Value: 30% vit. A, 34% Vit. C.

$200 WINNER
Mary Best Welter, St. Paul, Minn.

October
184

Peanut Butter 'N' Chocolate Soufflés

CHOCOLATE PUDDING GIVES A CREAMY
QUALITY (AND STABILITY) TO THESE
YUMMY SOUFFLÉS—

2 cups milk
½ cup peanut butter
*1 4-serving-size package regular chocolate
pudding mix*
3 slightly beaten egg yolks
1 teaspoon vanilla
3 egg whites
Whipped Cream

In a medium saucepan combine milk,
peanut butter, and pudding mix. Cook
and stir over medium heat till thickened
and bubbly. Remove from heat. Place
egg yolks in a large mixing bowl.
Gradually stir chocolate mixture into the
egg yolks. Stir in vanilla. Cover surface
of mixture with plastic wrap. Cool mixture about 15 minutes.

In a medium mixing bowl beat egg
whites till stiff peaks form. Fold into
partially cooled chocolate mixture.
Spoon into six *ungreased* 6-ounce custard
cups. Place cups in a 13x9x2-inch baking pan. Pour boiling water into baking
pan to a depth of one inch. Bake soufflés
in a 350° oven for 30 minutes or till centers shake slightly. Serve hot or chilled
with whipped cream and chopped
peanuts, if desired. Makes 6 servings.

Nutrition information per serving:
273 cal., 15 g total fat (4 g sat. fat), 113
mg chol., 451 mg sodium, 26 g carbo., 1
g fiber, 11 g pro. Daily Value: 21% vit.
A, 10% calcium, 5% iron.
$200 WINNER
Rai Arrant, San Francisco, Calif.

◆ Peanut Butter n' Chocolate Soufflés

Choco-Peanut Butter Pie

THIS PIE WILL REMIND YOU OF PECAN PIE
BUT WITH THE FLAVOR OF PEANUTS AND
CHOCOLATE—

3 eggs
1 cup light corn syrup
½ cup sugar
⅓ cup chunky-style peanut butter
½ teaspoon vanilla
½ cup semisweet chocolate pieces
Pastry for single-crust pie
Whipped dessert topping (optional)
Semisweet chocolate pieces (optional)
Chopped peanuts (optional)
continued on page 186

◆ Choco Peanut Butter Pie

continued from page 185

For filling, in a mixing bowl beat eggs lightly with a rotary beater or a fork till combined. Stir in corn syrup, sugar, peanut butter, and vanilla. Mix well. Sprinkle the ½ cup chocolate pieces over the bottom of an unbaked pastry-lined 9-inch pie plate. Pour filling into pie shell. Cover edge of pie with foil. Bake in a 375° oven for 20 minutes. Remove foil. Bake for 15 to 20 minutes more or till knife inserted near the center comes out clean. Cover and chill to store for up to 48 hours. Garnish with whipped topping, remaining chocolate pieces, and peanuts, if desired. Makes 10 servings.

Nutrition information per serving: 360 cal., 15 g total fat (3 g sat. fat), 64 mg chol., 143 mg sodium, 53 g carbo., 1 g fiber, 6 g pro. Daily Value: 3% vit. A, 0% vit. C, 3% calcium, and 17% iron.

$100 WINNER
Wanda Miller, Marion, Ind.

Creamy Turkey Pie

CREAM CHEESE AND COTTAGE CHEESE GIVE THIS TURKEY-MUSHROOM PIE A DELICIOUS, RICH FLAVOR—

1 pound ground raw turkey* or ground turkey sausage
½ cup chopped onion
1 3-ounce package cream cheese, cubed
1 4½-ounce jar sliced mushrooms drained
1 package (10) refrigerated biscuits
1 egg
1 cup cream-style cottage cheese
1 tablespoon all-purpose flour

In a large skillet cook turkey or turkey sausage and onion till meat is browned. Drain off fat. Stir in cream cheese till combined; add mushrooms. Set aside.

◆ Creamy Turkey Pie

For crust, lightly grease a 9-inch pie plate. Unwrap biscuits and separate. Arrange biscuits in pie plate, pressing onto the bottom and up sides of the plate, extending biscuits about ½-inch above pie plate. With kitchen scissors, cut edge of biscuits at half-inch intervals, if desired. Spoon turkey mixture into shell, spreading evenly.

In blender container or food processor bowl combine egg, cottage cheese, and flour. Cover and blend or process till smooth. Spoon over turkey mixture. Bake, uncovered, in 350° oven for 25 to 30 minutes or till edges are browned and filling is set. Let stand 5 to 10 minutes before cutting into wedges. Garnish with tomato and chives, if desired. Makes 6 main-dish servings.

*Note: If using ground turkey, add ¼ teaspoon *each* of *salt* and *pepper* to meat mixture.

Nutrition information per serving: 288 cal., 15 g total fat (6 g sat. fat), 85 mg chol., 716 mg sodium, 21 g carbo., 1 g fiber, 19 g pro. Daily Value: 10% vit. A, 5% vit. C, 4% calcium, and 13% iron.

$100 WINNER
David L. Huston, Waukegan, Ill.

November

Cookies

America's 15 Favorite
Appetizers and Snacks

American Heritage Desserts

Prize Tested Recipes

Cookies
Over 30 tempting holiday gems

By Lisa Holderness

Orange Spice Houses

Spumoni Slices and Brown Sugar Hazelnut Rounds

Snowball Christmas Trees

5-Way Fudge Brownies

Sour Cream Cutouts

189

Orange Spice Houses

USE COOKIE CUTTERS OR STENCILS TO CUT THIS BUTTERY DOUGH INTO QUAINT HOUSES AND BARNS.

3½ cups all-purpose flour
1 teaspoon finely shredded orange peel
1 teaspoon baking powder
1 teaspoon ground cinnamon
½ teaspoon salt
½ teaspoon ground ginger
¼ teaspoon ground cloves
1½ cups butter, softened
2 cups packed brown sugar
1 beaten egg
1 recipe Confectioners' Icing (optional)
(see recipe, page 193)
1 recipe Decorator Frosting (optional)
(see recipe, page 193)
Candies for decorating, such as colored hard candies; tiny mints; mini jelly beans, halved; gumdrops; and candy canes (optional)

In a mixing bowl stir together the flour, orange peel, baking powder, cinnamon, salt, ginger, and cloves; set aside. In a medium mixer bowl beat the butter with an electric mixer on medium to high speed for 30 seconds. Add the

brown sugar; beat till fluffy. Add the egg; beat well. Gradually beat or stir in flour mixture. Dough will be stiff.

To make your own house or barn stencil, use poster board or sturdy paper. The height from the roof top to floor should be about 3 inches and the width about 2½ inches. Or, use 3- to 4-inch house-shaped cookie cutters to cut the dough.

On a well-floured pastry cloth, roll one-third of the dough to ¼-inch thickness. Place your house or barn stencil on the dough and cut around the stencil using a small sharp knife. Or, cut dough using cookie cutters.

With a floured metal spatula, transfer cookies to ungreased cookie sheets, placing them about 2½ inches apart. Bake in a 375° oven about 8 minutes or till edges are light brown. Remove cookies and cool thoroughly on wire racks. Repeat with remaining dough.

Decorate house cookies with the Confectioners' Icing, Decorator Frosting, and assorted candies as desired. Makes about 60 cookies.

Nutrition facts per plain cookie:
93 cal., 5 g total fat (3 g sat. fat), 16 mg chol., 68 mg sodium, 12 g carbo., 0 g fiber, 1 g pro.

Spumoni Slices

PISTACHIO, PEPPERMINT, AND CHOCOLATE ALL ROLLED INTO ONE COOKIE!

2½ cups all-purpose flour
1½ teaspoons baking powder
½ teaspoon salt
1 cup margarine or butter
1½ cups sugar
1 egg
1 teaspoon vanilla
¼ teaspoon peppermint extract
5 drops red food coloring
¼ cup ground pistachio nuts or almonds
5 drops green food coloring
1 ounce unsweetened chocolate, melted and cooled
Sugar (optional)

In a medium mixing bowl stir together flour, baking powder, and salt; set the mixture aside.

In a large mixing bowl beat margarine or butter with an electric mixer on medium speed for 30 seconds. Add the 1½ cups sugar and beat till fluffy. Add egg and vanilla; beat just till combined. Slowly add the flour mixture, beating on medium speed till combined.

Divide dough into 3 equal portions. To one portion of the dough, stir in peppermint extract and red food coloring. To another third of the dough, stir in the pistachio nuts and green food coloring. To remaining dough, stir in melted chocolate.

Divide each portion of dough in *half* (you should have 6 portions total). On waxed paper shape each portion into a 10-inch roll. Lift and smooth the waxed paper to help shape the roll. Gently press 1 roll of pistachio dough and one roll of chocolate dough together, lengthwise, keeping the round shapes intact. Gently press 1 roll peppermint dough atop, lengthwise, making a shape similar to a triangle. Repeat with remaining 3 rolls.

Wrap each roll in waxed paper or plastic wrap. Chill for 2 to 48 hours or till firm enough to slice. (Or, wrap dough in foil; freeze for up to 3 months. Thaw in refrigerator before slicing.)

Using a thin-bladed knife, slice a tricolored roll of the dough into ¼-inch-thick slices. Rotate the roll as you slice to avoid flattening the roll. Place cutouts 1 inch apart onto ungreased cookie sheets. Sprinkle with sugar, if desired. Bake in a 350° oven for 10 to 12 minutes or till edges are firm and light brown. Cool on cookie sheets for 1 minute. Transfer cookies to a wire rack to cool completely. Repeat with remaining tricolored roll. Makes about 60 cookies.

Snowball Christmas Trees: Prepare plain dough for Spumoni Slices as directed. Tint ½ cup dough with *brown food coloring* to use as tree trunks. Tint remaining dough with *green food coloring.*

Roll green dough into small balls (about ½ inch each). Assemble trees on ungreased baking sheets. For each tree, start with 1 ball for the top of the tree. Attach 2 balls in a row below it. Continue attaching balls in rows, adding one more each time so the tree resembles a triangle, stopping after you get a row of five balls. Roll brown dough into small balls. Attach a brown ball to the middle of the last row for the tree trunk.

Bake in a 325° oven for 12 to 15 minutes. Carefully remove from baking sheets and cool on wire racks. To decorate, pipe tinted or white Confectioners' Icing (see page, 193) on trees to resemble garland and sprinkle with decorative candies. Or, sprinkle with edible glitter, if desired. Makes about 30 trees.

Nutrition facts per Spumoni Slice: 70 cal., 4 g total fat (1 g sat. fat), 4 mg chol., 55 mg sodium, 9 g carbo., 0 g fiber, 1 g pro.

Brown-Sugar Hazelnut Rounds

½ cup shortening
½ cup margarine or butter
2½ cups all-purpose flour
1¼ cups packed brown sugar
1 egg
1 teaspoon vanilla
½ teaspoon baking soda
¼ teaspoon salt
¾ cup toasted ground hazelnuts or pecans
⅓ cup toasted finely chopped hazelnuts or pecans (optional)
Milk chocolate, melted (optional)
⅓ recipe Confectioners' Icing made with maple flavoring, orange juice, or vanilla (optional) (see recipe, page 193)
Toasted, finely chopped hazelnuts or almonds (optional)

In a large mixing bowl beat shortening and margarine or butter with an electric mixer on medium to high speed about 30 seconds or till softened. Add about *1 cup* of the flour to the shortening mixture. Add brown sugar, egg, vanilla, baking soda, and salt. Beat till thoroughly combined, scraping sides of bowl occasionally. Beat or stir in the remaining flour and the ¾ cup ground nuts.

On waxed paper, shape dough into two 10-inch rolls. Lift and smooth the waxed paper to help shape the roll. If desired, roll one of the logs in the ⅓ cup chopped nuts. Wrap each in waxed paper or plastic wrap. Chill for 4 to 48 hours or till firm enough to slice. (Or, wrap dough in foil and freeze for up to 3 months; thaw in the refrigerator before slicing and baking.)

Using a thin-bladed knife, cut dough into ¼-inch-thick slices. Place slices 1 inch apart on ungreased cookie sheets. Bake in a 375° oven 10 minutes or till edges are firm. Remove cookies; cool.

To decorate with melted chocolate, dip cookies without nuts on the edges in melted chocolate, dipping about half of the cookie. Or, drizzle melted chocolate over cookies (with or without nuts on edges) rather than dipping them. Sprinkle with some of the finely chopped nuts or pipe Confectioners' Icing in a design over the chocolate. To decorate cookies with Confectioners' Icing, with a spoon drizzle the icing atop some of the cookies. Sprinkle with chopped nuts, if desired. Makes about 60 cookies.

Nutrition facts per plain cookie: 74 cal., 4 g fat (1 g sat. fat), 4 mg chol., 40 mg sodium, 8 g carbo., 0 g fiber, 1 g pro.

Sour Cream Cutouts

STARS, BELLS, TREES, ORNAMENTS, AND MORE—YOUR COLLECTION OF CUTOUTS IS LIMITED ONLY BY YOUR ASSORTMENT OF COOKIE CUTTERS AND YOUR IMAGINATION.

½ cup margarine or butter
⅓ cup shortening
2½ cups all-purpose flour
1 cup sugar
⅓ cup dairy sour cream
1 egg
1 teaspoon vanilla
1 teaspoon finely shredded lemon peel
(optional)
¾ teaspoon baking powder
½ teaspoon ground mace
¼ teaspoon baking soda
Dash salt
1 recipe Confectioners' Icing (optional)
(see recipe, page 193)
1 recipe Decorator Frosting (optional)
(see recipe, page 193)
Decorative candies (optional)

In a large mixing bowl beat the margarine or butter and shortening with an electric mixer on medium to high speed about 30 seconds or till softened. Add about *half* of the flour to the margarine and shortening. Then add the sugar, sour cream, egg, vanilla, lemon peel, baking powder, mace, baking soda, and salt. Beat till thoroughly combined, scraping sides of bowl occasionally. Beat or stir in the remaining flour.

Divide dough in *half*. Cover; chill 1 to 2 hours or till easy to handle. (Or, wrap in foil and freeze for up to 3 months. Thaw in refrigerator.)

On a well-floured pastry cloth, roll each half of dough (keep remaining portion chilled) to ⅛- to ¼-inch thickness. Using cookie cutters dipped in flour, cut dough into desired shapes. With a wide spatula, transfer cookies to ungreased cookie sheets, placing them ½ inch apart.

Bake in a 375° oven for 7 to 8 minutes or till edges are firm and bottoms are very light brown. Remove cookies and cool on wire racks. If desired, decorate with Confectioners' Icing, Decorator Frosting, and assorted decorative candies. Makes about 4 dozen, 2½-inch cookies.

Anise Cutouts: Prepare Sour Cream Cutouts as directed, *except* substitute ½ teaspoon *anise extract* for the ground mace and omit the lemon peel. Decorate as directed.

Nutrition facts per plain cookie: 72 cal., 4 g total fat (1 g sat. fat), 5 mg chol., 34 mg sodium., 9 g carbo., 0 g fiber, 1 g pro.

Five-Way Fudge Brownies

CHOOSE FROM FIVE FABULOUS VERSIONS OF THESE DENSE, CHOCOLATE BROWNIES.

½ cup margarine or butter
2 ounces unsweetened chocolate
1 cup sugar
2 eggs
1 teaspoon vanilla
⅔ cup all-purpose flour
1 recipe Chocolate Glaze (optional)
(see recipe, page 193)
Pecan halves (optional)

In a medium saucepan melt margarine or butter and chocolate over low heat. Stir in sugar, eggs, and vanilla. Beat lightly by hand just till combined. Stir in flour. Spread batter in a greased 9x9x2-inch baking pan. Bake in a 350° oven for 20 minutes. Cool on a wire rack. Spread Chocolate Glaze over the cooled brownies, if desired. Cut into bars. Makes 16.

Caramel Nut Goodies: Prepare Fudge Brownies as directed, *except* stir ½ cup chopped *pecans* into the batter before spreading in the greased pan. Sprinkle batter with ½ cup *miniature semisweet chocolate pieces*. Bake as directed. In a small saucepan combine one 6¼-ounce package *vanilla caramels* and 2 tablespoons *milk*. Cook and stir over medium-low heat till smooth. Drizzle caramel atop brownies. Cool completely.

Peanut Butter Brownies: Prepare Fudge Brownies as directed. For frosting, in a medium mixing bowl beat ¼ cup *peanut butter* till fluffy. Gradually add 1 cup sifted *powdered sugar*, beating well. Beat in ¼ cup *milk* and 1 teaspoon *vanilla*. Gradually beat in about ½ cup additional sifted powdered sugar to make of spreading consistency. Spread frosting atop brownies and sprinkle with ¼ cup finely chopped *dry roasted peanuts*. Cut into bars.

Chocolate Chunk Brownies: Prepare Fudge Brownies as directed, *except* stir one 2.2-ounce *bar milk chocolate*, coarsely chopped, and one 2.2-ounce *vanilla-flavored bar with almonds* (Alpine bar), coarsely chopped, into the batter.

Crème de Menthe Brownies: Prepare Fudge Brownies as directed, *except* omit vanilla. Stir ¼ teaspoon *mint extract* into batter. Bake as directed. For frosting, in a medium mixing bowl beat ¼ cup *margarine or butter* till fluffy. Gradually add 1 cup sifted *powdered sugar*. Beat in 2 tablespoons green *crème de menthe*. Gradually beat in about ½ cup sifted *powdered sugar* to make of spreading consistency. Spread atop brownies. In a small heavy saucepan melt 1 ounce *semisweet chocolate* over low heat. Drizzle over brownies. Let chocolate set, then cut into bars.

Nutrition facts per Fudge Brownie: 143 cal., 8 g total fat (2 g sat. fat), 27 mg chol., 75 mg sodium, 17 g carbo., 0 g fiber, 2 g pro.

Decorator Frosting

THIS FROSTING HAS A FLUFFY, THICK TEXTURE.

In a large mixer bowl beat ⅔ cup *margarine or butter* with an electric mixer on medium speed 30 seconds to soften. Gradually add 4 cups sifted *powdered sugar*, beating well. Beat in 2 tablespoons *milk, lemon juice, or orange juice*, and 1 teaspoon *vanilla*. Frosting will be thick but easy to pipe.

To tint frosting, stir in *food coloring* for desired color. To use more than one color, divide frosting into small bowls; stir a different color into each bowl. Makes 2 cups.

Nutrition facts per teaspoon: 28 cal., 1 g total fat (0 g sat. fat), 0 mg chol., 15 mg sodium, 4 g carbo., 0 g fiber, 0 g protein.

Chocolate Glaze

In a medium saucepan cook and stir 3 tablespoons *margarine or butter*, 2 tablespoons *unsweetened cocoa powder*, and 2 tablespoons *milk* till mixture comes to a boil. Remove from heat. Stir in 1½ cups sifted *powdered sugar* and ½ teaspoon *vanilla* till smooth. Makes about ⅔ cup.

Nutrition facts per teaspoon: 31 cal., 1 g total fat (0 g sat. fat), 0 mg chol., 13 mg sodium, 5 g carbo., 0 g fiber, 0 g protein.

Confectioners' Icing

USE THIS ICING TO SPREAD, DRIZZLE, OR PIPE ATOP COOKIES. IT WILL BE THINNER IN CONSISTENCY THAN THE DECORATOR FROSTING.

In a medium mixing bowl stir together 3 cups sifted *powdered sugar* and 1 tablespoon *lemon juice* or *orange juice* or other flavorings such as 1½ teaspoons *vanilla*, 1 teaspoon *maple flavoring*, or ½ teaspoon *peppermint extract*. Add enough milk to make of spreading or drizzling consistency.

To tint icing, stir in *food coloring* for desired color. To use more than one color, divide icing into small bowls and stir a different color into each bowl. Makes about 1 cup.

Nutrition facts per teaspoon: 26 cal., 0 g total fat (0 g sat. fat), 0 mg chol., 1 mg sodium, 7 g carbo., 0 g fiber, 0 g protein.

After the cookies have completely
cooled, they are ready to be decorated.
(See pages 188 and 189 for decorating
ideas.) Prepare Decorator Frosting and
Confectioners' Icing (see recipes, page
193); divide each into bowls and tint as
desired. (Paste food coloring gives more
intense color and does not thin the icing
or frosting as compared to liquid food
coloring.) Also, gather the candies you
plan to use for decorating. Organize the
candies into little dishes according to
kinds.

With a small clean paint brush (used
for food only) or a thin flexible metal
spatula, paint or spread Confectioners'
Icing on cookies, if desired. Allow this
base icing to slightly dry. Continue decorating by piping additional icing or
frosting. Position the decorative candies
or the sprinkles before the icing or frosting sets.

To pipe icing or frosting, use several
pastry bags (try the disposable type). Fill
each bag with a different color and fit
with a small round tip or star tip. Or,
spoon icing or frosting into a clean, sturdy plastic bag and snip a small hole in
the corner of the bag to pipe.

America's 15 Favorite
Appetizers & Snacks

By Lisa Holderness

Choose from this scrumptious
collection of party stars to
make your holiday gatherings
shine above the rest. You'll
find the flavors you love, plus
plenty of make-ahead tips,
timesaving ingredients, and
garnishing ideas.

Golden Phyllo Triangles

IF YOU WOULD LIKE TO USE ONLY ONE
OF THE FILLINGS, DOUBLE THE FILLING
RECIPE.

12 sheets frozen phyllo dough, thawed
(18x14-inch sheets)
½ cup margarine or butter, melted
1 recipe Cajun Pork Filling
1 recipe Five-Spice Beef Filling
Additional melted margarine or butter
1 recipe Apricot Dipping Sauce (optional)

Lightly brush *1 sheet* of phyllo dough
with some of the melted margarine or
butter. Place another sheet of phyllo
dough on top of the first sheet, then
brush with margarine or butter. Cover
remaining phyllo with a damp towel to
keep moist; set aside.

Cut the 2 layered sheets crosswise into
6 equal strips. For each triangle, spoon
1 rounded teaspoon of the Cajun Pork
Filling or Five-Spice Beef Filling about
1 inch from one end of one of the strips.
Starting at the same end of the phyllo

strip, fold one of the points over the filling so it lines up with the other side of the strip, forming a triangle. Continue folding like a flag in a triangular shape, using the entire strip of phyllo dough. Repeat 5 more times with the remaining sheets of phyllo dough, margarine or butter, and fillings.

At this point, you can place the unbaked triangles in a covered freezer container and freeze for up to 2 months. Place triangles (if frozen, do not thaw) on a baking sheet, then brush with the additional melted margarine or butter. Bake in a 375° oven for 15 minutes or till golden. Serve warm with Apricot Dipping Sauce, if desired. Makes 36 appetizers.

Cajun Pork Filling: In a medium skillet cook 8 ounces *ground pork* till no longer pink; drain. Add 1 teaspoon *Cajun seasoning*; cook 1 minute more. Stir in ½ cup *soft-style cream cheese*, ⅓ cup shredded *carrot*, and a few dashes bottled *hot pepper sauce*. Mix well. Makes about 1 cup filling.

Five-Spice Beef Filling: In a medium skillet cook 8 ounces *ground beef* and ¼ cup finely chopped *onion* till beef is no longer pink and onion is tender; drain. Add 1 teaspoon *five-spice powder* and cook mixture for 1 minute more.

Stir in 3 tablespoons *apricot preserves*, 1 *egg yolk*, and 1 tablespoon *vinegar*. Makes about 1 cup filling.

Apricot Dipping Sauce: In a 1-cup glass measure combine ½ cup *apricot preserves* and 1 tablespoon *hoisin sauce*. Stir in 1 tablespoon thinly sliced *green onion* and 2 to 3 fresh or bottled *kumquats*, thinly sliced and seeded, or

½ teaspoon finely shredded *orange peel*. Micro-cook on 100% power (high) for 45 to 60 seconds or till bubbly. Stir before serving. Serve warm with Golden Phyllo Triangles. Makes ⅔ cup.

Nutrition facts per triangle with Cajun Pork Filling: 81 cal., 6 g total fat (2 g sat. fat), 13 mg chol., 83 mg sodium, 5 g carbo., 0 g fiber, 3 g pro.

Golden Phyllo Triangles

Stuff these familiar bundles of flaky pastry with a fiery Cajun filling or go Oriental with a five-spice filling.

Polynesian Meatballs

1 beaten egg
¼ cup fine dry bread crumbs
2 tablespoons snipped fresh cilantro or parsley
2 cloves garlic, minced
¼ teaspoon salt
⅛ teaspoon ground red pepper
1 pound lean ground beef
¼ cup finely chopped peanuts
1 fresh pineapple or 2 papayas, peeled and cut into bite-size chunks, or one 20-ounce can pineapple chunks (juice pack), drained
1 recipe Sweet-and-Sour Sauce or 1¼ cups bottled sweet-and-sour sauce

In a medium mixing bowl combine egg, bread crumbs, cilantro or parsley, garlic, salt, and red pepper. Add the beef and peanuts. Mix well. Shape into 1-inch meatballs. Place in a 15x10x1-inch shallow baking pan. Bake in a 350° oven for 20 minutes or till no longer pink. Drain. Remove from oven. (To make ahead, cool meatballs, then cover and chill for up to 48 hours.)

Thread a pineapple or papaya chunk and a meatball on a wooden toothpick. Return to the shallow baking pan. Repeat with remaining fruit and meatballs. Brush with some of the Sweet-and-Sour Sauce. Bake 5 to 8 minutes more or till heated through. (For chilled meatballs, bake 10 minutes.) In a small saucepan heat remaining sauce till bubbly. Brush meatballs and fruit with additional sauce before serving. Serve any remaining sauce in a bowl alongside meatballs. Makes 36 appetizer skewers.

Sweet-and-Sour Sauce: In a small saucepan stir together ½ cup packed *brown sugar* and 4 teaspoons *cornstarch*. Stir in ½ cup *chicken broth*; ⅓ cup *red wine vinegar*; 2 tablespoons *corn syrup*; 2 tablespoons *soy sauce*; 1 clove *garlic*, minced; and 2 teaspoons grated *gingerroot*. Cook and stir till thickened and bubbly. Cook 2 minutes more. Use immediately or cover and chill for up to 1 week. If chilled, heat through before using. Makes about 1¼ cups.

Nutrition facts per appetizer skewer: 59 cal., 2 g total fat (1 g sat. fat), 14 mg chol., 102 mg sodium, 7 g carbo., 0 g fiber, 3 g pro. Daily Value: 0% vit. A, 3% vit. C, 0% calcium, 3% iron.

Smoked Salmon Quiches

⅓ cup chopped fresh mushrooms
1 tablespoon finely chopped green onion
1 teaspoon lemon juice
1 teaspoon margarine or butter
3 egg yolks
½ cup milk
1 3-ounce package thinly sliced smoked salmon (lox-style), cut up
1 recipe Swiss Cheese Pastry (see recipe, right)
Fresh dill sprigs (optional)

In a skillet cook mushrooms, onion, and lemon juice in hot margarine or butter 2 to 3 minutes or till vegetables are tender. Remove from heat; drain any excess liquid.

In a small mixing bowl beat egg yolks slightly. Stir in milk. Stir in mushroom mixture and salmon. Cover and chill for 30 minutes.

On a lightly floured surface roll Swiss Cheese Pastry into a 16-inch circle. Using a 3-inch biscuit cutter, cut pastry into 18 rounds. Fit rounds into generously greased 1¾-inch muffin cups, pleating dough, as necessary, to fit. Fill each pastry cup with a scant tablespoon of filling.

Bake in a 375° oven 35 minutes. Cool in pan for 5 minutes. Remove from pans. Top with dill sprigs. Serve warm. Makes 18 quiches.

Nutrition facts per quiche: 85 cal., 6 g total fat (2 g sat. fat), 38 mg chol., 80 mg sodium, 6 g carbo., 0 g fiber, 3 g pro. Daily Value: 6% vit. A.

Swiss Cheese Pastry

1 cup all-purpose flour
1 tablespoon snipped fresh dill or ½ teaspoon dried dillweed
⅓ cup shortening
¼ cup shredded Swiss cheese
2 to 3 tablespoons cold water

In a mixing bowl combine flour, dill, and ¼ teaspoon *salt*. With a pastry blender or 2 forks, cut in shortening till the pieces are the size of small peas. Stir in cheese. Sprinkle *1 tablespoon* of the water over part of the mixture and gently toss with a fork. Push dough to the side of the bowl. Repeat, adding enough of the remaining water till all is moistened. Form dough into a ball. Use for the Smoked Salmon Quiches.

◆ Polynesian Meatballs   ◆ Smoked Salmon Quiches   ◆ Mini Pepperoni Calzones

Mini Pepperoni Calzones

*1 10-ounce package refrigerated pizza
dough
1 recipe Pepperoni Pizza Filling
1 beaten egg
2 teaspoons water
2 to 3 tablespoons shredded Parmesan
cheese (optional)*

Unroll pizza dough. On a lightly
floured surface roll dough into a
15-inch square. Cut into twenty-five
3-inch squares. Spoon a slightly rounded
teaspoon of Pepperoni Pizza Filling atop
each dough square. Brush edges of each
dough square with water. Lift one corner
of each square and stretch dough over
the filling to the opposite corner, making
a triangle. Press edges together and seal
well with fingers or a fork.

Arrange calzones on a greased baking
sheet. Prick tops with a fork. Mix egg
and water, brush over calzones.

Bake in a 425° oven 10 to 12 minutes
or till golden. During the last 3 minutes
of baking time, sprinkle with Parmesan
cheese, if desired. Let stand for 5 minutes before serving. Makes 25 calzones.

Pepperoni Pizza Filling: In a small
bowl stir together ⅓ cup finely chopped
pepperoni, ¼ cup finely chopped *green
pepper*, ¼ cup *pizza sauce*, 2 tablespoons
finely chopped *onion*, and ½ teaspoon
dried *Italian seasoning*, crushed. Use
immediately or cover and chill for up to
24 hours. Makes ¾ cup filling.

***Nutrition facts per Mini Pepperoni
Calzone:*** 43 cal., 2 g total fat (1 g sat.
fat), 10 mg chol., 99 mg sodium, 5 g
carbo., 0 g fiber, 2 g pro. Daily Value:
1% vit. A, 3% vit. C, 1% calcium, 6%
iron.

Mini Broccoli Calzones: Prepare
Mini Pepperoni Calzones as directed
except use the following broccoli filling.
In a small bowl stir together ½ cup finely
chopped *broccoli*, ⅓ cup *soft-style cream
cheese with chives and onion*, 2 tablespoons diced *pimiento*, 1 tablespoon
grated *Parmesan cheese*, ½ teaspoon finely
shredded *lemon peel*, and dash *pepper*.
Use immediately or cover and chill for
up to 24 hours. Makes ⅔ cup filling.

***Nutrition facts per Mini Broccoli
Calzone:*** 39 cal., 2 g total fat (1 g sat.
fat), 12 mg chol., 55 mg sodium, 5 g
carbo., 0 g fiber, 1 g pro. Daily Value:
1% vit. A, 3% vit. C, 0% calcium, 2%
iron.

Gorgonzola-Onion Tarts

A unique combination that's hard to beat—gutsy Gorgonzola cheese and caramelized onions in a quick-fix herb crust.

Gorgonzola-Onion Tarts

1 11-ounce package piecrust mix
1 teaspoon dried chervil or marjoram leaves, crushed
¼ cup margarine or butter
1 tablespoon brown sugar
1 teaspoon vinegar
2 medium onions, quartered lengthwise and thinly sliced (about 1⅓ cups)
4 ounces Gorgonzola or blue cheese, crumbled (1 cup)
2 eggs
¼ teaspoon white or black pepper
⅓ cup half-and-half or light cream
3 tablespoons dry white wine or chicken broth
2 tablespoons snipped fresh parsley

Prepare piecrust mix according to package directions except stir chervil or marjoram into dry ingredients. Roll dough into a ball. Divide dough into 8 pieces. Place each piece of dough into a greased 4-inch tart pan with a removable bottom.* Using your fingers, press dough in the bottom and up the sides of each tart pan. Line pastry in each tart pan with heavy foil or a double thickness of regular foil. Place on a baking sheet. Bake in a 425° oven for 5 minutes. Remove foil. Continue baking for 5 to 7 minutes or till pastry is nearly done. Transfer baking sheet to a wire cooling rack. Decrease oven temperature to 375°.

Meanwhile, for filling, in a large skillet combine margarine or butter, brown sugar, and vinegar. Cook and stir over medium heat about 1 minute or just till blended. Add onions. Cook, uncovered, over low heat for 10 to 12 minutes or till onions are tender and light brown, stirring occasionally.

In a mixing bowl beat cheese, eggs, and pepper with an electric mixer on low speed till combined (cheese will still be lumpy). Stir in onion mixture, half-and-half or cream, and wine, mixing well with a spoon.

Ladle filling equally into the 8 pre-baked crusts on baking sheet. Sprinkle with parsley. Carefully return filled pans on the baking sheet to a 375° oven. Bake for 20 to 25 minutes or till tarts are slightly puffed and a knife inserted near centers comes out clean. Let cool for 15 minutes on a wire rack. Carefully remove sides. Serve warm. Makes 8 tarts (16 appetizer servings).

*Note: For one large tart, prepare piecrust mix according to package directions *except* use ½ *package* (1⅓ cups) piecrust mix and stir ½ *teaspoon* dried chervil or marjoram, crushed, into dry ingredients. Roll crust on a lightly floured surface to an 11-inch circle. Fit into a 9-inch tart pan and trim edges. Prebake crust as above; bake tart in a 375° oven about 20 minutes or till a knife inserted near center comes out clean.

Nutrition facts per appetizer serving: 198 cal., 14 g total fat (4 g sat. fat), 33 mg chol., 283 mg sodium, 13 g carbo., 0 g fiber, 4 g pro. Daily Value: 6% vit. A.

Swiss Fondue

Fondue is back. Swirl chunks of toasted bread or assorted vegetables in an irresistible blend of Swiss cheese and white wine.

Swiss Fondue

NUTTY-SWEET EMMENTALER AND SMOOTH-MELTING GRUYÈRE, BOTH SWISS-TYPE CHEESES, COMBINE WITH CHERRY-FLAVORED KIRSCH IN THIS FAVORITE HOT CHEESE DIP.

3 cups shredded Gruyère or Swiss cheese
2 cups shredded Emmentaler, Gruyère, or Swiss cheese
3 tablespoons all-purpose flour
Herb bread or French bread, cut into 1-inch cubes; pre-cooked broccoli or cauliflower flowerets*; and/or bias-sliced carrots

1½ cups dry white wine
¼ cup milk
2 tablespoons kirsch or dry sherry
⅛ teaspoon ground nutmeg
⅛ teaspoon white pepper
Paprika (optional)

Bring shredded cheeses to room temperature; toss with flour and set aside. If using bread cubes, place on a baking sheet; toast in a 350° oven for 5 to 7 minutes or till crisp and toasted; set aside.

In a large saucepan heat wine over medium heat till small bubbles rise to the surface. Just before wine boils, reduce the heat to low and stir in the cheese mixture, a little at a time, stirring constantly and making sure the cheese is melted before adding more. Stir till the mixture bubbles gently.

Stir in milk, kirsch or sherry, nutmeg, and white pepper. Transfer cheese mixture to a fondue pot. Keep mixture bubbling gently over a fondue burner.** Sprinkle with paprika, if desired. Serve with toasted bread cubes, broccoli or cauliflower flowerets, and/or carrots for dippers. Makes 3 cups fondue (12 appetizer servings).

*Note: To precook the broccoli or cauliflower flowerets, in a saucepan bring a small amount of water to boiling. Add broccoli or cauliflower and simmer, covered, for 3 minutes or till crisp-tender. Drain and rinse with cold water.

**Note: If mixture becomes too thick, stir in a little more milk.

Nutrition facts per serving with toasted bread cubes: 322 cal., 16 g total fat (9 g sat. fat), 49 mg chol., 341 mg sodium, 21 g carbo., 1 g fiber, 18 g pro. Daily Value: 15% vit. A, 0% vit. C, 42% calcium, 8% iron.

Bacon and Tomato Potato Skins

6 large baking potatoes
2 teaspoons cooking oil
1 teaspoon chili powder
Several dashes bottled hot pepper sauce
⅔ cup chopped Canadian-style bacon or
chopped, cooked turkey bacon
1 medium tomato, finely chopped
2 tablespoons finely chopped green onion
4 ounces cheddar cheese or lower-fat
cheddar cheese, shredded (1 cup)
½ cup dairy sour cream (optional)

Scrub potatoes thoroughly and prick with a fork. Arrange on a microwave-safe plate. Micro-cook, uncovered, on 100% power (high) for 17 to 22 minutes or till almost tender, rearranging once. (Or, bake potatoes in a 425° oven for 40 to 45 minutes or till tender.) Cool.

Halve each potato lengthwise. Scoop out the inside of each potato half, leaving about a ¼-inch-thick shell. Cover and chill the leftover fluffy white part of potatoes for another use. Combine the cooking oil, chili powder, and hot pepper sauce. With a pastry brush, brush the insides of the potato halves with the oil mixture. Cut the potato halves in half lengthwise. Return to the baking sheet. Sprinkle potato quarters with bacon, tomato, and green onion. Top with cheese. To make ahead, cover and chill for up to 24 hours.

Bake in a 450° oven for 10 to 12 minutes or till cheese is melted and potato quarters are heated through. Serve with sour cream, if desired. Makes 24 wedges.

Nutrition facts per potato wedge: 70 cal., 2 g total fat (1 g sat. fat), 8 mg chol., 107 mg sodium, 9 g carbo., 0 g fiber, and 3 g pro. Daily Value: 2% vit. A, 13% vit. C, 3% calcium, and 1% iron.

Seven-Layer Southwestern Dip

3 cups shredded lettuce
1 15-ounce can black beans, rinsed
and drained
½ cup chopped red and/or yellow
sweet pepper
¼ cup sliced green onions
1 8-ounce carton dairy sour cream or
lower-fat dairy sour cream
2 finely chopped jalapeño peppers
1 teaspoon shredded lime peel
1 8-ounce jar (1 cup) chunky salsa
½ of a medium avocado, halved, seeded,
peeled, and coarsely chopped
⅔ cup shredded cheddar cheese, Monterey
Jack cheese, or lower-fat cheddar cheese
⅓ cup chopped pitted ripe olives
1 tablespoon snipped fresh cilantro or
parsley (optional)
1 recipe Homemade Tortilla Chips or one
16-ounce package tortilla chips

Line a 12-inch platter with the shredded lettuce. Stir together black beans, sweet pepper, and green onion. Spoon atop lettuce, leaving a lettuce border. Dollop sour cream atop bean mixture; gently spread in a smooth layer atop beans, leaving a border. Sprinkle with jalapeño pepper and lime peel.

Drain excess liquid from salsa. Stir in avocado; spoon atop sour cream layer, leaving a border. Sprinkle cheese atop. Top with a layer of chopped ripe olives and sprinkle with cilantro or parsley, if desired. Serve immediately or cover; chill up to 6 hours. Serve with Homemade Tortilla Chips or purchased chips. Makes about 32 appetizer servings.

Homemade Tortilla Chips: Cut ten *6-inch flour tortillas* into wedges. Place in single layers on ungreased baking sheets. Bake in a 350° oven about 10 to 15 minutes or till dry and crisp.

Nutrition facts per appetizer serving: 66 cal., 4 g total fat (2 g sat. fat), 6 mg chol., 87 mg sodium, 7 g carbo., 1 g fiber, 3 g pro. Daily Value: 7% vit. A, 15% vit. C, 4% calcium.

◆ Bacon and Tomato Potato Skins

◆ Seven-Layer Southwestern Dip

◆ White Bean Dip with Toasted Pita Chips

In a food processor bowl or blender container combine beans, almonds, garlic, lemon juice, olive oil, salt, and ground red pepper. Cover and process or blend till almost smooth. Add bread crumb mixture. Blend till smooth. Stir in the 2 teaspoons oregano or basil. Cover and chill for several hours or overnight to blend flavors.

To serve, place in a bowl lined with kale leaves; sprinkle with fresh basil or oregano leaves, if desired. Serve with sweet pepper shapes and Toasted Pita Chips. Makes 2 cups dip (32 servings).

Nutrition facts per serving of dip: 22 cal., 1 g total fat (0 g sat. fat), 0 mg chol., 23 mg sodium, 2 g carbo., 1 g fiber, 1 g pro. Daily Value: 0% vit. A, 1% vit. C, 0% calcium, 1% iron.

Toasted Pita Chips

5 large pita bread rounds, split in half horizontally
2 tablespoons cooking oil or melted margarine
Paprika (optional)

Using small star and circle cookie cutters cut pita round halves into stars and circles. (Or, with a knife, cut each pita round half into 6 wedges.) Arrange in a single layer on baking sheets. Brush pita shapes lightly with oil or margarine and sprinkle with paprika, if desired.

Bake in a 350° oven for 12 to 15 minutes or till crisp and golden brown. Makes about 60 pita chips.

Nutrition facts per pita chip: 13 cal., 1 g total fat (0 g sat. fat), 0 mg chol., 18 mg sodium, 2 g carbo., 0 g fiber, 0 g pro. Daily Value: 0% vit. A, 0% vit. C, 0% calcium, 0% iron.

White Bean Dip with Toasted Pita Chips

¼ cup soft bread crumbs
2 tablespoons dry white wine or water
1 red and/or yellow sweet pepper (optional)
1 15- to 19-ounce can cannellini beans or great northern beans, drained and rinsed
¼ cup toasted slivered almonds
3 cloves garlic, minced
2 tablespoons lemon juice
2 tablespoons olive oil (preferably extra-virgin)
¼ teaspoon salt

⅛ teaspoon ground red pepper
2 teaspoons snipped fresh oregano or basil or ½ teaspoon dried oregano or basil, crushed
Purple kale leaves (optional)
Fresh basil or oregano leaves (optional)
1 recipe Toasted Pita Chips (see recipe, right)

Combine bread crumbs and wine or water; set aside to soak. Cut sweet pepper into triangles or 1-inch-wide strips, if desired; set aside.

November
201

Appetizer Cheesecake

¼ cup margarine or butter, melted
6 sheets frozen phyllo dough
(18x14-inch sheets), thawed
½ of a 6-ounce jar marinated artichoke
hearts
3 8-ounce packages cream cheese, softened
1¼ cups crumbled feta cheese (5 ounces)
½ teaspoon dried oregano, crushed
¼ teaspoon garlic powder
3 eggs
¼ cup sliced green onions
Plum tomato slices (optional)
Whole Greek or ripe olives (optional)
Fresh basil leaves (optional)

Brush bottom and sides of a 9-inch springform pan with some of the margarine or butter. Cut sheets of phyllo into 13-inch rounds. Ease one sheet in pan off-center so that phyllo extends 3 inches up sides of pan. Brush with margarine or butter. Repeat with remaining phyllo and margarine or butter, placing sheets off-center to cover bottom and sides of pan. Make 2 slits in the center of phyllo for steam to escape.

Bake in a 400° oven 9 to 10 minutes or till lightly golden. Cool on a wire rack. Decrease oven to 325°.

Drain and chop artichokes, reserving 2 tablespoons of the marinade. Set aside.

In a large mixer bowl beat cream cheese till smooth. Add feta, oregano, and garlic powder. Beat well. Add eggs; beat just till blended. *Do not overbeat.* Stir in artichoke hearts, reserved marinade, and onion. Pour into crust. Bake in a 325° oven 35 to 40 minutes or till center is soft set and sides stay firm when gently shaken. Cool.

Cover; chill for 2 hours or for up to 24 hours. Serve slightly chilled or at room temperature. To serve, remove from pan; top with plum tomato slices, whole olives, and basil leaves, if desired. Cut into wedges. Makes 14 appetizer servings.

Nutrition facts per appetizer serving: 307 cal., 27 g total fat (15 g sat. fat), 120 mg chol., 501 mg sodium, 9 g carbo., 0 g fiber, 9 g pro. Daily Value: 31% vit. A, 2% vit. C, 13% calcium, 8% iron.

Pastry-Wrapped Brie with Wild Mushrooms

1½ cups sliced mixed fresh mushrooms
(such as shiitake, oyster, button, and
brown mushrooms)
2 teaspoons margarine or butter
1 tablespoon dry sherry, dry red wine, or
beef broth
1 teaspoon Worcestershire sauce
¾ teaspoon snipped fresh tarragon or
chervil or ⅛ teaspoon dried tarragon or
chervil leaves, crushed
Dash pepper
2 tablespoons fine dry bread crumbs
1 17¼-ounce package frozen puff pastry
(2 sheets), thawed
2 3¼- or 4¼-inch rounds Brie
(8 ounces each)
1 beaten egg
1 tablespoon water
Apple and pear wedges (optional)

For mushroom filling, in a medium skillet cook mushrooms in hot margarine or butter till tender. Stir in the sherry, red wine, or broth; Worcestershire sauce; herb; and pepper. Cook, uncovered, 1 minute more or till liquid is evaporated, stirring occasionally. Remove from heat. Stir in bread crumbs. Cool.

On a lightly floured surface, unfold one sheet of puff pastry. Cut out a 9- to 9½-inch circle, saving trimmings. Spread half of the mushroom filling in the middle of the pastry to a circle the size of the Brie. Place one Brie round atop mushroom filling.

Combine beaten egg and water; brush some of the mixture atop pastry circle, around Brie. Wrap the pastry up and over the Brie, folding and pleating to cover the top of the Brie. Trim off excess pastry so that pleats are not too thick; press dough to seal. Carefully invert the Brie onto a greased shallow baking pan.

♦ Appetizer Cheesecake

♦ Jamaican Shrimp

♦ Pastry-Wrapped Brie
with Wild Mushrooms

Brush pastry with more of the egg mixture. If desired, cut reserved dough trimmings into shapes and use to decorate top pastry. Brush cutouts with egg mixture. Cut slits for escape of steam. Repeat with remaining sheet of pastry, mushroom filling, and Brie round. Chill both Brie rounds, covered, 2 to 4 hours.

Bake in a 400° oven for 20 to 25 minutes or till pastry is a deep golden brown. Let stand for 20 to 30 minutes before serving. Serve warm with apples and pears. Makes 8 servings per Brie.

Nutrition facts per serving: 244 cal., 18 g total fat (5 g sat. fat), 41 g chol., 311 mg sodium, 12 g carbo., 0 g fiber, 8 g pro.

Jamaican Shrimp

JAMAICAN COOKS USUALLY USE SCOTCH BONNET PEPPERS INSTEAD OF JALAPEÑO PEPPERS IN THEIR SPICY DISHES. THESE CAN BE SUBSTITUTED IN THIS RECIPE, IF AVAILABLE, BUT KEEP IN MIND THAT THEY ARE VERY HOT.

2 pounds fresh or frozen large shrimp
in shells
¼ cup salad oil
3 tablespoons white wine vinegar
2 tablespoons lime juice
1 jalapeño pepper, seeded and
finely chopped
1 tablespoon honey

2 teaspoons Jamaican Jerk Seasoning*
1 medium mango, peeled, pitted,
sliced, and halved crosswise
1 small lime, halved lengthwise and sliced
1 small red onion, quartered and
thinly sliced

In a large saucepan cook fresh or frozen shrimp, uncovered, in lightly salted boiling water for 1 to 3 minutes or till shrimp turn pink. Drain immediately and cool. Peel shrimp, leaving tails intact; devein. Place shrimp in a heavy plastic bag. At this point, you can seal the bag and chill for up to 24 hours.

For marinade, in a screw-top jar combine salad oil, white wine vinegar, lime juice, jalapeño pepper, honey, and the Jamaican Jerk Seasoning. Cover and shake well to mix; pour over shrimp in plastic bag. Cover and chill for 1 hour, turning bag occasionally.

To serve, drain shrimp, reserving marinade. In a large serving bowl, layer shrimp, mango, lime slices, and onion, repeating till all are used. Drizzle reserved marinade atop. Makes 10 to 12 appetizer servings.

*Note: To make your own Jamaican Jerk Seasoning, combine 2 teaspoons *onion powder*, 1 teaspoon *sugar*, 1 teaspoon *ground thyme*, 1 teaspoon *salt*, ½ teaspoon *ground allspice*, ¼ teaspoon *ground cinnamon*, and ¼ teaspoon *ground red pepper*.

Nutrition facts per appetizer serving: 102 cal., 3 g total fat (1 g sat. fat), 105 mg chol., 334 mg sodium, 7 g carbo., 1 g fiber, 11 g pro. Daily Value: 12% vit. A, 18% vit. C, 2% calcium, 13% iron.

Vegetable Nachos with Cilantro Cream

ONE CHIP WILL SURELY LEAD TO ANOTHER WHEN PILED HIGH WITH THIS ZESTY BEAN-AND-VEGETABLE TOPPING.

½ cup dairy sour cream or lower-fat dairy sour cream
2 tablespoons finely snipped fresh cilantro or parsley
1 small zucchini, quartered lengthwise and thinly sliced (1 cup)
½ cup shredded carrot
⅓ cup sliced green onion
1½ teaspoons ground cumin
4 teaspoons cooking oil
1 15-ounce can pinto beans, drained and rinsed
4 cups tortilla chips (4 ounce)
1 4-ounce can diced green chili peppers, drained, or 2 fresh jalapeño peppers, seeded and sliced
4 ounces shredded cheddar cheese (1 cup)
½ cup seeded and chopped tomato
Salsa (optional)

For cilantro cream, in a small mixing bowl stir together sour cream and cilantro or parsley; cover and set aside.

In a large skillet cook zucchini, carrot, onion, and cumin in hot oil for 3 to 4 minutes or till vegetables are crisp-tender. Stir in beans.

Spread tortilla chips about one layer deep on an 11- or 12-inch ovenproof platter or on a baking sheet. Spoon bean mixture over chips. Sprinkle with peppers and cheese. Bake in a 350° oven for 5 to 7 minutes or till cheese melts.

To serve, carefully transfer chips to a platter, if baked on a baking sheet. Top

◆ Vegetable Nachos with Cilantro Cream

chips with dollops of cilantro cream and sprinkle with tomatoes. If desired, pass salsa. Makes 8 appetizer servings.

Nutrition facts per appetizer serving: 234 cal., 14 g total fat (6 g sat. fat), 21 mg chol., 426 mg sodium, 21 g carbo., 4 g fiber, 9 g pro. Daily Value: 36% vit. A, 13% vit. C, 13% calcium, 9% iron.

Bruschetta

TO SAVE TIME ON THE DAY OF A PARTY, MAKE THE TOASTS AND TOPPINGS THE DAY BEFORE. JUST BEFORE SERVING, ASSEMBLE THE BRUSCHETTA AND HEAT THROUGH.

1 cup pitted ripe olives
2 teaspoons balsamic or red wine vinegar
1 teaspoons capers, drained
1 teaspoon olive oil
2 cloves garlic, minced

◆ Bruschetta

Bruschetta

All the rage in restaurants and homes across America, tomato- and olive-topped slices of crusty bread deliver plenty of hearty Italian taste.

2 medium red and/or yellow tomatoes,
chopped (1 cup)
⅓ cup thinly sliced green onion
1 tablespoon olive oil
1 tablespoon fresh snipped basil or oregano
or 1 teaspoon dried basil
or oregano leaves, crushed
⅛ teaspoon pepper
1 8-ounce loaf French bread (baguette)
with sesame seed
2 tablespoons olive oil
½ cup grated or shredded
Parmesan cheese

For the olive paste, in a blender container or food processor bowl combine olives, vinegar, capers, the 1 teaspoon olive oil, and garlic. Blend or process till a nearly smooth paste forms, stopping and pushing mixture down as necessary. If desired, cover and chill the mixture for up to 2 days.

For the tomato topper, in a small bowl stir together chopped tomatoes, green onion, the 1 tablespoon olive oil, basil or oregano, and pepper. If desired, cover and chill for up to 2 days.

For the toasts, cut bread into ½-inch-thick slices. Brush both sides of each slice lightly with the 2 tablespoons olive oil. Place on an ungreased baking sheet.

Bake toasts in a 425° oven for about 5 minutes or till crisp and light brown, turning once. If desired, transfer the cooled toasts to a storage container. Cover and store the toasts at room temperature for up to 24 hours.

To assemble, spread each toast with a thin layer of olive paste. Top each with about 2 tablespoons tomato topper; sprinkle with Parmesan cheese. Return slices to the ungreased baking sheet.

Bake in a 425° oven for 2 to 3 minutes or till cheese starts to melt and toppings are heated through. Serve warm. Makes about 24.

Nutrition facts per Bruschetta: 62 cal., 4 g total fat (1 g sat. fat), 2 mg chol., 120 mg sodium, 6 g carbo., 0 g fiber, and 2 g pro. Daily Value: 1% vit. A, 3% vit. C, 3% calcium, and 2% iron.

American Heritage Desserts

By Lisa Holderness

America's best-loved desserts ring rich with history, sentiment, and flavor. Many of these hand-me-down recipes are welcome finales to holiday celebrations. This luscious sampling comes from the all-new *Better Homes and Gardens Heritage of America Cookbook.*

Southern pecan pie

Every Southern cook has a cherished pecan pie recipe. For double pecan flavor, this Georgian version calls for nuts in the crust and filling.

Pralines

Named after the French aristocrat Cesar du Plessis Pralin, brown sugar pralines are a mainstay in the South.

Huguenot apple-pecan torte

The seventeenth century French Huguenots, who settled in South Carolina, were famed for their cooking. This French apple cake is still an American favorite.

Huguenot Apple-Pecan Torte

THIS NUTTY CAKE MIXES TOGETHER QUICKLY IN THE BLENDER OR FOOD PROCESSOR.

2 tablespoons all-purpose flour
1 teaspoon baking powder
1 teaspoon finely shredded lemon peel
4 eggs
¾ cup sugar
1 teaspoon vanilla
2½ cups pecans
1 cup water
1 tablespoon lemon juice
2 cups sliced, peeled apple
1 cup whipping cream
2 tablespoons sugar
Toasted pecan halves (optional)

Stir together flour, baking powder, and lemon peel; set aside.

In a blender container or food processor bowl place eggs, the ¾ cup sugar, and vanilla. Cover and blend or process till smooth. Add the 2½ cups pecans. Blend or process about 1 minute or till nearly smooth. Add the flour mixture and blend or process just till combined. Spread the batter evenly into 2 greased and floured 8x1½-inch round baking pans.

Bake in a 350° oven for 20 to 25 minutes or till lightly browned. Cool on wire racks for 10 minutes. Remove from pans; cool thoroughly on racks.

Meanwhile, in a skillet heat water and lemon juice to boiling. Add apple slices. Reduce heat. Cover; simmer 2 to 3 minutes or just till tender. Drain apple slices.

In a medium bowl beat whipping cream and the 2 tablespoons sugar till soft peaks form. Place a torte layer on a cake plate. Spread about *half* of the whipped cream evenly over layer. Arrange apple slices in a single layer on whipped cream, using as many as needed to cover surface and reserving remaining for top. Top with second torte layer. Spread remaining whipped cream on top of second torte layer. Arrange remaining apple slices and, if desired, pecan halves on top. Chill 1 to 2 hours. Makes 12 servings.

Nutrition facts per serving: 311 cal., 26 g total fat (6 g sat. fat), 98 mg chol., 24 g carbo., 55 mg sodium, 5 g pro.

Southern Pecan Pie

LUSCIOUS PECAN-AND-CARAMEL FILLING IN A FLAKY PASTRY IS HARD TO BEAT. NO WONDER IT'S STILL A FAVORITE AFTER ALL THESE YEARS.

1¼ cups all-purpose flour
⅓ cup shortening
¼ cup finely chopped pecans
3 to 4 tablespoons cold water
3 eggs
1 cup corn syrup
⅔ cup sugar
⅓ cup margarine or butter, melted
2 tablespoons bourbon whiskey
1 tablespoon all-purpose flour
1 teaspoon vanilla
1½ cups pecan halves
Whipped cream

For pastry, in a mixing bowl combine the 1¼ cups flour and ¼ teaspoon *salt*. Cut in shortening till pieces are the size of small peas. Stir in chopped pecans. Sprinkle 1 tablespoon of the water over part of the mixture; gently toss with a fork. Push to side of bowl. Repeat till all is moistened. Form dough into a ball.

On a lightly floured surface, flatten dough slightly with your hands. Roll dough from center to edges, forming a circle about 12 inches in diameter. Wrap pastry around a rolling pin. Unroll pastry onto a 9-inch pie plate. Ease pastry into pie plate, being careful not to stretch pastry. Trim pastry to ½ inch beyond edge of pie plate; fold under extra pastry. Make a fluted edge. Do not prick the pastry.

For filling, in a mixing bowl beat eggs lightly with a rotary beater till combined. Stir in corn syrup, sugar, margarine or butter, the 1 tablespoon flour, the bourbon, and vanilla. Mix well. Stir in the pecan halves.

Place pastry-lined pie plate on oven rack. Pour filling into pastry-lined pie plate. Cover edge of pie with foil. Bake in a 350° oven for 25 minutes. Remove foil; bake 20 to 25 minutes more or till a knife inserted near center comes out clean. Cool. Serve with whipped cream. Cover and chill to store. Makes 8 servings.

Nutrition facts per serving: 608 cal., 36 g total fat (5 g sat. fat), 80 mg chol., 69 g carbo., 204 mg sodium, and 7 g pro.

◆ Blackberry Pie with Hazelnut Glaze   ◆ Apple-Cherry Pie

Pralines

FOR GIFT GIVING, WRAP THESE SOUTHERN-STYLE CANDIES INDIVIDUALLY IN COLORFUL CELLOPHANE OR PLASTIC WRAP AND PLACE THEM IN TINS OR DECORATIVE GIFT BOXES.

1½ cups granulated sugar
1½ cups packed brown sugar
1 cup half-and-half or light cream
3 tablespoons margarine or butter
2 cups pecan halves

Butter the sides of a heavy 2-quart saucepan. In the saucepan combine sugar, brown sugar, and half-and-half. Cook over medium-high heat to boiling, stirring constantly with a wooden spoon to dissolve sugars. (This should take 6 to 8 minutes.) Avoid splashing the mixture on sides of the pan.

Carefully clip a candy thermometer to pan. Cook over medium-low heat, stirring occasionally, till thermometer registers 234° (soft-ball stage). Mixture should boil at a moderate, steady rate over entire surface. Reaching soft-ball stage should take 18 to 20 minutes.

Remove pan from heat. Add margarine or butter but do not stir. Cool, without stirring, to 150°. (This should take about 30 minutes.) Remove thermometer; stir in nuts. Beat vigorously with a wooden spoon till candy is just beginning to thicken but is still glossy. This should take 2 to 3 minutes.

Drop about 2 tablespoons candy at a time from a large serving spoon onto baking sheets lined with waxed paper, forming 3-inch pralines. If candy becomes too stiff to drop, stir in a few drops of *hot water*. When cool, store in a

tightly covered container. Makes 15 large pralines.

Nutrition facts per praline: 269 cal., 14 g total fat (2 g sat. fat), 6 mg chol., 37 g carbo., 32 mg sodium, and 2 g pro.

Blackberry Pie with Hazelnut Glaze

4 cups fresh or frozen
unsweetened blackberries
¾ cup sugar
¼ cup all-purpose flour
½ teaspoon finely shredded lemon peel
Pastry for Double-Crust Pie
(see recipe, right)
1 recipe Hazelnut Glaze (optional)

If using frozen blackberries, before adding, let stand for 15 to 30 minutes or till the berries are partially thawed but still icy. In a mixing bowl combine sugar, flour, and lemon peel. Add fresh or frozen blackberries; toss gently till coated.

Transfer berry mixture to a pastry-lined 9-inch pie plate. Add top crust; cut slits in top crust. Trim, seal, and flute edge. To prevent overbrowning, cover edge of pie with foil.

Bake in a 375° oven for 25 minutes for fresh berries (50 minutes for frozen berries). Remove foil. Bake for 20 to 25 minutes more for fresh berries (20 to 30 minutes for frozen berries) or till top is golden. If desired, top hot pie with Hazelnut Glaze. Cool. Makes 8 servings.

Hazelnut Glaze: In a small saucepan combine ⅓ cup packed *brown sugar* and 3 tablespoons *half-and-half or light cream.* Cook and stir over low heat till sugar melts. Stir in ⅓ cup chopped toasted *hazelnuts.* Pour over hot pie.

Nutrition facts per serving: 450 cal., 21 g total fat (5 g sat. fat), 2 mg chol., 61 g carbo., 139 mg sodium, 5 g pro.

Apple-Cherry Pie

2 cups fresh or frozen pitted tart
red cherries
1 cup sugar
2 tablespoons all-purpose flour
1 teaspoon ground cinnamon
¼ teaspoon ground nutmeg
3 cups peeled, cored, and thinly
sliced apples
Pastry for Double-Crust Pie
(see recipe, right)
2 tablespoons margarine or butter

1 tablespoon milk
½ teaspoon sugar
Dash ground cinnamon

If using frozen cherries, let stand at room temperature 30 minutes or till partially thawed. Combine the 1 cup sugar, flour, the 1 teaspoon cinnamon, and nutmeg; set aside.

In a large bowl combine cherries and apple slices. Add sugar mixture. Toss to coat. Transfer to pastry-lined 9-inch pie plate. Dot fruit with margarine or butter. Adjust top crust. Seal and flute edge. If desired, cut decorative shapes from dough scraps. Brush the back sides of the shapes with milk and arrange on the top crust. Cut slits in the top crust. Brush top crust with milk. Combine the ½ teaspoon sugar and the dash cinnamon; sprinkle over crust. Cover edge with foil.

Bake in a 375° oven for 25 minutes (50 minutes if using frozen cherries). Remove foil. Bake for 20 to 25 minutes more or till the top is golden and fruit is tender. Makes 8 servings.

Nutrition facts per serving: 439 cal., 21 g total fat (5 g sat. fat), 0 mg chol., 61 g carbo., 160 mg sodium, 4 g pro.

Pastry for Double-Crust Pie

USE THIS TRADITIONAL HOMEMADE PASTRY FOR THE BLACKBERRY PIE WITH HAZELNUT GLAZE, THE APPLE-CHERRY PIE, OR ANY DOUBLE-CRUST PIE.

2 cups all-purpose flour
½ teaspoon salt
⅔ cup shortening or lard
6 to 7 tablespoons cold water

In a mixing bowl stir together flour and salt. Cut in shortening or lard till pieces are the size of small peas. Sprinkle *1 tablespoon* of the water over part of the mixture; gently toss with a fork. Push to side of bowl. Repeat till all is moistened. Divide dough in half. Form each half of dough into a bowl.

On a lightly floured surface, flatten each ball of dough slightly with your hands. Roll out dough from center to edges, forming a circle about 12 inches in diameter. Wrap pastry around a rolling pin. Unroll pastry onto a 9-inch pie plate. Ease pastry into pie plate, being careful not to stretch pastry. Trim pastry even with rim of pie plate.

For top crust, repeat rolling remaining dough. Cut slits to allow steam to escape. Fill pastry in pie plate with desired filling. Place the top crust on filling. Trim top crust to ½ inch beyond edge of plate. Fold the top crust under bottom crust; flute edge. Bake as directed in the pie recipe.

Prize Tested Recipes®

Blackened Shrimp Stroganoff

THIS CAJUN TWIST ON STROGANOFF RELIES ON SPICY BLACKENED SEASONING FOR FLAVOR—

1 pound fresh or frozen shrimp in shells
1 tablespoon olive oil or cooking oil
2 tablespoons blackened seasoning
8 ounces fresh mushrooms, sliced (3 cups)
1 shallot, chopped (1 tablespoon)
1 tablespoon margarine or butter
⅔ cup dry vermouth or white wine
½ cup dairy sour cream
1 tablespoon cornstarch
½ of a 12-ounce jar roasted red sweet peppers, drained and cut into thin strips
1 tablespoon drained capers (optional)
Hot cooked fettuccine or rice

Peel and devein shrimp, reserving shells. For shrimp broth, place shells in saucepan with 2 cups *water*. Bring to boiling; reduce heat. Simmer, uncovered, 10 minutes. Strain broth; discard shells. (Or, use 1 cup *chicken broth* instead.) In small bowl combine shrimp and oil. Add blackened seasoning, stirring to coat shrimp; set aside.

In a 10-inch skillet cook mushrooms and shallot in hot margarine or butter till tender. Remove from skillet. In skillet cook and stir shrimp over medium-high heat about 2 minutes or till shrimp turn pink. Remove from skillet. Add vermouth to skillet. Boil, uncovered, till reduced to ¼ cup (2 to 3 minutes). Stir together sour cream and cornstarch; stir in *1 cup* of the shrimp broth or chicken broth. Add to skillet. Cook and stir till thickened and bubbly. Cook 1 minute more. Add shrimp, red peppers, mushroom mixture, and capers, if desired. Heat through. Season to taste with salt. Serve over pasta or rice. Makes 4 servings.

◆ Blackened Shrimp Stroganoff

Nutrition facts per serving: 381 cal., 16 g total fat (6 g sat. fat), 148 mg chol., 640 mg sodium, 39 g carbo., 3 g fiber, 20 g pro. Daily Value: 35% vit. A, 135% vit. C.

$200 WINNER
Ben Vernia, Nashville, Tenn.

Cranberry Bread Pudding

ORANGE JUICE AND CRANBERRIES MAKE A
PERFECT FLAVOR MATCH IN THIS OLD-
FASHIONED FAVORITE—

1 small orange
2 cups fresh cranberries
1⅔ cups sugar
½ teaspoon almond extract
3 eggs
2 cups whipping cream, half-and-half, or
light cream
¼ cup all-purpose flour
8 ounces rich egg bread or 8 slices firm-
textured white bread

Peel off just the rind of the orange
using a vegetable peeler, reserving peel
but not the pith. Peel remaining pith
from fruit; discard. Section orange. In a
food processor bowl process peel and
sections till chopped. Add cranberries;
process till coarsely chopped. Transfer to
a bowl. Stir in ⅔ cup sugar and extract.
Beat remaining sugar, eggs, cream, and
flour till smooth. For egg bread, cut into
½-inch-thick slices. Trim crusts; discard.
Cut slices diagonally. Arrange *half* the
bread in a greased 2-quart square baking
dish. Spread cranberry mixture over
bread. Pour *half* the egg mixture over
cranberries. Top with remaining bread;
pour remaining egg mixture atop. Bake
in a 325° oven 65 minutes or till knife
comes out clean. Makes 12 servings.

Nutrition facts per serving: 329 cal.,
17 g total fat, 108 mg chol., 128 mg
sodium.

$200 WINNER
Marilou Robinson, Portland, Oreg.

◆ Cranberry Bread Pudding

Cranberry Ice-Cream Pie

THE MORTENS TRANSFORMED ICE
CREAM INTO A HOLIDAY DESSERT BY
ADDING CRANBERRY SAUCE—

2 chocolate-flavored crumb pie shells
1 quart vanilla ice cream, softened
1 16-ounce can whole cranberry sauce
1 tablespoon Grand Marnier or orange
liqueur
1 8-ounce carton frozen whipped dessert
topping, thawed
2 tablespoons toasted sliced almonds
Additional whole cranberry sauce thinned
with orange juice

Place pie shells in freezer while preparing filling. For filling, in a large bowl use
a large spoon to mix ice cream, cranberry
sauce, and Grand Marnier or orange

continued on page 212

◆ Cranberry Ice-Cream Pie

continued from page 211

liqueur till combined. Spoon filling into chilled pie shells. Freeze at least 4 hours or till firm. Pipe or dollop whipped topping atop pies and sprinkle with almonds. Cover; return to freezer till serving time. For easier cutting, remove pie from freezer 5 to 10 minutes before serving. To serve, spoon cranberry sauce over each serving, if desired. Makes 12 servings (2 pies).

Note: You may freeze the pies wrapped tightly in freezer wrap, up to 2 months, if desired. To serve, place in the refrigerator for 10 to 20 minutes before needed.

Nutrition facts per serving: 345 cal., 16 g total fat (4 g sat. fat), 20 mg chol., 232 mg sodium, 49 g carbo., 1 g fiber, 3 g pro. Daily Value: 5% vit. A, 2% vit. C, 5% calcium, and 4% iron.

$100 WINNER
Mike and Linda Morten, Katy, Tex.

Spiced Shrimp Pilau

PILAU (PIH-low) OR PILAF, A RICE-BASED DISH, USUALLY CONTAINS A VARIETY OF INGREDIENTS—

1 pound fresh or frozen medium shrimp in shells, peeled and deveined
1 teaspoon grated gingerroot
1 teaspoon ground coriander
½ teaspoon five-spice powder
½ teaspoon paprika
¼ teaspoon ground cumin
¼ teaspoon ground turmeric
3 tablespoons margarine or butter
1 tablespoon olive oil or cooking oil
¼ cup finely chopped onion
3 cloves garlic, minced
1 fresh chili pepper (such as Anaheim), seeded and chopped
1½ cups long grain rice

◆ Spiced Shrimp Pilau

3¼ cups water or chicken broth
3 green onions, sliced

In a large bowl combine shrimp, gingerroot, coriander, five-spice powder, paprika, cumin, and turmeric. Cover. Let stand at room temperature while preparing rice. In a large saucepan heat margarine or butter and oil till margarine or butter is melted. Add onion, garlic, and chili pepper. Cook till onion is tender, about 5 minutes. Add rice. Add water (plus ½ teaspoon *salt* if using water) or chicken broth. Bring to boiling; reduce heat. Simmer, covered, for

10 minutes or till rice is nearly done. Stir in shrimp mixture. Return to boiling; reduce heat. Cook, covered, about 5 minutes more or till shrimp turn pink and rice is tender. To serve, spoon onto a serving platter. Garnish with green onions and *cilantro,* if desired. Makes 4 main-dish servings.

Nutrition facts per serving: 442 cal., 13 g total fat (2 g sat. fat), 131 mg chol., 548 mg sodium, 59 g carbo., 1 g fiber, 20 g pro. Daily Value: 19% vit. A, 27% vit. C.

$100 WINNER
Vera Prasad, Jamaica Hills, N.Y.

December

Delicious Memories

Prize Tested Recipes

Delicious Memories

BY JULIA MALLOY

"Holiday celebrations just wouldn't be the same without our cherished family recipes," claimed many readers in their heartwarming letters. The recipes they sent in response to our request for favorites were luscious and full of love. We think you'll find this cross-country sampling of holiday foods irresistible.

Cranberry Raisin Pie

"WE GREW UP ON MAINE'S LITTLE CRANBERRY ISLAND, SO IT'S NO SURPRISE THAT CRANBERRIES FOUND THEIR WAY INTO A LOT OF FAMILY RECIPES. THIS PIE HAS BEEN A FAVORITE FOR FOUR GENERATIONS."

—MAUREEN BRYANT COSTELLO, SOUTH PORTLAND, MAINE

¼ cup margarine or butter
1 cup chopped cranberries
1 cup chopped raisins
1 cup sugar
3 tablespoons all-purpose flour
1 teaspoon vanilla
1 recipe Pastry for Lattice-Top Pie
Coarse sugar

For filling, combine ½ cup *boiling water* and margarine; stir till melted. Stir in cranberries, raisins, sugar, flour, and vanilla. Set aside.

On a floured surface, flatten *one ball* of pastry dough. Roll to a 12-inch circle. Transfer to a 9-inch pie plate. Trim to ½ inch beyond edge. Roll remaining dough into a 10-inch circle. Cut into ½-inch-wide strips.

Spread filling in pastry. Weave strips atop to make a lattice top. Press ends of strips into rim of crust. Fold bottom pastry over strips; seal and flute edge. Sprinkle with coarse sugar. Cover the edge with foil. Bake in a 375° oven for 25 minutes. Remove foil; bake for 20 to 25 minutes more or till crust is golden. Cool on a wire rack. Makes 8 servings.

Pastry for Lattice-Top Pie: In a bowl stir together 2 cups all-purpose *flour* and ½ teaspoon *salt.* Cut in ⅔ cup *shortening or lard* till pieces are size of small peas. Sprinkle 1 tablespoon of *cold water* over part of mixture; gently toss with a fork. Push to side of bowl. Repeat with 5 to 6 more tablespoons cold water till all is moistened. Divide dough in half. Form each half into a ball.

Nutrition facts per slice: 477 cal., 23 g total fat (5 g sat. fat), 204 mg sodium, 66 g carbo., 2 g fiber, 4 g pro. Daily Value: 7% vit. A, 4% vit. C, 1% calcium, 12% iron.

Lady Baltimore Cake

"I FIRST TASTED THIS CAKE IN ALABAMA ON MY VERY FIRST JOB. NOW THAT I LIVE IN LOUISIANA, I USE LOCALLY GROWN PECANS AND FIGS IN MY FILLING."

—SANDRA DAY, LAFAYETTE, LA.

2½ cups all-purpose flour
2 cups sugar
1 teaspoon baking powder
1 teaspoon finely shredded orange peel
½ teaspoon baking soda
⅛ teaspoon salt
1⅓ cups buttermilk or sour milk
½ cup shortening, margarine, or butter, softened
1 teaspoon vanilla
4 egg whites
1 cup raisins
8 dried figs, snipped (½ cup)
¼ cup brandy
1 cup toasted chopped pecans
⅓ cup finely chopped candied red or green cherries
⅓ cup finely chopped candied pineapple or mixed candied fruits and peels
1 recipe Seven-Minute Frosting (see recipe, page 216)

continued on page 216

Lady Baltimore Cake

Cranberry-Raisin Pie

continued from page 214

In a bowl stir together flour, sugar, baking powder, orange peel, baking soda, and salt. Add buttermilk, shortening, and vanilla. Beat for 30 seconds, scraping sides of bowl. Beat for 2 minutes, scraping bowl often. Add egg whites; beat for 2 minutes more, scraping bowl.

Pour batter into 3 greased and floured 8x1½-inch round baking pans; spread evenly. Bake in a 350° oven about 30 minutes or till a toothpick inserted near center comes out clean. Cool cake layers for 10 minutes. Loosen from sides; remove from pans. Cool on wire racks. (At this point, you may cover and freeze the cake for up to 6 months.)

For filling, in a medium bowl combine raisins, figs, and brandy; let stand at room temperature about 2 hours or till brandy is absorbed, stirring occasionally. Stir in the pecans, fruits, and about *one-third (1½ cups)* of the Seven-Minute Frosting.

To assemble, place one cake layer on a platter; spread *half* of the filling on top. Add another cake layer and the remaining filling. Top with the remaining cake layer. Frost with the remaining frosting. Serve within 2 hours. Makes 12 servings.

Nutrition facts per slice: 572 cal., 15 g total fat (2 g sat. fat), 1 mg chol., 212 mg sodium, 103 g carbo., 3 g fiber, 7 g pro. Daily Value: 9% vit. C, 6% calcium, 12% iron.

Seven-Minute Frosting

STIR SOME OF THIS GLOSSY DIVINITY-LIKE FROSTING INTO THE FILLING FOR LADY BALTIMORE CAKE AND SAVE THE REST FOR THE TOP AND SIDES. IT CAN TAKE A WHILE TO BEAT, SO USE A STURDY PORTABLE ELECTRIC MIXER OR A FREE-STANDING MIXER.

1½ cups sugar
⅓ cup cold water
2 egg whites
¼ teaspoon cream of tartar or 2 teaspoons light corn syrup
1 teaspoon vanilla

In the top of a double boiler combine sugar, cold water, egg whites, and cream of tartar or corn syrup. Beat for 30 seconds or till mixed.

Place over boiling water (upper pan should not touch water). Cook, beating constantly with the electric mixer on high speed, about 7 minutes or till frosting forms stiff peaks. Remove from heat; add vanilla. Beat for 2 to 3 minutes more or till frosting is of spreading consistency.

Christmas Wreath Salad

THIS FESTIVE FENNEL-PEPPER SALAD IS SO PRETTY, YOU CAN USE IT AS YOUR HOLIDAY TABLE CENTERPIECE.

—PAT ELTISTE, PLAYA DEL REY, CA

2 large fennel bulbs
2 to 4 red sweet peppers
1 head Bibb or Boston lettuce, torn (5 cups)
1 bunch watercress (1 cup)
¼ cup olive oil

3 tablespoons balsamic vinegar
½ teaspoon fennel seed, crushed
¼ teaspoon salt
⅛ teaspoon pepper

Discard outer layers of fennel; slice fennel into thin strips, discarding core. Halve peppers lengthwise; remove seeds. Slice peppers into thin half rings.

To assemble, arrange lettuce and watercress on 6 plates. Arrange fennel and red pepper on greens.

For dressing, in a screw-top jar combine oil, vinegar, fennel seed, salt, and pepper. Cover and shake well to mix. Drizzle dressing over salad. Makes 6 side-dish servings.

Nutrition facts per serving: 122 cal., 9 g total fat (1 g sat. fat), 134 mg sodium, 10 g carbo., 1 g fiber, 2 g pro. Daily Value: 6% vit. A, 61% vit. C, 4% calcium, 3% iron.

Baked Ham with Apple Stuffing

"OUR CHILDHOOD MEMORIES DICTATE THE MENU FOR OUR OWN HOLIDAY CELEBRATION—THERE HAS TO BE STUFFING. THIS FRUITY STUFFING IS A FAVORITE, ESPECIALLY WHEN SERVED WITH A REAL COUNTRY-STYLE HAM."

—PAT WARD, PENNSAUKEN, N.J.

1 4- to 5-pound ham, shank half
10 cups whole-grain bread, cut into ½-inch cubes (about 13 slices)
1½ cups chopped onion
1½ cups chopped celery (3 stalks)
⅓ cup margarine or butter
3 cups coarsely shredded apple (about 3 medium)

Christmas Wreath Salad

Baked Ham with
Apple Stuffing

Caramel-Sweet-Potato Casserole

Caramel-Sweet-Potato Casserole

"BELIEVE IT OR NOT, THE ROOTS OF THIS RECIPE STEM FROM THE DAYS OF MAKING BABY FOOD FOR MY CHILDREN. THROUGHOUT THE YEARS I'VE EMBELLISHED IT, EVEN ADDING A RICH CARAMEL TOPPING. MY 'BABIES,' NOW 18 AND 23, REQUEST IT FOR OUR HOLIDAY DINNER EVERY YEAR."

—LINDA VERILLO, NORTH BERGEN, N.J.

1 egg
½ cup evaporated milk
3 cups mashed, cooked sweet potatoes
(4 medium)
2 tablespoons margarine or butter
½ cup snipped pitted whole dates
2 tablespoons maple syrup or
maple-flavored syrup
2 tablespoons margarine or butter

In a medium mixing bowl use a fork to beat egg; stir in milk. Add sweet potatoes; stir till smooth.

In a large skillet melt the 2 tablespoons margarine or butter. Add dates; cook and stir for 2 minutes. Stir in sweet potato mixture. Spoon mixture into a 1½-quart casserole.

For topping, heat maple syrup and remaining 2 tablespoons margarine or butter till melted; pour over sweet potato mixture. Bake in a 350° oven for 25 to 30 minutes or till hot. Makes 6 side-dish servings.

Nutrition facts per serving: 287 cal., 10 g total fat (6 g sat. fat), 62 mg chol., 124 mg sodium, 46 g carbo., 6 g fiber, 5 g pro. Daily Value: 267% vit. A, 48% vit. C, 8% calcium, 6% iron.

½ cup dried cherries, dried cranberries,
or raisins
¼ cup snipped parsley
1 teaspoon ground cinnamon
1 to 1¼ cups chicken broth or low-sodium
chicken broth
Apple slices (optional)

Place ham, fat side up, on a rack in a roasting pan. Score top. Insert a meat thermometer. Roast in a 350° oven for 1 to 2 hours or till thermometer reaches 140°.

Arrange bread in a shallow pan; toast alongside ham for 10 to 12 minutes or till crisp, stirring twice.

For stuffing, in a large skillet cook onion and celery in margarine about 5 minutes or till tender.

In an extra-large bowl combine the bread cubes; onion; celery; apple; cherries, cranberries, or raisins; parsley; and cinnamon. Add enough broth to moisten. Toss to mix.

Spoon stuffing into a 2½-quart casserole. Bake, covered, in a 350° oven for 45 to 50 minutes or till hot. Serve with ham. If desired, garnish with apple slices. Makes 12 to 14 servings.

Nutrition facts per serving with ham: 357 cal., 13 g total fat (3 g sat. fat), 63 mg chol., 1,871 mg sodium, 27 g carbo., 5 g fiber, 33 g pro. Daily Value: 7% vit. A, 52% vit. C, 4% calcium, 17% iron.

◆ Chilled Cranberry Soup

Chilled Cranberry Soup

"OUR FAMILY FELL IN LOVE WITH THIS WONDERFUL SOUP ON A MASSACHUSETTS VACATION SEVERAL YEARS AGO. MY KIDS NOW EXPECT IT AS PART OF OUR CELEBRATION EVERY YEAR AND CALL IT THEIR 'VACATION SOUP.' "

—PAT WARD, PENNSAUKEN, N.J.

4 cups fresh cranberries (1-pound)
3 cups water
1½ cups sugar
3 inches stick cinnamon
¼ teaspoon ground cloves
2 tablespoons lemon juice
1 tablespoon finely shredded orange peel
Orange peel curl (optional)
Mint leaves (optional)

In a 3-quart saucepan combine cranberries, water, sugar, cinnamon sticks, and cloves. Bring to boiling; reduce heat. Simmer, uncovered, about 5 minutes or till about *half* of the cranberries are popped.

Remove from heat. Stir in lemon juice and orange peel. Cool. Cover and chill for 4 to 24 hours. Before serving, remove cinnamon stick.

To serve, ladle into soup bowls. If desired, top each serving with orange peel and mint. Makes 6 to 8 (¾ cup) side-dish servings.

Nutrition facts per serving: 190 cal., 0 g total fat (0 g sat. fat), 0 mg chol., 4 mg sodium, 50 g carbo., 3 g fiber, 0 g pro. Daily Value: 0% vit. A, 20% vit. C, 1% calcium, 2% iron.

Vinarterta (Icelandic Christmas Cake)

THE SEVEN CAKE LAYERS FOR VINARTERTA (VEEN ah TER tah) ARE REALLY MORE COOKIELIKE THAN CAKELIKE. THE FRUITY FILLING SOFTENS THEM.

—ANNE S. LEWIS
SACRAMENTO, CA.

2 pounds pitted prunes (5½ cups)
3 cups water
¾ cup sugar
4½ cups all-purpose flour
2 teaspoons baking powder
½ teaspoon salt
¼ teaspoon ground cardamom
1 cup margarine or butter
1½ cups sugar
2 eggs
2 teaspoons vanilla
¼ cup half-and-half or light cream
1 recipe Vanilla Glaze
Red and green candied cherry halves (optional)

For filling, in a large saucepan combine prunes and water. Bring to boiling; reduce heat. Cover and simmer about 20 minutes or till prunes are very soft. Drain, reserving ½ *cup* of the liquid. Cool slightly.

In a blender container or food processor bowl combine *half* of the prunes and ¼ *cup* of the reserved liquid. Cover; blend or process till smooth; return to pan. Repeat with remaining prunes and liquid.

Stir the ¾ cup sugar into prunes. Cook and stir over low heat about 5 minutes or till the consistency of thick jam. Remove from heat; cool.

For cake, grease two 9x1½-inch round cake pans; line with 9-inch circles of waxed paper. Set aside.

In a bowl combine flour, baking powder, salt, and cardamom; set aside.

In a large bowl beat margarine or butter on medium speed for 30 seconds. Gradually add the 1½ cups sugar, beating till fluffy. Add eggs, one at a time, beating well after each. Beat in vanilla. Alternately add flour mixture and half-and-half to egg mixture, beating till combined. Divide into seven ⅔-cup portions.

For each cake layer, pat *one portion* of dough into a thin, even layer, covering the bottom of a prepared pan. Bake in a 350° oven for 12 to 15 minutes or till edges are light brown. Invert onto a wire rack; remove waxed paper. Grease and line pans with more waxed paper before baking remaining dough.

To assemble, place *one* cake layer on a serving platter; spread about ⅔ cup filling from center to edges. Top with a second cake layer and ⅔ cup more filling. Repeat with remaining cake layers and filling, ending with a plain cake layer on top. Spread Vanilla Glaze on the top of the cake, allowing some glaze to drizzle over sides. If desired, arrange red and green candied cherry halves around the top in the shape of a wreath. Cover and chill for 24 hours. Bring to room temperature before serving. To serve, cut into 3x1-inch slices. Makes 30 servings.

Vanilla Glaze: In a small bowl stir together 2 cups sifted *powdered sugar* and 1 teaspoon *vanilla*. Stir in enough *milk* (2 to 3 tablespoons) to make an icing of drizzling consistency. Makes 1 cup.

Nutrition facts per serving: 319 cal., 7 g total fat (2 g sat. fat), 16 mg chol., 117 mg sodium, 63 g carbo., 3 g fiber, 4 g pro. Daily Value: 13% vit. A, 2% calcium, 12% iron.

♦ Vinarterta (Icelandic Christmas Cake)

My grandparents came from Iceland, bringing with them recipes that would become family legacies—recipes such as my favorite dessert, Vinarterta. Now I bake it in my own home, even mini versions to give as Christmas gifts.
—Anne S. Lewis

Cranberry Pumpkin Bread

"AT OUR ANNUAL NEW YEAR'S DAY POTLUCK, MOM'S PUMPKIN BREAD AND CRANBERRY NUT BREAD WERE ALWAYS ON THE HELP-YOURSELF TABLE. I COMBINED THE TWO FLAVORS FOR MY OWN CHRISTMAS BREAD."

—LISA BLAIS, RUMFORD, R.I.

4 cups all-purpose flour
2 tablespoons baking powder
2 teaspoons ground cinnamon
½ teaspoon baking soda
½ teaspoon ground nutmeg
¼ teaspoon ground ginger
2 cups sugar
2 cups canned pumpkin
1 cup frozen egg product, thawed
(equivalent to 4 large eggs)
½ cup cooking oil
2 cups coarsely chopped cranberries
½ cup chopped toasted almonds
1 recipe Vanilla Icing (optional)

Grease two 9x5x3-inch loaf pans; set aside. In a medium bowl stir together flour, baking powder, cinnamon, baking soda, nutmeg, and ginger; set aside. In a large bowl combine sugar, pumpkin, egg product, and oil. Add flour mixture to pumpkin mixture; stir just till moistened. Fold in berries and almonds.

Pour batter into the prepared pans. Bake in a 350° oven for 60 to 65 minutes or till a wooden toothpick inserted near the centers comes out clean.

Cool for 10 minutes. Remove from pans; cool. Wrap and store overnight. If

◆ Cranberry Pumpkin Bread

desired, before serving, drizzle with Vanilla Icing. Makes 2 loaves (36 servings total).

Vanilla Icing: In a small bowl stir together ½ cup sifted *powdered sugar* and ½ teaspoon *vanilla*. Stir in enough *milk* (1 to 2 teaspoons) to make an icing of drizzling consistency. Makes 1 cup.

Nutrition facts per slice: 148 cal., 5 g total fat (1 g sat. fat), 0 mg chol., 29 mg sodium, 24 g carbo., 1 g fiber, 3 g pro. Daily Value: 30% vit. A, 2% vit. C, 1% calcium, 6% iron.

Down-South Stuffing

"GROWING UP IN A MILITARY FAMILY MEANT MOVING AROUND A LOT. LUCKILY FOR US, MOM EMBRACED THE PEOPLE AND FOOD OF EACH NEW PLACE, MAKING IT EASIER FOR US ALL TO ADJUST. IT WAS HER SOUTHERN STUFFING THAT HELPED TO CURE OUR NOT-SO-WELL-HIDDEN HOMESICKNESS ON OUR FIRST THANKSGIVING IN THE PHILIPPINES. ONCE DAD CARVED THE BIRD, WE DIDN'T PUT DOWN OUR FORKS UNTIL OUR PLATES WERE EMPTY—A SECOND TIME."

—JANIS VANDERVORT, PORTLAND, ORE.

¾ pound bulk pork sausage
¾ cup finely chopped onion
½ cup chopped green pepper
½ cup chopped celery (1 stalk)
½ cup margarine or butter
2 eggs
1 teaspoon poultry seasoning
⅛ teaspoon pepper
5 cups dry white bread cubes (7 slices)
5 cups crumbled corn bread*
¾ cup toasted chopped pecans
1 to 1½ cups chicken broth

◆ Down-South Stuffing

In a large skillet cook sausage till brown. Drain, reserving 2 tablespoons of the drippings. Set aside.

In same skillet cook onion, green pepper, and celery in hot margarine or butter till tender but not brown.

In a large bowl use a fork to beat eggs; stir in poultry seasoning and pepper. Add bread cubes and corn bread; toss till coated. Add sausage, reserved drippings, vegetables, and pecans. Add enough broth to moisten (¾ to 1 cup), tossing to mix well.

Use to stuff one 6- to 9-pound capon** or other bird. Place any remaining stuffing in a casserole; drizzle with enough of the remaining chicken broth (¼ to ½ cup) to make a stuffing of desired moistness. Bake, covered, in a 325° oven for 40 to 45 minutes or till hot. Makes 10 to 12 side-dish servings.

***Note:** For the corn bread, you can make your favorite recipe or use a packaged mix. For 5 cups, you'll need two 8½-ounce packages of mix.

****Note:** Smaller than a turkey, but bigger than a chicken, roasted capon is the perfect alternative for smaller holiday gatherings. These young male chickens generally weigh between 6 and 9 pounds.

Nutrition facts per serving of stuffing only: 352 cal., 24 g total fat (4 g sat. fat), 56 mg chol., 857 mg sodium, 28 g carbo., 1 g fiber, 9 g pro. Daily Value: 13% vit. A, 8% vit. C, 3% calcium, 10% iron.

Vetetable Latkes
—SALLY FINK, DES MOINES, IOWA

2 medium zucchini (6-ounces)
or 4 medium carrots, thinly sliced
1 egg
3 tablespoons dry curd cottage cheese
3 tablespoons Matzo meal
¼ teaspoon salt
⅛ teaspoon pepper
Cooking oil
Dairy sour cream (optional)

Place zucchini or carrots in a steamer basket; cover and steam over boiling water till very tender, allowing about 8 minutes for zucchini and 15 minutes for carrots. Drain; mash with a potato masher.

In a medium bowl beat egg; stir in zucchini or carrot, cottage cheese, Matzo meal, salt, and pepper. Heat a lightly oiled skillet or griddle over medium heat. Add the vegetable mixture, a rounded tablespoon at a time, spreading each patty to a 2½-inch circle. Cook about 4 minutes or till golden, turning once. If desired, serve with sour cream. Makes 10 latkes (5 side-dish servings).

Nutrition facts per serving: 93 cal., 7 g total fat (1 g sat. fat), 43 mg chol., 129 mg sodium, 6 g carbo., 1 g fiber, 3 g pro. Daily Value: 3% vit. A, 2% vit. C, 1% calcium, 3% iron.

◆ Vetetable Latkes

Hanukkah means cooking in oil, usually potato latkes. Not in our house. Instead of making potato latkes, our children help me prepare many different kinds of latkes, a tradition I hope they continue to cherish in the years to come.
—Sally Fink

Mormor's Syltkakor (Grandmother's Jelly Cookies)

Easy Apricot Foldovers

Butterscotc Fudge

Mincemeat Bars

Noels

Coffee Pecans

In 1966, with a newborn and not enough money to buy gifts, I
baked holiday treats for family and friends. Now grown, my "baby"
requests those same recipes year after year.
—Edna Bates Burger

Noels

"EVERY YEAR WHEN I TRAVEL HOME FOR CHRISTMAS, THIS DATE COOKIE IS ONE OF THE THINGS I CAN'T WAIT TO TASTE THE MOMENT I WALK IN THE DOOR."

—MARLENE BROWN, STUDIO CITY, CALIF. AND LORRAINE BROWN, ST. LOUIS PARK, MINN.

1¼ cups all-purpose flour
½ teaspoon baking soda
¼ teaspoon baking powder
¼ teaspoon salt
⅓ cup butter
¾ cup packed brown sugar
1 egg
1 teaspoon vanilla
½ cup dairy sour cream
1 8-ounce package pitted whole dates,
snipped (2 cups)
½ cup broken walnuts
1 recipe Butter Icing

In a small bowl stir together flour, baking soda, baking powder, and salt; set aside. In a medium bowl beat butter with an electric mixer on medium speed for 30 seconds. Gradually add brown sugar, beating on medium speed till fluffy. Add egg and vanilla; beat till combined.

Alternately add flour mixture and sour cream to egg mixture, beating on low speed just till combined. Stir in dates and walnuts. Drop by well-rounded teaspoons 2 inches apart onto an ungreased cookie sheet. Bake in a 400° oven for 8 to 10 minutes or till light brown. Cool on a wire rack. When cool, drizzle with Butter Icing. Makes 36 cookies.

Butter Icing: In a small bowl stir together 1 cup sifted *powdered sugar*, 2 tablespoons melted *butter*, and 1 teaspoon *vanilla*. Stir in enough *milk* (2 to 3 teaspoons) to make an icing of drizzling consistency.

Nutrition facts per cookie: 108 cal., 4 g total fat (2 g sat. fat), 14 mg chol., 60 mg sodium, 17 g carbo., 1 g fiber, 1 g pro. Daily Value: 3% vit. A, 0% vit. C, 1% calcium, 3% iron.

Mormor's Syltkakor (Grandmother's Jelly Cookies)

"THESE FILLED COOKIES COME FROM THE DECEMBER 1968 ISSUE OF *BETTER HOMES AND GARDENS*® MAGAZINE. THAT YEAR, MY MOTHER, SISTER, AND I ROLLED UP OUR SLEEVES AND PROCEEDED TO MAKE A DOZEN DIFFERENT COOKIES FROM AROUND THE WORLD, STARTING A TRADITION THAT CONTINUES TODAY. OUR FAVORITE IS SWEDISH MORMOR'S SYLTKAKOR (MOR MORZ SOOLT KAH KOR). EVEN WHEN WE CANNOT GET TOGETHER, MY MOTHER WILL BAKE BY HERSELF, THEN CAREFULLY PACK AND EXPRESS-MAIL A TIN OF THESE DELICIOUS MEMORY MAKERS TO US BOTH."

—VICTORIA KEENUM, ROANOKE, VA.

1 cup butter, softened
¾ cup sugar
1 egg
3 cups all-purpose flour
1 slightly beaten egg white
⅓ cup finely chopped almonds
1 tablespoon pearl sugar or granulated
sugar
¼ to ½ cup currant jelly

In a large bowl combine butter and ¾ cup sugar; beat on medium speed till fluffy. Add egg; beat well. Add flour to butter mixture; beat till combined. (If necessary, use a wooden spoon to stir in flour.)

Divide dough in half. On a lightly floured surface, roll *half* of the dough to ⅛-inch thickness. Using a star- or round-shaped cookie cutter, cut into 2½-inch stars or circles. Roll out second portion to ⅛-inch thickness; cut with a 2-inch star- or round-shaped cookie cutter. Using a ¾- or 1-inch cutter, cut a circle from center of smaller rounds. Reroll dough trimmings.

Brush tops of 2-inch shapes with egg white; sprinkle with almonds and/or the 1 tablespoon pearl sugar or granulated sugar. Arrange shapes on lightly greased cookie sheets; bake in a 375° oven for 7 to 9 minutes or till light brown on bottoms.

Transfer to wire racks; cool. Place a small amount of jelly in centers of 2½-inch cookies; top with 2-inch cookies, sugar and/or nut side up, and press together, showing jelly in center. Makes 3 to 3½ dozen.

Nutrition facts per cookie: 112 cal., 6 g total fat (3 g sat. fat), 20 mg chol., 56 mg sodium, 13 g carbo., 0 g fiber, 2 g pro. Daily Value: 5% vit. A, 0% vit. C, 0% calcium, 3% iron.

Coffee Pecans

"THE TIMEWORN RECIPE FOR THESE CAN-
DYLIKE NUTS HAS MOVED WITH OUR
FAMILY ALL OVER THE DEEP SOUTH,
TUCKED SAFELY IN THE BOTTOM DRAWER
OF AN ANTIQUE PINE CHEST. FROM
JANUARY TO NOVEMBER IT LIES THERE,
PATIENTLY WAITING FOR THAT EXCITING
DECEMBER DAY WHEN I PULL IT OUT FOR
ANOTHER ROUND OF HOLIDAY BAKING."

—EDNA BATES BURGER, COLUMBUS,
GEORGIA.

3 cups pecan halves
¾ cup packed brown sugar
⅓ cup granulated sugar
⅓ cup dairy sour cream (not low-fat
sour cream)
1 tablespoon instant coffee crystals
1 teaspoon vanilla

Place pecans in a shallow baking pan.
Bake in a 350° oven for 5 to 10 minutes
or till toasted, stirring occasionally.
Transfer pecans to a large, heat-proof
bowl. Keep warm.

Line a large shallow baking pan with
aluminum foil; grease foil with margarine or butter. Set aside.

Butter sides of a heavy 1-quart
saucepan. In the pan combine brown
sugar, granulated sugar, sour cream, and
coffee crystals. Cook and stir over medium heat to boiling. Carefully clip a
candy thermometer to the side of the
saucepan. Cook and stir over medium
heat till the mixture reaches soft-ball
stage (236° to 240°). (This should take
about 8 minutes from the point the mixture starts to bubble.)

Remove from heat. Remove the thermometer. Working quickly, stir in
vanilla. Pour over warm pecans in bowl.
Gently stir till nuts are coated.

Pour mixture onto the foil-lined pan.
With 2 forks, separate nuts. Cool till set.
Break up nuts as desired. Remove from
pan. Cover and store in the refrigerator
for up to 1 week. Makes 4 cups.

Nutrition facts per piece: 60 cal., 5 g
total fat (1 g sat. fat), 1 mg chol., 1 mg
sodium, 5 g carbo., 0 g fiber, 1 g pro.
Daily Value: 0% vit. A, 0% vit. C, 0%
calcium, and 1% iron.

Easy Apricot Foldovers

"JUST AS WINES AND FRIENDSHIPS
CHANGE WITH AGE, SO TOO DO RECIPES.
SINCE 1966, WHEN I STARTED MAKING
THESE PASTRIES, THE RECIPE HAS UNDER-
GONE A LOT OF CHANGES. ONE THING I
WILL NEVER CHANGE, THOUGH, IS MAK-
ING THE DOUGH FROM PIECRUST MIX.
IT'S JUST TOO EASY."

—EDNA BATES BURGER, COLUMBUS,
GEORGIA.

1 package piecrust mix (for 2-crust pie)
1 3-ounce package cream cheese, softened
2 tablespoons granulated sugar
2 tablespoons milk
1 teaspoon lemon extract

⅓ cup apricot, grape, or raspberry preserves
32 pecan halves
Powdered sugar

In a medium bowl combine piecrust
mix, cream cheese, sugar, milk, and
lemon extract. Stir with a fork till mixture forms a ball. Divide the dough in
half.

On a lightly floured surface, roll each
portion into a 10-inch square. With a
pastry wheel or knife, cut each large
square into sixteen 2½-inch squares.
Spoon *½ teaspoon* preserves in the center
of *each* square. Place a pecan half on top
of preserves on each. Moisten two opposite corners with water; bring corners up
over filling. Pinch corners tightly together to seal.

Arrange filled squares on a cookie
sheet. Bake in a 350° oven for 10 to 12
minutes or till golden. Transfer immediately to a rack to cool. Sift powdered
sugar over tops. Makes 32 cookies.

Nutrition facts per cookie: 86 cal., 5
g total fat (1 g sat. fat), 3 mg chol., 90
mg sodium, 9 g carbo., 0 g fiber, 1 g
pro. Daily Value: 1% vit. A, 0% vit. C,
0% calcium, and 2% iron.

Butterscotch Fudge

"UPON DISCOVERING MY SON'S ALLERGY TO CHOCOLATE, I HAD TO MODIFY MY FAMILY'S TRADITIONAL FUDGE TO BUTTERSCOTCH. NOW, EVEN THE CHOCOLATE-LOVERS IN MY FAMILY PREFER MY BUTTERSCOTCH VERSION. HOW DO I KNOW? I OVERHEARD MY HUSBAND TELL A GUEST, 'THIS IS THE BEST—BETTER THAN CHOCOLATE ANY DAY!' "

—CHRISTINA OSBORNE, HOUSTON, TEXAS

Nonstick spray coating
2 cups sugar
2 5-ounce cans evaporated milk
(1⅓ cups)
½ cup margarine or butter
2 12-ounce packages butterscotch pieces
1 13-ounce jar marshmallow creme
1 teaspoon vanilla
1½ cups toasted chopped pecans
½ cup butterscotch-flavored pieces
(optional)

Line a 13x9x2-inch baking pan with aluminum foil. Spray with nonstick coating; set aside.

Spray the sides of a 3-quart heavy saucepan. In the saucepan combine sugar, milk, and margarine or butter. Cook and stir over medium heat to boiling. Carefully clip a candy thermometer to side of pan. Cook and stir constantly over medium heat to 234°, soft-ball stage (about 15 minutes), scraping the bottom of the pan as you stir.

Remove the pan from heat; remove thermometer. Add the 2 packages of butterscotch pieces, marshmallow creme, and vanilla; stir till melted. Stir in *1 cup* of the pecans. Pour into the prepared baking pan, spreading evenly.

If desired, while fudge is still warm, sprinkle with remaining nuts and butterscotch pieces; press gently into top. Cool in the pan. Cover and chill in the refrigerator till firm. Remove fudge and foil from pan. Cut into 1-inch squares. Store in the refrigerator for up to 1 week. Makes 4½ pounds (117 pieces).

Nutrition facts per piece: 73 cal., 4 g total fat (2 g sat. fat), 1 mg chol., 19 mg sodium, 10 g carbo., 0 g fiber, 0 g pro. Daily Value: 1% vit. A.

Mincemeat Bars

"AS COUNTRY CHILDREN, MY SISTER AND I LOOKED FORWARD EVERY YEAR TO INVITING OUR CLASSMATES TO A HOLIDAY ICE-SKATING PARTY. AFTER THE FUN OF ICE-SKATING, WE WOULD RETURN HOME FOR MOM'S DELICIOUS MINCEMEAT BARS!"

—JESSIE F. HULBERT, JACKSON, MISS.

¾ cup water
1 9-oz. package condensed mincemeat
¾ cup shortening
½ cup granulated sugar
⅓ cup molasses
1¼ cups all-purpose flour
1½ cups rolled oats
Powdered sugar (optional)

For filling, in a saucepan bring water to boiling. Add mincemeat; reduce heat. Cover and simmer for 3 minutes, stirring often. Cool.

In a large bowl beat shortening with an electric mixer on medium speed for 30 seconds. Gradually add granulated sugar, beating till fluffy. Beat in molasses. Add flour; beat till combined. Use a wooden spoon to stir in oats.

Press half of the oatmeal mixture onto the bottom of a greased 9x9x2-inch baking pan. Spread mincemeat filling onto oatmeal mixture. Drop remaining mixture by teaspoonfuls onto filling. Bake in a 350° oven for 35 minutes or till light brown. Cool in the pan on a wire rack. If desired, sprinkle with powdered sugar. Cut into diamonds or bars. Makes 24 servings.

Nutrition facts per diamond or bar: 176 cal., 7 g total fat (2 g sat. fat), 0 mg chol., 71 mg sodium, 27 g carbo., 0 g fiber, 2 g pro. Daily Value: 0% vit. A, 0% vit. C, 1% calcium, 6% iron.

Calypso Pork

"EVERY YEAR, WE GATHER FOR A DELICIOUS POTLUCK DINNER BASED ON A DIFFERENT REGION OR COUNTRY. THE HOSTS PICK THE CUISINE, THEN EVERYONE PITCHES IN WITH A RECIPE. FOR OUR CARIBBEAN DINNER, THE MAIN DISH WAS OUR VERSION OF THE TRADITIONAL JAMAICAN 'JERK' PORK. ALTHOUGH IT IS USUALLY COOKED IN A PIT OR BARBECUE, WE ROASTED OURS IN THE OVEN."

—MABLE HOFFMAN, SAN DIEGO, CALIF.

3 green onions, sliced
1 fresh jalapeño or chili pepper*, rinsed, seeded, and chopped
1 tablespoon soy sauce
2 teaspoons grated gingerroot
2 teaspoons cooking oil

½ teaspoon salt

½ teaspoon ground allspice

¼ teaspoon ground cinnamon

¼ teaspoon ground nutmeg

1 5- to 6-pound boneless pork double loin
roast, rolled and tied

2 tablespoons cornstarch

1½ cups unsweetened pineapple juice

1 pineapple, cored, sliced, and cut
into wedges

1 large mango, seeded, peeled, and sliced
lengthwise

1 large papaya, peeled, halved, seeded, and
sliced lengthwise

2 limes, cut into thin wedges

2 cups watermelon balls

3 kiwi fruit, sliced

1 cup red raspberries

Hot cooked rice

14 to 16 ti leaves (optional)

Cracked peppercorns (optional)

Fresh cilantro (optional)

◆ Calypso Pork

In a blender container or food processor bowl, combine green onions, jalapeño or chili pepper, soy sauce, gingerroot, cooking oil, salt, allspice, cinnamon, and nutmeg. Cover and blend or process till smooth. Pat mixture onto all sides of roast. Cover and refrigerate about 8 hours or overnight.

Place meat on a rack in a shallow roasting pan. Insert a meat thermometer. Roast, uncovered, in a 325° oven for 2½ to 3½ hours or till meat thermometer registers 160°. Remove roast from pan, reserving drippings. Cover meat loosely with foil; let stand for 10 minutes.

Meanwhile, for sauce, place ¼ cup of the drippings in a medium saucepan. Stir in cornstarch. Add pineapple juice all at once. Cook and stir till thickened and bubbly. Cook and stir for 2 minutes more.

To serve, carve meat into slices; arrange on a serving platter with fruit. Serve with rice and sauce. If desired, serve on dinner plates lined with ti leaves; top each serving with cracked peppercorns and fresh cilantro. Makes 14 to 16 servings.

*Note: Because hot peppers contain volatile oils that can burn skin and eyes, avoid direct contact with the pepper as much as possible. Wear plastic or rubber gloves or work under cold running water. If your bare hands touch the peppers, wash your hands and nails well with soap and water.

Nutrition facts per serving: 436 cal., 13 g total fat (4 g sat. fat), 77 mg chol., 207 mg sodium, 51 g carbo., 3 g fiber, 28 g pro. Daily Value: 8% vit. A, 99% vit. C, 4% calcium, and 17% iron.

◆ Christmas Bread Tree and Wreath

Some recipes live on for decades. Since 1951, when my mother tore
these recipes from her new *Better Homes and Gardens* magazine,
these breads have been a mainstay of our holidays.
Thank you!
—Nancy Snyder

Christmas Bread Tree And Wreath

"ON CHRISTMAS MORNING, DAD WOULD SCRAMBLE THE EGGS, COOK THE BACON, AND WARM UP MOM'S CHRISTMAS BREADS. EACH OF US HAD OUR FAVORITE BREAD AND OFTEN MY BROTHER AND I WOULD FIGHT OVER THE LAST PIECE OF THE SUGAR PLUM TREE. CONTINUING THE FAMILY TRADITION, IT'S NOW MY HUSBAND WHO SCRAMBLES THE EGGS AND COOKS THE BACON ON CHRISTMAS MORNING, AND MY SONS AND DAUGHTER ARGUE OVER WHO GETS WHAT KIND OF BREAD. SOME THINGS ARE WORTH FIGHTING FOR."

—NANCY SNYDER, ANCHORAGE, ALASKA

5 to 5½ cups all-purpose flour
2 packages active dry yeast
1¼ cups milk
½ cup sugar
½ cup margarine or butter
½ teaspoon salt
2 eggs
1 teaspoon finely shredded lemon peel

In a large bowl stir together *2 cups of* the flour and the yeast. Set aside.

In a medium saucepan heat and stir milk, sugar, margarine or butter, and salt till warm (120° to 130°) and margarine is almost melted. Add milk mixture to flour mixture; add eggs and lemon peel. Beat on low speed for 30 seconds, scraping bowl. Beat on high speed for 3 minutes. Using a spoon, stir in as much remaining flour as you can.

Turn dough out onto a lightly floured surface. Knead in enough of the remaining flour to make a moderately stiff dough that is smooth and elastic (6 to 8 minutes total). Shape into a ball. Place in a lightly greased bowl; turn once to grease surface. Cover and let rise in a warm place till double (about 60 minutes). (Or, cover and let rise in the refrigerator overnight.)

Punch dough down. Turn out onto a lightly floured surface. Divide into 4 portions. Cover; let rest for 10 minutes. Shape and bake into desired shapes below.

Poinsettia Wreath: In a small bowl soak ⅔ cup diced mixed *candied fruits and peels* in enough boiling water to cover for 5 minutes. Drain. Cut up big pieces.

Combine *2 portions* of the dough. On a lightly floured surface, roll dough to a 16x12-inch rectangle (about ¼ inch thick). Brush with 3 tablespoons melted *margarine or butter*. Drain fruit; sprinkle over dough. Sprinkle with 3 tablespoons *sugar*. From one of the short sides, roll up jelly-roll style; seal edges. Cut diagonally into eight or nine 1-inch-thick slices plus the 2 ends.

On a greased baking sheet arrange slices, cut side down, in a 9-inch circle, overlapping edges. Place ends in center. Cover; let rise till double (30 minutes).

Sprinkle the top with coarse sugar, if desired. Bake in a 350° oven for 15 minutes. Cover edge with foil, leaving center uncovered. Bake about 10 minutes more or till center rolls are golden. Transfer to a wire rack to cool. Makes 1 cake (24 servings).

Nutrition facts per piece: 109 cal., 4 g total fat (2 g sat. fat), 18 mg chol., 62 mg sodium, 17 g carbo., 2 g pro. Daily Value: 3% vit. A, 4% iron.

Sugar Plum Tree: Divide *1 portion* of dough into 4 equal parts. On a lightly floured surface, roll each part into a long ½-inch-thick rope. Transfer to waxed paper. Brush with 3 tablespoons melted *margarine or butter*. Combine ¼ cup *sugar* and 1 teaspoon finely shredded *orange peel*; spread evenly onto paper. Roll each rope in orange peel mixture. Twist each strand.

To make a tree, on a slightly greased baking sheet, starting at the top of the tree, zigzag dough strand back and forth into wider and wider lengths. When you reach the end of one piece, attach another and continue the zigzag, ending with a curl to shape the trunk. Sprinkle with any leftover sugar-orange-peel mixture. Cover; let rise in a warm place till almost double (about 30 minutes).

Bake in a 350° oven for 15 minutes. Cover with foil and bake for 10 minutes more. Transfer to a wire rack to cool. Decorate with Orange Icing and candied cherry halves. Makes 1 coffee cake (12 servings).

Orange Icing: Combine 1 cup sifted *powdered sugar* and 1 teaspoon *vanilla*. Stir in enough *orange juice* (2 to 3 teaspoons) to make an icing of drizzling consistency. Makes about 1 cup.

Nutrition facts per serving: 143 cal., 4 g total fat (3 g sat. fat), 20 mg chol., 67 mg sodium, 25 g carbo., 2 g pro. Daily Value: 4% vit. A, 2% vit. C, 1% calcium, 4% iron.

◆ Lefse

◆ Light Fruitcake

Light Fruitcake

"I LOVED MY MOTHER'S FRUITCAKE SO MUCH THAT SHE BAKED A LARGE VERSION FOR MY WEDDING AND HAD THE LOCAL BAKERY DECORATE IT WITH MARZIPAN YELLOW ROSES. EVEN THOUGH I MAKE IT AT HOLIDAY TIME, I STILL THINK OF IT AS MY WEDDING CAKE."

—BEATRICE SCHOTT, SEATTLE, WASH.

9 eggs
2 cups margarine or butter
3 cups light raisins (1 pound)
2 cups diced candied green citron
2 cups candied red cherries
4 cups all-purpose flour
1 teaspoon baking powder
2¼ cups sugar
2 teaspoons finely shredded lemon peel
¼ cup lemon juice
Brandy or fruit juice

Bring eggs and margarine or butter to room temperature. Grease and lightly flour three 8x4x2-inch or five 7x3x2-inch loaf pans; set aside.

In a large bowl combine raisins, citron, and cherries; add 2 cups of the flour. Toss gently to coat fruit; set aside.

In a small mixing bowl stir together remaining 2 cups flour and baking powder; set aside.

In an extra-large bowl beat margarine or butter with a freestanding electric mixer on medium speed for 30 seconds. (Portable mixers are not recommended.) Gradually add sugar, beating on medium to high speed about 6 minutes or till very light and fluffy. Add lemon peel and juice. Add eggs, one at a time, beating well after each, scraping sides of bowl often. Gradually add flour mixture to butter mixture, beating on low to medium speed just till combined. Stir in fruit mixture.

Divide batter evenly among prepared pans. Bake in a 325° oven till done, allowing 70 minutes for the 8x4x2-inch pans and 55 minutes for the 7x3x2-inch pans.

Cool cakes in pans on a wire rack for 10 minutes. Remove from pans. Cool thoroughly on the wire rack.

To moisten and store, wrap cakes in brandy- or fruit-juice-moistened 100% cotton cheesecloth. Wrap with foil. Store in the refrigerator for 2 to 8 weeks. Remoisten cheesecloth about once a week, or as needed. Makes 3 medium loaves or 5 small loaves (24 servings).

Nutrition facts per serving: 449 cal., 18 g total fat (10 g sat. fat), 121 mg chol., 184 mg sodium, 71 g carbo., 1 g fiber, 5 g pro. Daily Value: 17% vit. A, 2% vit. C, 2% calcium, and 10% iron.

Lefse

"WITH THE FLOUR FLYING, MY PARENTS AND I PREPARED FOR THE HOLIDAYS BY PILING UP NORWEGIAN LEFSE ROUNDS TO THE TUNE OF BING CROSBY'S 'SILVER BELLS.' MY FATHER WAS OF GERMAN EXTRACTION, BUT HE COULD FLIP LEFSE WITH THE BEST OF THEM."

—MARGARET A. HAAPOJA, BOVEY, MINNESOTA

1¾ pounds russet potatoes
2 cups all-purpose flour
½ cup margarine or butter, softened
¼ cup whipping cream or half-and-half
1 teaspoon salt
½ cup margarine or butter, softened (optional)
Sugar (optional)
Ground cinnamon (optional)

Peel and cut up potatoes. In a large saucepan cook, covered, in lightly salted boiling water for 20 to 25 minutes or till tender; drain. Squeeze potatoes through a potato ricer or mash with a potato masher in a large mixing bowl. (You should have 4 cups mashed potatoes.) Cover and chill.

Add flour, the ½ cup margarine or butter, whipping cream, and salt to chilled potatoes. Beat with an electric mixer on medium speed till mixture is combined. Divide dough into 16 portions.

On a lightly floured pastry cloth, use a lefse rolling pin (with a textured surface) or regular rolling pin (covered with a rolling pin cover) to roll 1 portion of dough into a 9- or 10-inch circle. Place a lefse griddle or regular griddle over medium heat. Carefully transfer lefse to griddle. Cook for 1 to 2 minutes on each side, turning when golden brown spots appear. Transfer to a wire rack to cool. Repeat with remaining dough to make 16 lefse total. Freeze lefse or serve immediately.

To freeze, layer waxed paper between lefse. Wrap in freezer wrap or place in a freezer container. Cover and freeze for up to 3 months. To thaw, let stand at room temperature about 30 minutes.

To serve, if desired, spread lefse with ½ cup softened margarine or butter; sprinkle with sugar and cinnamon. Roll or fold; slice into 4 or 5 slices. Makes about 64 pieces.

Nutrition facts per piece: 152 cal., 7 g total fat (4 g sat. fat), 21 mg chol., 196 mg sodium, 19 g carbo., 1 g fiber, 2 g pro. Daily Value: 6% vit. A, 5% vit. C, 0% calcium, 5% iron.

Prize Tested Recipes.

Holiday Prune Butter Bread

SWIRLS OF HONEY-SCENTED PRUNE BUT-
TER EARN THIS WHEAT BREAD TOP
HONORS.

*1 cup lightly packed, pitted prunes
(about 8 ounces)
1 teaspoon lemon juice
2 tablespoons honey
3 to 3½ cups all-purpose flour
1 package active dry yeast
1 teaspoon ground cardamom
1 cup milk
½ cup margarine or butter
⅓ cup sugar
3 eggs
1 teaspoon vanilla
2 cups whole wheat flour
1 cup chopped walnuts
2 teaspoons ground cinnamon
1 tablespoon margarine or butter, melted*

◆ Holiday Prune Butter Bread

For prune butter, in a saucepan combine prunes, lemon juice, and ¾ cup
water; bring to boiling. Reduce heat.
Simmer, covered, 40 minutes. Remove
from heat; stir in honey. Cool. Place in a
food processor bowl. Process till smooth.
Cover and cool.

In a bowl stir together *2 cups* of the
all-purpose flour, yeast, and cardamom.
Heat milk, ½ cup margarine or butter,
sugar, and ¾ teaspoon *salt* till warm
(120° to 130°). Add to flour mixture
along with eggs and vanilla. Beat with an
electric mixer on low speed for 30 seconds. Beat on high 3 minutes. Stir in
whole wheat flour and as much remaining all-purpose flour as you can. On a
floured surface, knead in enough
remaining all-purpose flour to make a
moderately stiff dough. Place in a
greased bowl. Cover; let rise till double.
Turn out onto a floured surface. Divide
in half. Cover; let rest 10 minutes. Roll

♦ Pork with Cranberry Sauce

each half into a 12x7-inch rectangle. Spread each with ½ *cup* prune butter to within 1 inch of edges. Sprinkle with nuts and cinnamon. Roll up; seal. Place loaves, seam down, in greased 8x4x2-inch loaf pans. Cover; let rise till double. Bake in a 350° oven 30 to 35 minutes or till bread sounds hollow when tapped. Remove from pans. Brush with margarine. Serve with remaining prune butter. Makes 2 loaves (32 servings).

Nutrition facts per serving: 156 cal., 6 g fat, 21 mg chol., 103 mg sodium, 22 g carbo. 2g fiber, 4 g pro. Daily Value: 6% vit A, 0% vit. C, 2 % calcium, 8% iron.

$200 WINNER

Cecilia Pestlin, Talent, Oreg.

Pork with Cranberry Sauce

To use dried herbs instead of fresh, substitute one-third the amount of fresh.

1 3- to 5-pound pork loin center rib roast, backbone loosened
½ cup fine dry bread crumbs
2 tablespoons snipped fresh sage
2 tablespoons snipped fresh thyme
1 tablespoon snipped fresh oregano
1 tablespoon snipped fresh basil
2 tablespoons margarine or butter, melted
1 teaspoon pepper
2 tablespoons honey
1 16-ounce can whole cranberry sauce
¼ cup lemon juice

Trim fat from meat. With a sharp knife, score top of meat into a shallow diamond pattern. Place roast, rib side down, in a roasting pan. Insert a meat thermometer. Roast in a 350° oven, uncovered, 1 hour. Combine bread crumbs, herbs, margarine or butter, pepper, and ½ teaspoon *salt*. Brush meat with honey. Pat herb mixture over pork. Continue roasting 30 to 45 minutes or till thermometer registers 160° to 170°. Reserve *2 tablespoons* pan drippings. Cover roast; let stand 15 minutes. For sauce, in a saucepan combine cranberry sauce, lemon juice, and reserved drippings. Cook over medium heat till heated through. To serve, slice roast between ribs. Pass sauce. Serves 8 to 10.

Nutrition facts per serving: 326 cal., 13 g fat, 290 g sodium, 64 mg chol., 21 g pro.

$200 WINNER

Harriet Nelson-Jones, Inglewood, Calif.

♦ Cheese-Stuffed Chicken In Phyllo

Cheese-Stuffed Chicken In Phyllo

A tantalizing mixture of spinach, four cheeses, nutmeg, and cumin makes up the filling.

8 skinless, boneless chicken breast halves (1½ pounds)
4 cups chopped fresh spinach
1 cup chopped onion
2 tablespoons olive oil or cooking oil
½ of an 8-ounce package cream cheese, cubed and softened
1 cup shredded mozzarella cheese (4 ounces)
½ cup crumbled feta cheese (2 ounces)
½ cup shredded cheddar cheese
1 beaten egg yolk
1 tablespoon all-purpose flour
½ teaspoon ground nutmeg
½ teaspoon ground cumin
16 sheets phyllo dough (18x14-inch rectangles)
⅔ cup margarine or butter, melted

Place each chicken breast half between two sheets of heavy plastic wrap; pound with the flat side of a meat mallet till ⅛ inch thick. Season with salt and pepper; set aside.

continued on page 234

continued from page 233

In a large skillet cook spinach and onion in hot oil till onion is tender. Remove from heat. Stir in cream cheese till blended. Stir in remaining cheeses, egg yolk, flour, nutmeg, and cumin. Place about ¼ *cup* of the spinach mixture on each chicken breast half; roll up jelly-roll style (it's not necessary to seal ends). Place one sheet of phyllo on work surface (keep remaining sheets covered with a damp towel to prevent drying out). Brush with some of the melted margarine or butter. Place another phyllo sheet on top of first; brush with margarine. Place one chicken roll near a short side of the phyllo; roll chicken and phyllo over once to cover chicken. Fold in long sides; continue rolling from short side. Place in a shallow baking pan. Repeat with remaining chicken, phyllo, and margarine. Brush with margarine. Bake, uncovered, in a 350° oven for 30 to 35 minutes or till chicken is no longer pink. Makes 8 servings.

Nutrition facts per serving: 541 cal., 33 g total fat (18 g sat. fat), 150 mg chol., 661 mg sodium, 33 g carbo., 1 g fiber, 30 g pro. Daily Value: 54% vit. A, 15% vit. C, 19% calcium, 21% iron.

$100 WINNER
Carole Nerlino, Venice, Fla.

Festive Holiday Brioches

IF YOU LIKE, MAKE THESE ROLLS THE NIGHT BEFORE AND CHILL THEM TILL MORNING.

1 package active dry yeast
¼ cup warm water (105° to 115°)
½ cup margarine or butter, softened
⅓ cup sugar

◆ Festive Holiday Brioches

4 cups all-purpose flour
½ cup milk
4 eggs
½ cup dried cranberries or cherries
½ cup chopped candied citron
¼ cup currants
1 tablespoon sugar

Soften yeast in the warm water. In a mixing bowl beat the margarine or butter, ⅓ cup sugar, and 1 teaspoon *salt* till fluffy. Add *1 cup* of the flour and the milk to the sugar mixture. Separate one of the eggs. Add the yolk and 3 whole eggs to the beaten mixture. (Chill remaining egg white.) Add softened yeast to flour mixture and beat well. Stir in cranberries, citron, and currants. Stir in remaining flour. Place in a greased bowl. Cover; let rise in a warm place till double (about 2 hours), then refrigerate dough for 6 hours. (Or, omit 2-hour rise and refrigerate dough overnight.) Stir

dough. Turn out onto a floured surface. Divide dough into 4 equal portions. Set 1 portion aside. Divide remaining 3 portions into 8 pieces each. Roll into balls. Place into well-greased muffin cups. Divide remaining dough into 24 pieces, shape into small balls. With thumb, make an indentation in middle of each large ball. Press a small ball into each indentation. Mix reserved egg white and 1 tablespoon sugar. Brush over rolls. Cover; let rise in a warm place till nearly double (about 45 minutes). Bake in a 375° oven 15 minutes or till golden. Remove from pans; cool. Makes 24.

Nutrition facts per brioche: 151 cal., 5 g total fat (3 g sat. fat), 46 mg chol., 149 mg sodium, 23 g carbo., 1 g fiber, 3 g pro. Daily Value: 5% vit. A, 1% calcium, 7% iron.

$100 WINNER
Joanne Lewis Sears, South Laguna, Calif.

Index

Index

Tips

Metric Cooking Hints

By making a few conversions, cooks in Australia, Canada, and the United Kingdom can use the recipes in Better Homes and Gardens® *1994 Best Recipes Yearbook* with confidence. The charts on this page provide a guide for converting measurements from the U.S. customary system, which is used throughout this book, to the imperial and metric systems. There also is a conversion table for oven temperatures to accommodate the differences in oven calibrations.

Volume and Weight: Americans traditionally use cup measures for liquid and solid ingredients. The chart (top right) shows the approximate imperial and metric equivalents. If you are accustomed to weighing solid ingredients, here are some helpful approximate equivalents.
● 1 cup butter, caster sugar, or rice = 8 ounces = about 250 grams
● 1 cup flour = 4 ounces = about 125 grams
● 1 cup icing sugar = 5 ounces = about 150 grams
 Spoon measures are used for smaller amounts of ingredients. Although the size of the tablespoon varies slightly among countries. However, for practical purposes and for recipes in this book, a straight substitution is all that's necessary.
 Measurements made using cups or spoons should always be level, unless stated otherwise.

Product Differences: Most of the ingredients called for in the recipes in this book are available in English-speaking countries. However, some are known by different names. Here are some common American ingredients and their possible counterparts:
● Sugar is granulated or caster sugar.
● Powdered sugar is icing sugar.
● All-purpose flour is plain household flour or white flour. When self-rising flour is used in place of all-purpose flour in a recipe that calls for leavening, omit the leavening agent (baking soda or baking powder) and salt.
● Light corn syrup is golden syrup.
● Cornstarch is cornflour.
● Baking soda is bicarbonate of soda.
● Vanilla is vanilla essence.

Useful Equivalents

1/8 teaspoon = 0.5 ml	2/3 cup = 5 fluid ounces = 150 ml
1/4 teaspoon = 1 ml	3/4 cup = 6 fluid ounces = 175 ml
1/2 teaspoon = 2 ml	1 cup = 8 fluid ounces = 250 ml
1 teaspoon = 5 ml	2 cups = 1 pint
1/4 cup = 2 fluid ounces = 50 ml	2 pints = 1 litre
1/3 cup = 3 fluid ounces = 75 ml	1/2 inch = 1 centimetre
1/2 cup = 4 fluid ounces = 125 ml	1 inch = 2 centimetres

Baking Pan Sizes

American	Metric
8x1½-inch round baking pan	20x4-centimetre sandwich or cake tin
9x1½-inch round baking pan	23x3.5-centimetre sandwich or cake tin
11x7x1½-inch baking pan	28x18x4-centimetre baking pan
13x9x2-inch baking pan	32.5x23x5-centimetre baking pan
2-quart rectangular baking dish	30x19x5-centimetre baking pan
15x10x2-inch baking pan	38x25.5x2.5-centimetre baking pan (Swiss roll tin)
9-inch pie plate	22x4- or 23x4-centimetre pie plate
7- or 8-inch springform pan	18- or 20-centimetre springform or loose-bottom cake tin
9x5x3-inch loaf pan	23x13x6-centimetre or 2-pound narrow loaf pan or paté tin
1½-quart casserole	1.5-litre casserole
2-quart casserole	2-litre casserole

Oven Temperature Equivalents

Farenheit Setting	Celsius Setting*	Gas Setting
300°F	150°C	Gas Mark 2
325°F	160°C	Gas Mark 3
350°F	180°C	Gas Mark 4
375°F	190°C	Gas Mark 5
400°F	200°C	Gas Mark 6
425°F	220°C	Gas Mark 7
450°F	230°C	Gas Mark 8
Broil		Grill

Electric and gas ovens may be calibrated using Celsius. However, increase the Celsius setting 10 to 20 degrees when cooking above 160°C with an electric oven. For convection or forced-air ovens (gas or electric), lower the temperature setting 10°C when cooking at all heat levels.